MW00783516

Practical Mapping for Applied Research and Program Evaluation

Sara Miller McCune founded SAGE Publishing in 1965 to support the dissemination of usable knowledge and educate a global community. SAGE publishes more than 1000 journals and over 800 new books each year, spanning a wide range of subject areas. Our growing selection of library products includes archives, data, case studies and video. SAGE remains majority owned by our founder and after her lifetime will become owned by a charitable trust that secures the company's continued independence.

Los Angeles | London | New Delhi | Singapore | Washington DC | Melbourne

Practical Mapping for Applied Research and Program Evaluation

Bernadette Wright

Meaningful Evidence, LLC

Steven E. Wallis

Foundation for the Advancement of Social Theory

Capella University, School of Social and Behavioral Sciences

Los Angeles | London | New Delhi
Singapore | Washington DC | Melbourne

FOR INFORMATION:

SAGE Publications, Inc.
2455 Teller Road
Thousand Oaks, California 91320
E-mail: order@sagepub.com

SAGE Publications Ltd.
1 Oliver's Yard
55 City Road
London EC1Y 1SP
United Kingdom

SAGE Publications India Pvt. Ltd.
B 1/I 1 Mohan Cooperative Industrial Area
Mathura Road, New Delhi 110 044
India

SAGE Publications Asia-Pacific Pte. Ltd.
18 Cross Street #10-10/11/12
China Square Central
Singapore 048423

Acquisitions Editor: Helen Salmon
Editorial Assistant: Megan O'Heffernan
Production Editor: Andrew Olson
Copy Editor: Karin Rathert
Typesetter: C&M Digitals (P) Ltd.
Proofreader: Alison Syring
Indexer: Robie Grant
Cover Designer: Dally Verghese
Marketing Manager: Susannah Goldes

Copyright © 2020 by SAGE Publications, Inc.

All rights reserved. Except as permitted by U.S. copyright law, no part of this work may be reproduced or distributed in any form or by any means, or stored in a database or retrieval system, without permission in writing from the publisher.

All third party trademarks referenced or depicted herein are included solely for the purpose of illustration and are the property of their respective owners. Reference to these trademarks in no way indicates any relationship with, or endorsement by, the trademark owner.

Printed in the United States of America

Library of Congress Cataloging-in-Publication Data

Names: Wright, Bernadette, author. | Wallis, Steven E., author.

Title: Practical mapping for applied research and program evaluation / Bernadette Wright, Meaningful Evidence, LLC, Steven E. Wallis, Capella University; ASK MATT Solutions.

Description: Los Angeles : SAGE, 2020. | Includes bibliographical references and index.

Identifiers: LCCN 2018058598 | ISBN 9781544323343 (pbk. : alk. paper)

Subjects: LCSH: Evaluation research (Social action programs) | Results mapping.

Classification: LCC H62 .W6775 2020 | DDC 001.4—dc23
LC record available at https://lccn.loc.gov/2018058598

This book is printed on acid-free paper.

19 20 21 22 23 10 9 8 7 6 5 4 3 2 1

CONTENTS

Preface   xv

Overview and Map of the Book   xix

Acknowledgments   xxv

About the Authors   xxvii

Chapter 1 • Three Dimensions of Knowledge for Solving Complex Problems: Meaning, Data, & Logic   1

Chapter 2 • Meaning: A Collaborative Mapping Approach   33

Chapter 3 • Data: Mapping From Related Research and Materials   69

Chapter 4 • Mapping From Your Own Research   101

Chapter 5 • Logic: Evaluating the Structure of Maps   139

Chapter 6 • Collaborating With Other Researchers   169

Chapter 7 • Communication, Collaboration, and Action   199

Appendix A: Advanced Strategies for Making Maps More Useful   233

Appendix B: Sample Report   249

Appendix C: Some Research Methods for Building Better Maps   261

Glossary   283

Index   289

DETAILED CONTENTS

Preface   xv

Overview and Map of the Book   xix

Acknowledgments   xxv

About the Authors   xxvii

Chapter 1 • Three Dimensions of Knowledge for Solving Complex Problems: Meaning, Data, & Logic   **1**

Toward Better Maps for Solving Complex Problems   2

Three Dimensions of Knowledge   6

    Meaning—The First Dimension   **6**

        Just Because Everyone Believes It Doesn't Make It True   8

    Data—The Second Dimension   **9**

        Data—Just the Facts   10

    Logic—The Third Dimension   **11**

        Causality   12

        It Sounds Good in Theory, but There Are Limits to Logic   14

Putting the Dimensions Together   15

        Test-Drive   16

    • **Knowledge Appraisal Matrix**   **17**

    • **Class Activity 1.1. Evaluating Evidence**   **19**

Right of Way: Research Ethics   22

    Institutional Review Boards   **24**

        Community IRB   25

Chapter 1 Key Points   25

Frequently Asked Questions   25

Further Exploration   26

    The Wicked Complexity of Problems Facing the World   27

    The Explosion of Information   27

    The Disconnect Between Research and Practice   27

    The Low Rates of Success in Using Data for Making Decisions   28

    Unanticipated Consequences From Policies and Programs   28

    Human-Centered Design, Complexity, and Systems Thinking in Research and Evaluation   28

    Three Dimensions of Knowledge   29

    Techniques for and Practical Examples of Knowledge Mapping and Logic Models   29

Practical Example: After-School Programs   30
Right of Way: Research Ethics   30

Chapter 2 • Meaning: A Collaborative Mapping Approach   33

The Road Ahead   34
    Collaboration Over Consensus   35
    Relevance   36

Uses for Collaborative Mapping   37

Milestones on the Road to Collaborative Mapping   39
    Stage 1. Preparation for the Mapping Session   **39**
      Choose a Map Topic   39
      Invite Stakeholders   40
      Arrange Logistics   42
    • Class Activity 2.1. Practicing Facilitation for Choosing a Topic   **44**
    Stage 2. The Collaborative Mapping Session   **44**
      Start With Introductions and Orientation   44
      Begin Mapping   45
      Encourage Transformative Concepts   47
      Encourage Loops   47
      Continue Mapping   47
    • Class Activity 2.2. Collectively Creating a Map   **49**
    Stage 3. From Mapping to Action   **50**
      Assess Options for Action   50
      Find Opportunities for Collaboration   51
      Commit to Action   51
    Stage 4. Road Trip   **52**
      Meet Monthly   52
      Share the Results   53
      Revisit the Map Each Year   54
      Circling Back to the Leadership Team   54
    • Class Activity 2.3. Considering Options Presented by Maps   **55**

Dealing With Difficult Dynamics   55
    Gravity and Money   **55**
    Off Topic   **56**
    "Special" Situation   **56**
    Super Talkers   **56**
    Premature Decision   **57**
    Super Connectors   **57**
    Unstructured Conversation   **57**
    Power Dynamics   **58**
    Working With People With Disabilities   **58**

Gamified Approach to Collaborative Mapping   59
    The ASK MATT Game   **59**

Case Study: Mapping a Regional Energy Coalition   61

Chapter 2 Key Points   63

Frequently Asked Questions   63

Further Exploration   64
   Action Research   64
   Facilitation and Change   65
   Importance of Involving Many Stakeholders   65
   Importance of Incorporating Many Views   66
   Equity in Participation: Disabilities and Power   66
   Strategic Planning for Nonprofits   66
   Strategic Planning for Businesses   66
   Serious Play   67

Chapter 3 • Data: Mapping From Related Research and Materials   69

Uses for Mapping From Existing Research   70

Steps to Mapping From Existing Research   71
  Step 1. Searching for and Choosing Existing Studies   **73**
    Determining Your Study Inclusion Criteria   73
    Deciding Where to Search   74
    Scanning Search Results and Selecting Studies   76
  Step 2. Creating a Table of Studies   **77**
  Step 3. Extracting and Organizing Knowledge From Studies   **79**
    Extract Knowledge From Studies   79
    Organize Study Findings   81
  Step 4. Assessing Research Quality   **82**
    Study Appraisal Checklist   83
  Step 5. Mapping the Knowledge From Studies   **85**
    Mapping Propositions in Studies   85
    Integrating Multiple Maps   87
  • **Class Activity 3.1. Creating Maps From Related Studies**   **87**

Mapping From Program Materials   89

Case Study: Mapping From Program Materials   90
    Creating an Initial Knowledge Map From Program Materials   90
    Clarifying and Refining a Map From Program Materials   93
  • **Class Activity 3.2. Mapping From Program Materials**   **93**

Chapter 3 Key Points   95

Frequently Asked Questions   95

Further Exploration   97
   Techniques for Reviewing Related Research   97
   Issues to Consider in Reviewing Related Research   97
   Guidelines for Reporting and Conducting Reviews of Related Research   97
   Assessing the Quality of Evidence From Related Research   98
   Techniques for Mapping From Related Research   98
   Case Study: NMAC Strong Communities Project   98
   Case Study: Map of an Academic Research Institution's Strategic Plan   99
   Example of Mapping From Related Research   99

Chapter 4 • Mapping From Your Own Research   **101**

The Road Ahead   102

Developing Research Questions for Better Maps   102

   **Research Questions for Measuring Concepts and Connections
on Your Map**   **105**

   Research Questions for Expanding Maps   **106**

Specifying Methods to Answer Your Research Questions   108

   • Class Activity 4.1. Thinking About Multiple Methods   **111**

Focus on Conducting Interviews   113

   Who to Interview   **114**

   Participant Recruitment and Logistics   **115**

     Strategies for Recruiting Interview Participants   115

     Interview Format and Location   118

     Interview Timing   118

     Interviewers   119

     Techniques for Capturing Interview Data   119

   Procedures for Protecting Participants   **120**

   Your Interview Discussion Guide   **120**

   • Class Activity 4.2. Interview Practice   **126**

Organizing Your Research Findings   127

Reporting and Presenting Your Research   128

   Finding and Mapping Propositions of Your Research Findings   **128**

   • Class Activity 4.3. Mapping From Research Findings   **132**

   Visualizing Data on Your Map   **134**

Chapter 4 Key Points   135

Frequently Asked Questions   135

Further Exploration   136

   Developing Useful Research Questions   136

   Interview and Focus Group Methods   137

   Sampling   137

   Knowledge Mapping From Interviews   137

   Case Study: Howard University PAC-Involved Evaluation   137

   Approaches to Logic Models, Theories of Change, and so Forth   138

Chapter 5 • Logic: Evaluating the Structure of Maps   **139**

The Well-Built Road   140

Our Evolving Understanding of Knowledge Maps   140

   From Inference to Structure   143

   Early Techniques for Understanding Structure for Knowledge   144

   • Class Activity 5.1. Choosing a Topic   **145**

Measuring the Structure of Maps   145

   Evaluating the Structure of Knowledge Maps   146

   Test-Drive   146

   • Class Activity 5.2. Evaluating the Structure of a Map   **148**

Comparing and Improving Maps 148
    Four Quadrants 150
    Now, Moving On 153
Case Study: Evaluating The Structure of Entrepreneurship Theories 153
    Introduction and Problem Statement 154
    Method and Sample 154
    Results and Insights 155
    Limitations and Conclusions 157
More Views of Structure 157
    Loops 157
    Leverage Points 158
    Clustering 159
    • **Class Activity 5.3. Clustering and Categorization** **160**
    Abstraction/Categorization 160
    Deconstruction 161
    Simplicity 161
    What? Not! 162
    Show the Invisible 162
    • **Class Activity 5.4. Gap Analysis** **163**
Chapter 5 Key Points 164
Frequently Asked Questions 164
Further Exploration 165
    History of Knowledge Mapping 165
    Many Approaches to Mapping 165
    Concepts and Circles 165
    Causality and Arrows 165
    Graphic Recording/Facilitation 165
    Integrative Complexity 165
    Structure of Maps, Models, and More 166
    Other Approaches to Structure Using Online Mapping Platforms 166
    Analyzing Structure for Policy and Programs 166
    Entrepreneurship—From the Case Study 167

Chapter 6 • Collaborating With Other Researchers **169**

The Fragmented World of Social Sciences 170
Putting The Pieces Together 172
Integration, Acceleration, Solution! 173
    A Cycle of Collaboration 174
Finding People, Finding Maps 177
    Steps to Integrating Maps 178
    Bridging and Explaining to Support Integration 179
    Showing the Results—and the Progress of Integration 181
Case Study: Collaboration Among Researchers 182
    Rearview Mirror 183
    On-Ramp 183

Surrounding Scenery	184
Bumpy Road Ahead	184
Alternate Route	184
Speed Bumps	187
Easy Street	187
Test-Drive	188
The Road Does Not End Here	190
• **Class Activity 6.1. Integrating Multiple Maps**	**192**
Challenges to Interdisciplinary Collaboration	193
Chapter 6 Key Points	195
Frequently Asked Questions	195
Further Exploration	196
Fragmentation of the Sciences Due to Soft or Ad Hoc Integration of Theories	196
Collaboration Among Researchers for Interdisciplinary Progress	197
Collaborative Research in Business	197
Some Sites About Supporting Collaboration in Communities	197
Some Sites About Learning to Collaborate Better in Teams	197
More Sources for Connecting With Researchers	198
Examples of Integrating Theories	198
Case Study for This Chapter	198
Test-Drive Resources	198
Chapter 7 • Communication, Collaboration, and Action	**199**
The Road Ahead	200
Tools for Making Maps	200
Low-Tech Tools	**200**
The ASK MATT Tabletop Game	202
Desktop Tools	**202**
Online Mapping Tools	**203**
Insightmaker.com	203
Stormboard.com	205
Kumu.io	206
Test-Drive—Mapping in Kumu	208
Creating a Map in Kumu	209
• **Class Activity 7.1. Creating an Online Map**	**213**
Making Presentations	216
Presenting Data With Maps	**216**
Submaps	217
Nested Maps	220
Guiding Conversations Around a Map	222
Collaborative Decisions	224
Action Planning	225
Short-Term and Long-Term Goals	226
Reporting Relationships	226
The End Is a New Beginning	227

Tracking Results   227
     Key Performance Indicators (KPI)   227
Chapter 7 Key Points   228
Frequently Asked Questions   228
Further Exploration   229
     Tools for Creating Maps   229
     Presentations   230
     Nested Maps   230
     Facilitating Decisions in Groups   231
     Tracking Results With Dashboards   231

Appendix A: Advanced Strategies for Making Maps More Useful   **233**
Bridges   233
Time   234
Core and Belt   235
Looking for Sub-Structures   236
     Atomistic Structure   **236**
     Linear Structure   **236**
     Circular Structure   **237**
     Branching Structure   **238**
     Transformative Logic Structure   **238**
Travelling From Optimism to Reality   238
Scale of Abstraction   240
Reducing Redundancy   242
Unanticipated Consequences   243
Inter-Mapper Consistency   244
Off the Shelf   245
Further Exploration   246
     Time   246
     Core and Belt   247
     Looking or Sub-Structures   247
     Scales of Abstraction   247
     Unanticipated Conseqeunces   247
     Inter-Mapper Consistency   247
     Off-the-Shelf   247

Appendix B: Sample Report   **249**

Appendix C: Some Research Methods for Building Better Maps   **261**
Research Strategies For Finding Data   262
     Reviewing Existing Quantitative Data   262
     Closed-Ended Survey Questions   262
     Delphi Method   263
     Quantitative Observation   265

Quantitative Meta-Analysis   265
    Randomized Experiments   265
    Quasi-Experiments   267
    Before-and-After (Pre-Post) Design   268
    Retrospective Pre-Post Design   269
    Cost Analysis Studies   269
    Social Network Analysis   270
    Statistical Modeling   270

Research Strategies For Creating and Expanding Maps   272
    Interviews   273
    Focus Groups   273
    Review of Narrative Documents   273
    Qualitative Observation   274
    Open-Ended Survey Questions   274
    Case Study   275
    Causal Link Monitoring   275
    Contribution Analysis   276

Further Exploration   278
    Research Strategies and Example Studies 278
    Statistical Modeling and Computer Simulation Resources 280

Glossary   **283**
Index   **289**

PREFACE

WHO IS THIS BOOK FOR?

Collectively, we face seemingly impossible problems like war, poverty, crime, injustice, and hunger. These "wicked" problems have been with us for thousands of years and exist on every level of society, from our immediate communities to the global stage. If you are interested in understanding and resolving those problems, this book is for you.

Whether you are aiming to be a researcher, program evaluator, manager, executive, or policy wonk, this book will show you how to better understand and more successfully address the problems of today's world.

WHY IS THIS BOOK SPECIAL?

Previous approaches to teaching (and learning) about social research and program evaluation might tell you that we can find better solutions to the vast problems of the world if we could obtain more/better *data*. On the other hand, books by practitioners might tell you that we can solve these problems if everyone would recognize that these problems are relevant and *meaningful* to their daily lives and work together collaboratively to solve them. We agree with both of those perspectives (and include them in this book); we also recognize that something more is required.

Scholars and practitioners are increasingly finding that when our research results are better structured—when their concepts are more *logically* interconnected—that knowledge is more useful for understanding and resolving problems. And importantly, we have learned how to measure this logic structure and show how *useful* this knowledge will be. This breakthrough provides a new and powerful approach to generating more effective knowledge for solving pressing problems. This research textbook is the first to provide this innovative and useful approach.

One of our objectives in writing this book is to help readers become more effective researchers as quickly and easily as possible. So this book provides a practical "nuts and bolts" approach to conducting research and evaluating programs to support their continued improvement. This book is designed to empower the next generation of researchers and practitioners to more readily reach their highest goals.

Providing clear, direct, and concise instruction (including examples and illustrations) on tools for synthesizing research within and between disciplines, this book will enable students to combine data from both qualitative and quantitative research methods, from studies across disciplines, and from both stakeholder experience and academic research.

WHAT KINDS OF COLLEGE COURSES?

This book is focused on research. So teachers and students in a wide range of courses may find this book useful. More specifically, this book looks at how to use research to evaluate (and improve) social programs (including the improvement of operations within organizations), and similarly, how research can inform the creation and evaluation of policy. Areas of useful application include (but are by no means limited to) the following:

- Population health

- Human services

- Public safety

- Community well-being

- Social justice and equity

- Education

- Housing

- Economic development

Importantly, this book is focused on creating knowledge maps (KMs) and evaluating those maps for their potential usefulness on three critical dimensions. Because of this innovative approach and focus, this book makes a great secondary text for courses on research, program evaluation, program planning, and policy evaluation. Similarly, it is a good supplementary text to support students in courses that have a research component (but where research is not the focus), such as a class project. This includes research courses in psychology, sociology, policy, business, and others. This book can certainly serve as a primary text for an introductory research course at the undergraduate or graduate level. And it is useful as a resource for researchers and practitioners working in the field.

INCREASING RELEVANCE

Numerous articles have pointed out that prevailing evaluation methods have not been as useful as they could be for advancing better solutions to social problems. As a result, researchers and policy and program people are increasingly calling for better ways of understanding and solving issues in the world. In response, program evaluators are shifting to approaches that take into account the real-world complexity of the issues that programs are addressing.

In short, a significant shift has begun in how social research is conducted to address highly complex problems—a shift that is necessary to make research more useful and effective in supporting practical decision-making, policy choices, and program improvement.

Whether you are an undergraduate, graduate, academic scholar, program director, or established research professional, the methods presented here will help you have a greater impact in making the world a better place, one where we set aside prejudice and fear while working (and playing) toward a more optimistic future.

In the next section, you will find an Overview and Map of the Book, explaining the structure and scope of this book.

OVERVIEW AND MAP OF THE BOOK

This is a book for the bold—those individuals who are not only *willing* but also *eager* to explore the farthest limits of human understanding.

In writing this book, we were reminded of the excitement and danger of this adventurous field.

You can be writing on a topic (yes, this one, for example) that you know well. You may even be an expert, with your name known around the world. Then, suddenly, a colleague mentions something. A name, an article, an old idea. In a flash, you realize that the old idea might be related to the new ideas you are working on. Down the rabbit hole you go. Researching, reading, talking, studying, investigating, contemplating, synthesizing, creating, and so on.

There is a danger. Are you going in the right direction? How far should you venture forward before trying to find your way back? Many scholars have been lost this way—as if Alice were unable to escape from Wonderland.

Walking this fine line, you keep your focus—trekking through the literature, following references from one publication to another, emailing scholars around the world, asking for clarification around their ideas, and finding still more. You test your ideas by conducting research in the field, interviewing people and facilitating groups from various communities and organizations.

The number of files on your computer keeps increasing. The piles on your desk get higher. The books, articles, and interview results become an almost insurmountable mountain. Here is another danger. Do you give up? No. You synthesize those piles of evidence. You integrate the views you have collected. You reduce that incomprehensible mountain into a climbable hill.

Exhausted, you stand at the border of a new land. From the top of the hill, you gaze out over green fields of future possibilities under the blue skies of your imagination.

What will happen when people read the results of your research? What happens when they follow your lead and climb that hill? Managers, leaders, and people of every description see the benefit of your research. They understand how following your ideas will lead them to better lives.

Slowly, at first, they move forward. Then, with growing confidence in your work, they advance, working, striving, to make better lives for themselves and a better world.

In this book, you will learn how to be that explorer, how to make **maps that** others may follow, how to change the way people see the world so that they can change the world.

We welcome you to this exciting profession and look forward to reading about the results of your adventures in research.

Excelsior!

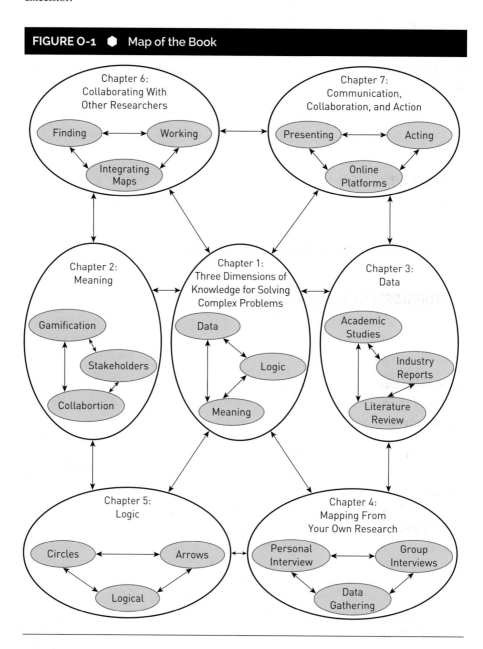

FIGURE 0-1 ● Map of the Book

OVERVIEW

This book is designed to provide clear instructions on how to conduct effective social research. Research that may be used to evaluate and improve social programs, policies, organizations, communities, nations, and more for the general purpose of improving the human condition. By focusing on the basic methods that work best, our goal in writing this book is to help you become a better researcher.

Importantly, you will learn critical skills for creating and evaluating knowledge maps. With those abilities, you can provide more effective research results to make a greater positive impact on the world.

To help you navigate through this book, we've provided a few icons. For example, watch for the "Travel Tips" sign for helpful advice.

TRAVEL TIP

Travel Tips are helpful hints to support your understanding and success.

You will also find "Definition" signs to explain key ideas.

STOP/REFLECTION/DISCUSSION

The text in the "Reflection/Discussion" box will point out some interesting things to consider and some challenging questions for conversation.

At the end of each chapter, you will find some Frequently Asked Questions (FAQs) as well as a list of additional reading to support your further exploration in whatever direction you may choose.

Chapter 1 talks about some of the seemingly impossible problems people seek to solve in the world, the three dimensions of knowledge for understanding and solving those problems, and how we can better connect research and practice for the benefit of all. Importantly, the three interconnected approaches to creating, evaluating, and improving knowledge maps are data, logic, and meaning.

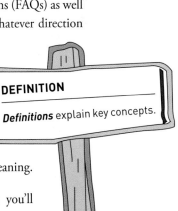

DEFINITION

Definitions explain key concepts.

Chapter 2 delves deeper into the mapping process. In this chapter, you'll discover how to work with groups to create meaningful maps for practical decision-making, tracking progress, and evaluating results. You'll learn how to plan and facilitate a successful collaborative mapping process.

In **Chapter 3**, you'll learn how you can create a map using knowledge from existing research, such as government reports, academic papers, books, articles in trade publications, and program materials. This mapping approach can be part of a literature synthesis or literature review.

Chapter 4 is about mapping from your own research. We provide an example in which we conducted research to evaluate a program, using a mix of several methods. Next, we delve deeply into conducting interviews, organizing data across methods, and using that data to create knowledge maps.

In **Chapter 5**, you will learn the importance of "structure" for knowledge maps and methods for evaluating the logic structure of knowledge maps. Importantly, understanding structure provides an innovative way to improve the usefulness and impact of your knowledge.

By the time we get to **Chapter 6**, you will have a good understanding of how to do effective research. So here we will expand our thinking to provide a brief history of "fragmentation" (increasingly narrow focus of researchers and increasing specialization of practitioners) along with its effect on research and practice. You will learn how to address highly complex problems by countering the effects of fragmentation by connecting with other researchers and integrating multiple knowledge maps.

Ready for action? Good. Because in **Chapter 7**, we will talk about using online platforms for creating knowledge maps, techniques for presenting maps to stakeholder groups, and techniques for supporting collaborative decisions and action.

For those who have developed a thirst for knowledge, **Appendix A** contains some advanced concepts and more directions for continuing your investigation into the field of research and knowledge mapping.

Appendix B provides a sample report—the kind you might provide to a client, other stakeholders, or your professors and fellow students.

Appendix C looks at the basics of a variety of research methods.

They say that if you know the vocabulary, you know the thing—for example, if you understood every word a lawyer might say, you would be well on your way to practicing law. Here, the **Glossary** contains many words you need to know.

The following figure shows a few key ideas we'll be using.

A FEW KEY IDEAS

Within each research project, you will have multiple *stakeholder groups*. For example, you might be a consultant conducting research for a client—a nonprofit organization that wants to better understand homelessness so they can improve their organization's

FIGURE O-2 🔶 A Few Key Ideas

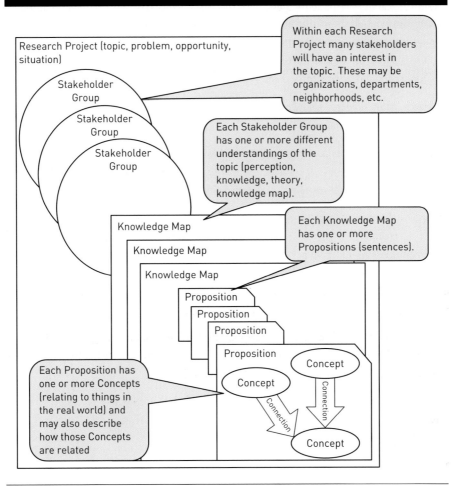

ability to help the homeless in their community. Stakeholder groups might include staff within the nonprofit, government agencies that provide funding to the nonprofit, other nonprofits in the community such as the local food bank, and the homeless community.

Your research might consist of interviewing members of each stakeholder group. As you do that, you will learn their many perspectives on the question of homelessness. The results of those interviews will provide the *propositions*—the sentences—that reflect the understanding of the stakeholders. For example, one might say that mental illness is an important cause of homelessness. Another might say that homelessness is caused by poor economic conditions. Each of those statements includes *concepts* (homelessness, mental illness, economic conditions). The statements also show how the concepts are *causally connected* (when changes in one concept result in change in another concept).

As you combine these propositions, you create a knowledge map—a clear presentation of your research results. With that map, the client can better understand the problem of homelessness. They will be able to see that solving the problem of homelessness will involve improving economic conditions and addressing issues of mental health. And they can use the map to communicate their new understanding with others in the community to support collaborative efforts at resolving the situation.

Research, stakeholders, knowledge maps, concepts, and causal connections. Got it? OK—lets go on to Chapter 1!

ACKNOWLEDGMENTS

The authors would like to acknowledge the editors and staff at SAGE Publishing for their tireless efforts; the expert reviewers for their careful reading and excellent suggestions; the many organizations and individuals we used as examples and case studies for their kind permission; our professional colleagues for their encouragement; and our loved ones (on our respective coasts) for putting up with us during the many months of concentrated writing.

The authors and SAGE would like to thank the following reviewers for their feedback:

Karen Allen, Indiana University Bloomington

Katrina Bledsoe, Claremont Graduate University

Doug Franklin, University of Illinois Springfield

Krisanna Machtmes, Ohio University

Robyn Maitoza, York College of Pennsylvania

Vanaja Nethi, Nova Southeastern University

John Ridings, The Institute for Clinical Social Work

Sandra Schrouder, Barry University

Mack Clayton Shelley II, Iowa State University

Sunyoung Shin, Indiana University

ABOUT THE AUTHORS

Bernadette Wright, PhD, is founder of Meaningful Evidence, where she helps nonprofits to use social research to make a bigger difference. She works with organizations in the areas of health, human services, housing, and education. She has delivered dozens of evaluation-related workshops and webinars at local, national, and international events. Before starting her own business, Dr. Wright was Consultant at The Lewin Group, where she conducted and managed research on aging and disability issues for federal clients. Before that, she was Policy Research Analyst at AARP Public Policy Institute, where she analyzed proposed legislation and regulations and developed publications on supportive services and community living. In her early career, she was Senior Evaluation Specialist at the Baltimore Mayor's Office of Employment Development. She earned her PhD in public policy/program evaluation from the University of Maryland. She is passionate about advancing equity and social justice.

Steven E. Wallis, PhD, is a Fulbright alumnus, international visiting professor, award-wining scholar, and Director of the Foundation for the Advancement of Social Theory. An interdisciplinary thinker, his publications cover a range of fields including psychology, ethics, science, management, organizational learning, entrepreneurship, and policy with dozens of publications, hundreds of citations, and a growing list of international co-authors. In addition, he supports doctoral candidates at Capella University in the Harold Abel School of Social and Behavioral Sciences. Following a career in corrosion control, he earned his PhD at Fielding Graduate University and took early retirement to pursue his passion – leveraging innovative insights to advance science for the betterment of the world. On those occasions when he is not striving to revolutionize the social sciences, he may be found fencing epee, playing chess, or riding his side-car rig "Igor."

THREE DIMENSIONS OF KNOWLEDGE FOR SOLVING COMPLEX PROBLEMS

Meaning, Data, & Logic

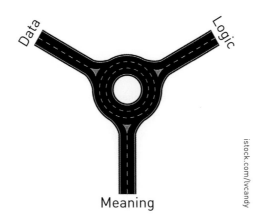

istock.com/lvcandy

To understand and resolve the big problems of the world, we conduct program evaluations and other applied research. In this chapter you will discover the following:

- How we can better connect research and practice for the benefit of all

- Three interconnected dimensions of useful/actionable knowledge

- Research ethics

TOWARD BETTER MAPS FOR SOLVING COMPLEX PROBLEMS

As practical researchers and program evaluators, our job is to provide new understandings that inform planning and action. We can think of those understandings as knowledge maps. Decision makers use those maps to develop new solutions and to improve existing solutions that address problems such as poverty, injustice, and public health.

> **DEFINITION**
>
> *Knowledge* is the understanding of a topic that potentially enables effective action. That understanding may be in our minds, communicated verbally, or in writing as text or diagrams.

We wrote this book to provide you with techniques for building better knowledge maps. This way, you can maximize the usefulness of your research and have a greater positive impact on the world.

In our attempt to understand the big problems of the world and make effective decisions to resolve those problems, we are like early ocean voyagers, navigating by simple lists of waypoints that we will encounter as we sail from our town to distant ports. These early proto-maps might look something like Figure 1.1.

Such a list of waypoints—or an itinerary—would not be as useful as a map.

> **DEFINITION**
>
> A *knowledge map* is a diagram representing knowledge. Knowledge maps make it easier to clarify logic, identify data, and confirm relevancies for making better decisions for reaching important goals.

Ancient cartographers were able to synthesize many of those itineraries to create the first simple maps. However, with so few facts, those maps contained many blank spaces (and occasionally listed the locations of dragons).

As time went on, those maps, tested and improved on voyage after voyage, formed a foundation of modern navigation, enabling safer and more reliable travel around the world. Today, we have Global Positioning Systems (GPS). A swarm of satellites backed by powerful computers tell your smart phone exactly where you are in the world—and how many minutes to the nearest coffee shop or pub. With more complete and more accurate maps, we can navigate our world with greater chances for success at safely reaching our desired destinations.

While geographic maps have improved, our knowledge maps for addressing big problems, such as poverty, injustice, and public health, have not. The

FIGURE 1.1 ● List of Waypoints for Navigators in Ancient Times

- Hometown
- Mountain
- Waterfall—fresh water
- Forest—good hunting
- Bigger mountain
- Other town

maps we make from research to guide program evaluations and other applied research projects have changed little since the early days of the field. Figure 1.2 shows a typical map (often called a logic model), which is used to show how a program is expected to function (adapted from figure in GAO, 2012, p. 11).

These kinds of simple maps may be useful for showing a few key things that a program is supposed to do. And they may be useful for showing what an evaluation of that program might want to measure. However, each is only a small scrap of a map, so there are many blank spaces.

Small maps have not been sufficient for dealing with problems such as poverty, hunger, injustice, war, and ignorance. Some call these problems "wicked," not because they are "evil," but because they are so very difficult that they defy understanding and so persistent that they defy all efforts to end them.

Generally, researchers have tried to understand these wicked problems in two ways. First, by involving more participants in the process. Second, by seeking more data—including "big data" approaches in which information is obtained from social media platforms, government data bases, and other sources that aggregate large amounts of data. Despite the explosion of information in terms of the number of studies and the amount of data, researchers have not

DEFINITION

Research is a scientific process of investigation and discovery that may include program evaluation and policy analysis. This book focuses on **applied research**, that is, research conducted to inform decisions and action to address social issues.

Here Be Dragons

istock.com/colevinyard

Map for sailors in olden days.

DEFINITION

Program evaluation is research conducted to provide information for shaping effective programs, policies, and other actions to purposefully bring about social or environmental change. Program evaluations explore a broad range of questions, such as whether a program is reaching its goals, what unanticipated impacts it is having, and how to design and implement action for the greatest chance of success. In practice, these studies are conducted by researchers from a variety of disciplines (e.g., sociology, education, public policy), and they are not always labelled as a "program evaluation." While program evaluations are conducted for the primary purpose of informing specific decisions, many also contribute to broader knowledge of the issue, which can benefit others in the field.

reached consensus on how to solve these problems, in part, because each study has served to create only a scrap of the larger picture.

Without a good way to make good maps, research is inefficient and we are unable to make progress toward solving our big problems.

In our observations of the field, most studies start almost from scratch, grounded in knowledge from just a few previous studies. It is like our practitioners are relying on an ancient hand-drawn map of a few well-worn paths. What we need is more like a GPS map that lets you quickly assess alternative routes and find the best path to achieving your goals, using the best available knowledge of all the waypoints and routes between them.

For practitioners to be able to better understand and solve complex problems, they need more than disconnected insights and data points. Because all those things in the real world are interconnected, practitioners need a map with more interconnections.

Like ancient mariners, we are sailing in dangerous waters with sadly simplistic maps. We are avoiding areas that warn us of (fictional) dragons, and we avoid the blank parts of the map because we fear that we might fall off the edge of the world. Fortunately, some scholars and practitioners are exploring new directions to redefine knowledge to better understand and resolve those wicked problems.

Emerging innovative approaches include the following:

- *Interdisciplinary research* to bring in more expertise

- *Human-centered design* to use a variety of research methods, make improvements, and then re-study the problem (and repeat)

- *Implementation science* to make the process of research, learning, and change an ongoing process

- *Systems thinking,* increasingly used to understand the world as an interconnected network

- *Mapping tools* to provide more realistic and interconnected diagrams—such as logic models, concept maps, theories of change, and mind maps—to provide a better picture of the situations we face

This book provides an approach to research that is both scientific and highly useful for addressing the seemingly unsolvable problems we face around the world and in our own communities. We do this by understanding what useful/actionable knowledge is in terms of three interrelated dimensions.

Map for driving in the 21st century.

FIGURE 1.2 ● A Fairly Typical Knowledge Map

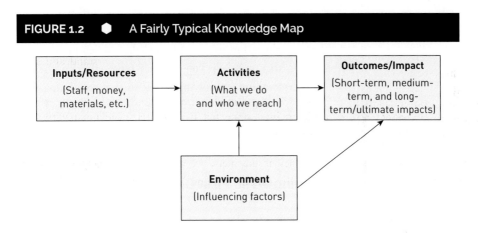

STOP/REFLECTION/DISCUSSION

On your own or in small groups, consider these questions:

- What are some local, national, or global issues on which two (or more) sides have disagreed over the best course of action?

- Do all sides agree on whether or not enough research has been conducted?

- How long has the problem gone on?

- Has progress been made in understanding and solving the problem? Why or why not?

DEFINITION

A **practitioner** is a person such as a worker, manager, supervisor, or leader who uses knowledge to make decisions and take action to accomplish goals.

DEFINITION

Meaning, as a dimension of knowledge, refers to the relevance and importance of the concepts on a knowledge map to the people involved and the situation at hand.

THREE DIMENSIONS OF KNOWLEDGE

We, as researchers (or knowledge cartographers), must improve the quality of our knowledge maps if we are to connect multiple scraps of maps, bridge the chasm between research and practice, and solve the wicked problems of the world. With a more effective process of creating and connecting maps, researchers can be clearer in their communication with practitioners. With better maps, practitioners can have better understanding and make better decisions so that they can better serve their constituents. Overall, this improves our collective ability to make effective decisions to reach our program and policy goals while avoiding unintended consequences.

There are three dimensions of knowledge. When properly put together, they will help you conduct more effective research for understanding and solving problems that seem impossibly complex. Those three dimensions are *meaning, data*, and *logic*. This section introduces those three dimensions. We will delve into them in more depth in following chapters.

Meaning—The First Dimension

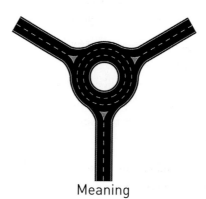

Meaning

In developing a knowledge map, the first step is to identify the *concepts* on the map that have *meaning* or relevance for the stakeholders.

A *concept* is something that relates to the real world but is held in our minds. For example, when we think about "income," "education," or "teachers," we are thinking in concepts of things that we believe are important or meaningful. A good knowledge map is one that includes many relevant concepts. A critical question for researchers to explore throughout the research process is, *"What concepts will we include when we make our map?"*

Answering that question starts with the person who decides to conduct a study and selects research questions to explore. When writing a paper for a class, your process might begin with you deciding what topic you want to study. Working as a program evaluator, you might receive an assignment to conduct a study to explore specific questions or topics—for example, to explore what effects an after-school program is having on students' academic performance. As such, your knowledge map might begin with concepts such as "participation in after-school programs" and "academic performance."

A typical next step is to learn all you can about your topic. You can find that kind of background material from talking with program managers and others involved in the program, reading program materials, and reviewing the existing academic literature and professional publications. From that information-gathering, you can find additional concepts to add to your knowledge map.

Good practical research includes the perspectives of all stakeholders (those with a vested interest in your subject of study). For a study on after-school programs, for example, stakeholders might include (but are not limited to) students, parents, teachers, school administrators, professional associations, advocacy organizations, experts, policymakers, and the public.

The more stakeholder groups that you include in your research, the more you are able to understand the broader picture—avoiding the "pothole" in your research road of having too narrow a focus. Also, the more stakeholder groups you include, the greater chances for success at getting the trust and cooperation needed for effective action.

DEFINITION

A *concept* is a part of a causal knowledge map (often shown inside a circle) that represents an idea or notion. The concept may be as concrete as in "apple" or as abstract as in "truth." Concepts may be simple as in "number of participants" or complex as in "left-handed monkeys with undiagnosed trauma." A concept is typically detectable, that is to say, empirically measurable, but this is not an absolute standard. Concepts are part of propositions. A concept is also called an "aspect" or "variable."

You can engage stakeholders and acquire concepts that stakeholders find meaningful in a variety of ways:

- Organize a collaborative mapping session for people to share their understanding of the issue and how to address it (as detailed in Chapter 2)

- Conduct individual or focus group interviews with stakeholders (Chapter 4)

- Hold a community forum for people to share their thoughts and ideas

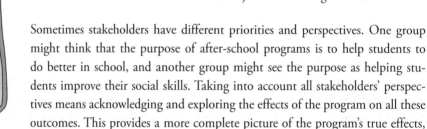

DEFINITION

A *stakeholder* is a person with a personal and/or professional interest in a situation, topic, or subject that is being studied or whose life may be impacted by that situation in the future. Your stakeholders may include, for example, advocates, family members, program managers, social service workers, researchers, funders, elected officials, and representatives of partnering organizations.

- Convene an advisory group of people with knowledge and experience in your topic to contribute ideas and feedback throughout a project

- Find what stakeholders have written or talked about through review of related literature and materials (Chapter 3), such as

    o Speeches

    o News articles

    o Press releases

    o Reports by agencies

    o Previous studies that elicited the perspectives of stakeholders

    o Other sources . . . just start looking around!

Sometimes stakeholders have different priorities and perspectives. One group might think that the purpose of after-school programs is to help students to do better in school, and another group might see the purpose as helping students improve their social skills. Taking into account all stakeholders' perspectives means acknowledging and exploring the effects of the program on all these outcomes. This provides a more complete picture of the program's true effects, enabling decision makers to make more informed decisions than if they only explored outcomes important to one stakeholder.

The greater number of knowledgeable stakeholders you can include, the more concepts you will have from those closest to the situation. That added information will strengthen the quality of your research and your ability to build a knowledge map that is useful to that community for understanding, collaborating, and working together to solve their shared problems.

TRAVEL TIP

TRAVEL TIP

More heads are better than one: While the focus of this section is on stakeholders and their perspectives, we also want you to remember that research is better (and often easier) when you work in collaboration with other researchers. For more on this, see Chapter 6.

Just Because Everyone Believes It Doesn't Make It True

There can be problems with relying only on meaning. You might do a very good job of accessing many stakeholder groups. And they all might agree that the concepts on the

istock.com/monkeybusinessimages

istock.com/skynesher

istock.com/FilippoBacci

Stakeholders as individuals, teams, and large groups

map are relevant. Sometimes, however, what "everyone knows to be true" turns out to be wrong. "Groupthink" can lead people down the wrong road. Also, people do not always know what effects their activities are having. Sometimes, our activities have unanticipated effects that we are not aware of. So for solving tough problems, we need more than a list of concepts that are relevant to people. We also need data.

Data—The Second Dimension

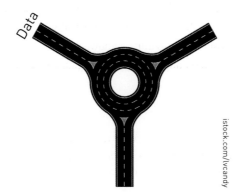

istock.com/Ivcandy

Concepts exist only in the mind. They could be very real, or they could be completely fictional. Data, on the other hand, can be measured, touched, or viewed. Data are the facts or information acquired by research and from experience. The notions of data and meaning overlap because studies can use methods such as interviews and surveys to collect data for understanding what's meaningful to people.

After you've identified the meaningful concepts for your preliminary map, the next step is to look for data related to those concepts. For example, if one of the concepts on your map is "attendance in after-school programs," the data may include the number of children in attendance—as determined by observation and/or a review of the school records.

Research data may be obtained from a variety of sources including the following:

- Your own data collection and analysis (surveys, interviews, experimental studies, etc.)

- Existing academic research (from books and journal articles)

- Industry sources (including reports from government agencies, associations, and other organizations)

- Online sources (such as websites of key organizations and government agencies)

- Expert knowledge (from informal conversations, expert workgroup meetings, interviews/surveys of experts)

- Presentations (professional conferences, webinars)

We will cover data in greater depth in Chapters 3 and 4.

A good way to strengthen your data is by gathering data using multiple methods. For example, to examine whether an after-school program helped students get better grades, you might conduct interviews with students, teachers, parents, and others to get their perspectives on how the program affected them and their perceptions of how it affected others. You could analyze administrative data that show the effects of the program on grades. You could also synthesize data from existing studies of similar programs.

TRAVEL TIP

The more sources of data you have to support your findings, the greater confidence you can have in those findings.

As you collect and analyze data throughout your study, you may discover additional meaningful concepts and relationships that you hadn't thought to consider. For example, you might expect that well-designed after-school programs help improve students' math and literacy skills but discover that the programs also help increase graduation rates.

Data—Just the Facts

In this section, we've provided a brief introduction to data (we will go into this topic in greater depth in Chapters 3 and 4). While data are important for making decisions, all observations and measurements have limitations. That's why practitioners need more than "just the facts" to plan effective action. Even if they know that A causes B (because that relationship is supported by many reliable facts), leaders still need to know how to make A happen! They need to know what others are doing to get to B (does C cause B?) and what affects does C have on all the other activities of the organization?

In addition, data may be misinterpreted by accident or on purpose. With sufficient manipulation, statistical results may be slanted in order to convince or confuse. So for solving tough problems, the data must be presented logically.

Logic—The Third Dimension

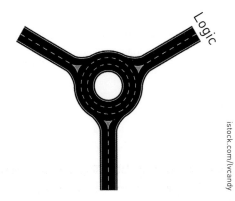

istock.com/lvcandy

> **DEFINITION**
>
> **Data** are the facts or information gained from research/measurement or from experience. Examples include survey results, interview results, and everything you see and hear.

Previously, we talked about maps as guides—because maps help you get where you want to go. For planning a cross-country road trip, for example, your map will be more useful if it includes more dots (locations of cities, points of interest, gas stations, etc.) and more lines (roads and highways connecting the dots). The more lines and dots on your map, the more options you have for places to visit and the more choices you have for what road to take to get there.

Maps with no lines (maps that do not show clear relationships between the dots) are not very useful. Consider, for example, a knowledge map that says, "After-school programs and students' academic performance are related." That does not tell us HOW they are related. It's like saying "Chicago is close to New York."

> **DEFINITION**
>
> **Logic** represents an understanding of the causal relationship between two or more things—basically the "arrows" we've been talking about in the book. **Logic structure** (or more simply, **structure**) is about the way those arrows interconnect (much more on this throughout this book).

It only brings up more questions, such as "How close, and in what direction?" A map with no lines does not provide useful guidance for how to solve the challenge of improving students' academic performance.

Knowledge maps work on much the same principle as the maps you use for driving. Instead of physical locations on a road map, we have concepts on

DEFINITION

Causality is seen any time two or more things change—and one of those is the cause of the other. For example, rain and sunlight cause plants to grow.

a knowledge map; instead of roads, we have arrows showing causal connections (changes in one thing lead to changes in another). Generally, the more concepts and arrows on your knowledge map, the more useful that map will be for understanding, making decisions, and resolving problems. Because everything in the real world is interconnected, the concepts on our maps must also be interconnected if they are to provide useful guides for decision-making.

When we talk about the *logic* of a knowledge map, we are talking about the causal connections between the concepts. This is a very different approach to logic than you might be used to. Often when people think that something "seems logical," they are thinking it "makes sense" or "seems reasonable." Instead, for this book, something is logical when we understand a causal connection—showing how changes in one thing cause changes in another.

Causality

When you are creating a knowledge map from your research, arrows are used to represent *causal* logic. Causal logic is necessary for any deep, scientific understanding of your research topic. And equally important for practitioners, decision makers must be able to look at a map and see how doing more (or less) of some actions will lead to changes in the world.

In this book, we will show causal relationships by using arrows. Typically, we will use arrows that have solid lines to represent "causes more." We will use arrows that have dashed lines to represent "causes less," as in Figure 1.3.

The simplest logic that provides an explanation is in the form of "A causes B" statements because these statements are made of a single cause and a single effect. Examples include "after-school programs improve students' academic performance" and "after-school

FIGURE 1.3   ⬢   Causal Arrows Show How More of One Thing Cause More or Less of Something Else

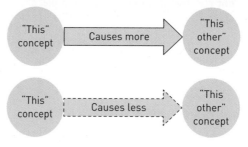

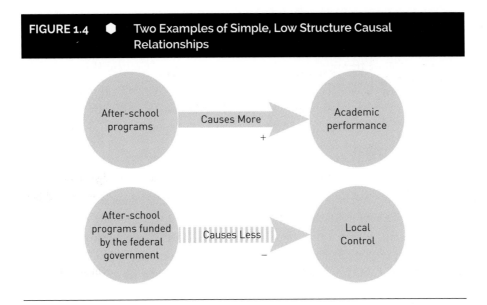

FIGURE 1.4 ⬡ **Two Examples of Simple, Low Structure Causal Relationships**

programs reduce local control of schools." Mapped out, these simple causal connections appear as two circles connected by an arrow as in Figure 1.4.

TRAVEL TIP

Note here that when we are talking about the dimension of logic, our focus is on the number of circles and what connections we see *between* the circles, not what is *inside* the circles.

TRAVEL TIP

One weakness of previous approaches to research was having too narrow a focus. Researchers would spend too much time, energy, and effort trying to decide if "A causes B." That is like having a map with only one road connecting two places of interest (and spending all your time studying that one road).

Instead of focusing our efforts on those small scraps of maps, we want to develop more useful explanations by creating maps with more circles and more causal arrows. For example, a broader study of after-school programs might include many things that contribute to school success, such as quality of teaching, attitudes toward school, dropout rates, and attendance.

Because focusing on the meaning and data may be distracting for our discussion on logic and structure, we will sometimes present maps that are more abstract. That helps us focus on what is *between* the circles rather than what is *inside* the circles.

For example, instead of saying what the concept "is," we write something like "Concept A" in the circle, as we did in Figure 1.5.

Notice here that we are using a more abstract representation—"Concept A" instead of, for example, "parental involvement." This abstract view helps you focus on the "structure" of the map—looking at the number of circles and the arrows connecting the circles—instead of looking at the concepts inside the circles.

It Sounds Good in Theory, but There Are Limits to Logic

While having multiple causal arrows is good, logic alone is not enough. An entertaining story, for example, might present many causal relationships and make us feel good, but it won't provide useful guidance for planning and action. For example, stories about Sherlock Holmes provide a rich, complex, and interconnected world where clues make sense and lead us to a better understanding of the crime, the motives, and (usually) the murderer. Indeed, one reason those stories have been so popular for so long is that they make sense. They provide logical explanations.

However, a highly logical fictional story does not provide useful direction for solving real problems. For highly useful knowledge maps in the real world, we need all three dimensions:

1. Concepts that are meaningful to the stakeholders

2. Data found by measuring the concepts

3. Logic supported by data that show causal connections

FIGURE 1.5 ⬡ Abstract Example of Concepts and Causal Connections

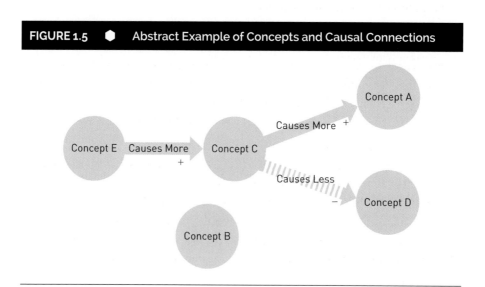

PUTTING THE DIMENSIONS TOGETHER

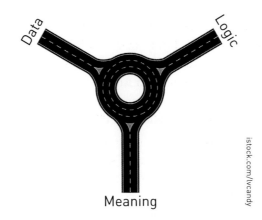

istock.com/Ivcandy

Many researchers and practitioners are calling for higher quality research for solving complex problems. However, they disagree on how to assess research quality. The most expensive and most time-consuming studies are not always the best quality.

We know that research is of higher quality when it is more useful for making decisions to solve complex problems. High quality research (among others)

- Helps managers make plans for effective action to reach meaningful goals

- Supports innovation

- Demonstrates the value of programs and services to funders and stakeholders

- Helps to shape effective public policy

- Provides useful direction for future studies

In this section, we will show how the three dimensions of knowledge (meaning, data, and logic) are interrelated and how you can evaluate each of them to be sure that you are conducting the highest quality research possible. In the following chapters, we will provide more advanced methods for evaluating research and building better knowledge maps.

You can see the interrelationship between meaning, data, and logic from a variety of perspectives. Stakeholders identify concepts that have meaning. Research provides data on those concepts and shows causal, logical relationships. By using knowledge maps, stakeholders find insights leading to effective decisions. Decisions lead to actions, including observable behavior. Reports based on those actions provide more data, raise awareness and understanding, and improve the quality of the map's logical structure. Most importantly, improving our maps helps to improve the human condition—the lives of people everywhere.

TRAVEL TIP

TRAVEL TIP

By using all three dimensions in your research, each piece helps you to avoid the limits of the others.

An important part of any research project is the ability to show that your efforts have resulted in a map that improves upon maps shown in previous research. A knowledge map helps you to show this on each of the three dimensions of knowledge.

- *Meaning*: Your knowledge map shows concepts and connections that are supported by more perspectives/stakeholders than previous maps.

- *Data*: The concepts and connections in your knowledge map are supported by better quality and quantity of data.

- *Logic*: Your knowledge map contains new concepts and connections (circles and arrows) not shown in previous maps.

An easy and effective way to evaluate the quality of existing research and to show the quality of your planned research is to use the Knowledge Appraisal Matrix (Table 1.1).

To use the matrix, start by considering a map, then mark or circle the appropriate boxes on the matrix that best reflect how well the study might meet each consideration.

You can use the matrix to evaluate the *results* of existing studies. You can also use the matrix to quickly evaluate (and show directions for improving) research projects that you are planning.

Test-Drive

Let's take a simple hypothetical example and walk through it one step at a time. Then we'll go into a more complex example.

In this scenario, a white paper published by a major think tank states the following:

> In an interview with a leading expert on after-school programs, sociologist Dr. Mary Smith told us, "My research provides the best answers to this important question. We just completed a major study in which we interviewed hundreds of teachers, faculty, and parents in New York City. Their priorities are to increase after-school programs because funding is available, students are important, and our society needs this kind of support."

Figure 1.6 shows a knowledge map of that story.

KNOWLEDGE APPRAISAL MATRIX

This matrix provides a quick-and-easy appraisal of research projects.

We will show you how to use the matrix in the Test-Drive section. You can use the matrix to compare research results for the following demonstration and class activity.

TABLE 1.1 ● Knowledge Appraisal Matrix

		LEVELS OF QUALITY		
DIMENSIONS OF KNOWLEDGE		**Level 1**	**Level 2**	**Level 3**
	1. Logic (arrows between concepts/ circles)	Map has one or no causal connections.	Map has more than one causal arrow connecting concepts.	Most or all concepts are connected by two or more arrows.
	2. Meaning (concepts within circles)	Concepts (in circles) on map are relevant to one knowledgeable person or stakeholder group.	Concepts on map are accepted as relevant to the topic by multiple stakeholder groups.	Concepts are accepted by general consensus across the entire field of study.
	3. Data (facts or information relating to concepts and arrows on the map)	Facts for one or more concepts have been found from one reliable study or research method.	Facts for multiple concepts have been found from multiple reliable studies or methods.	Most or all of the concepts have data from multiple reliable studies or methods.

Source: Adapted from Wright and Wallis (2017).

Download an electronic version of this handout at https://practicalmapping.com

Looking at the Knowledge Appraisal Matrix (Table 1.1), we can identify the level of quality for each dimension of knowledge.

First, looking at the dimension of *meaning*, you will notice that the researcher is a sociologist. That would count as one knowledgeable person. You will also notice that her research drew on insights from other groups (teachers, faculty, and parents). That is a fairly good number of stakeholder groups but does not include everyone who might be interested. Other stakeholder groups could be included (students, community members, elected officials, etc.). Research might also be done by other sociologists and by professionals in other fields

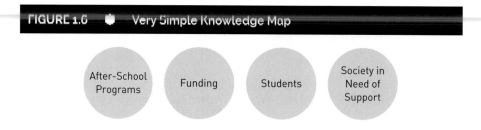

FIGURE 1.6   ⬡   Very Simple Knowledge Map

After-School Programs   Funding   Students   Society in Need of Support

(e.g., economists, psychologists, policy analysts). So we would rate that research at a Level 2 for meaning. To get to Level 3, we'd need to increase the number of stakeholder groups, which would probably result in an increase in the number of meaningful concepts. Also, we would need to share the map widely with the field and reach consensus that the map contains all meaningful concepts. We will look into stakeholders more in Chapter 2.

On the dimension of *data*, while the map is supported by interviews, there does not seem to be a lot of data. Although there may be more data that we haven't accessed, it seems that the researcher was only able to identify some top priorities. So we would rate the data as Level 1. The level of data could be improved by including more methods besides

TABLE 1.2   ⬡   Marked-Up Knowledge Appraisal Matrix

DIMENSIONS OF KNOWLEDGE		LEVELS OF QUALITY		
		Level 1	**Level 2**	**Level 3**
	1. Logic (arrows between concepts/circles)	Map has one or no causal connections.	Map has more than one causal arrow connecting concepts.	Most or all concepts are connected by two or more arrows.
	2. Meaning (concepts within circles)	Concepts (in circles) on map are relevant to one knowledgeable person or stakeholder group.	Concepts on map are accepted as relevant to the topic by multiple stakeholder groups.	Concepts are accepted by general consensus across the entire field of study.
	3. Data (facts or information relating to concepts on the map)	Facts for one or more concepts have been found from one reliable study or research method.	Facts for multiple concepts have been found from multiple reliable studies or methods.	Most or all of the concepts have data from multiple reliable studies or methods.

Source: Adapted from Wright and Wallis (2017).

interviews and by adding findings from more studies by researchers across disciplines (psychology, social work, etc.). We will further explore how to evaluate the quality and quantity of data in Chapters 3 and 4.

Last, let's look at logic. You will note that nothing in that white paper identifies a causal relationship. So for logic, we would rate this as Level 1. The logic can be improved by adding more causal connections between the concepts (if, of course, they are supported by data). We will explore logic further in Chapter 5.

Table 1.2 shows a Knowledge Appraisal Matrix that we've marked up to reflect the analysis.

You can see in the boxes to the right of each marked circle directions for improving the quality of each dimension of knowledge. Those boxes show what new research we could conduct that would improve understanding of and ability to address the big problems of the world.

CLASS ACTIVITY 1.1

Evaluating Evidence

In this section, we provide a hypothetical example, based on real events, to help you understand how to use mapping and to evaluate the quality of mapped research based on the three dimensions presented in this chapter. As you read the study, note how meaning, data, and logic are represented. Then, use the Knowledge Appraisal Matrix (Table 1.3) to evaluate the quality of the knowledge map (Figure 1.6). Afterwards, consider the questions for reflection and discussion and describe how you could conduct a better research project.

Background: A national debate has emerged over whether or not to continue funding for a billion-dollar program that provides support for after-school activities for children across the United States. Both sides present their perspectives. Opponents of the program say it should be cut because it doesn't have enough evidence to support its continued operation. Advocates for the program say it has enough evidence.

Your Role: A political organization hires you to conduct an independent analysis of the evidence from one recent study of the program. Your task is to read the following study and describe some of its strengths and weaknesses (your findings will be used to inform the organization's advocacy strategies).

The Study: In the study, the U.S. General Accountability Office (GAO, 2017) examined what was known about the effectiveness of after-school programs funded by the Department of Education's 21st Century Community Learning Centers (21st Century) grants program. GAO reviewed findings from a total of

(Continued)

(Continued)

ten studies—four state program evaluations and six other studies that examined student outcomes.

- Of the four state evaluations that GAO reviewed, three found that after-school programs had a positive effect on school-day attendance. One of the studies that GAO reviewed, which was a meta-analysis of 30 studies, also found a positive effect of after-school programs on school attendance.

- Two of the state evaluations found that after-school programs had a positive effect on school-day discipline (reducing disciplinary problems). The Texas evaluation showed that centers that taught students face-to-face rather than via computer and those that focused on general learning strategies rather than on specific subject area skills were associated with fewer disciplinary incidents.

- None of the 10 studies in GAO's review found consistently better scores in either math or reading in program participants' state assessments.

Figure 1.7 presents a map created from the key findings of the GAO study. In the figure, each arrow shows which of the study(ies) that GAO reviewed provided evidence for that arrow (more on this kind of presentation in Chapter 7).

FIGURE 1.7 ● Knowledge Map of GAO (2017) Study of 21st Century After-School Programs

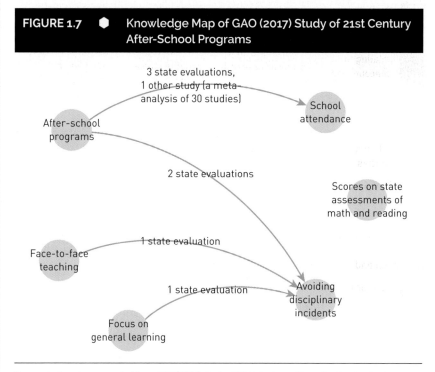

Source: Authors' map created from GAO (2017) study of 21st Century after school programs.

Instructions: Consider Figure 1.7 and circle the appropriate boxes on the Knowledge Appraisal Matrix on Table 1.3.

TABLE 1.3 ⬡ Knowledge Appraisal Matrix for You to Use in Evaluating the GAO 2017 Study on After-School Programs			
	LEVELS OF QUALITY		
DIMENSIONS OF KNOWLEDGE	**Level 1**	**Level 2**	**Level 3**
1. Logic (arrows between concepts/circles)	Map has one or no causal connections.	Map has more than one causal arrow connecting concepts.	Most or all concepts are connected by two or more arrows.
2. Meaning (concepts within circles)	Concepts (in circles) on map are relevant to one knowledgeable person or stakeholder group.	Concepts on map are accepted as relevant to the topic by multiple stakeholder groups.	Concepts are accepted by general consensus across the entire field of study.
3. Data (facts or information relating to concepts and arrows on the map)	Facts for one or more concepts have been found from one reliable study or research method.	Facts for multiple concept have been found from multiple reliable studies or methods.	Most or all of the concepts have data from multiple reliable studies or methods.

By evaluating the research of others and your own research, you can explain to your audience (client, employer, professor, etc.) the strengths, limitations, and opportunities for future research.

Download an electronic version of this handout at https://practicalmapping.com

STOP/REFLECTION/DISCUSSION

Reflect on and discuss the results of your assessment from Class Activity 1.1.

Compare your assessment with that of others in the class.

- What was similar or different between your assessments?
- If they were different in any way, why do you think they were different?
- What research could you conduct (that would be added to the research presented in Class Activity 1.1) to reach higher levels of knowledge on each dimension?

RIGHT OF WAY: RESEARCH ETHICS

In this section, we'll talk about ethics and why it is very important that we protect the participants of any research work we do. Simply put, if we fail in that task, the consequences can be terrible.

istock.com/3D_generator

A well-known example of an unethical study is the U.S. Public Health Service Syphilis Study at Tuskegee, Alabama. The study began in the hopes of being able to justify more treatment programs for African Americans. Local physicians were asked to withhold treatment from half the men in the study to provide a comparison with the men in the study who were receiving treatment.

In a terrible breach of ethics, the participants in the study were told that they were being treated for "bad blood" when, in truth, half the men in the study were not receiving the treatment needed for their condition.

The ethical failures became worse when the study continued even after penicillin became a widely used, effective treatment. Concerns were raised about the study; however, officials at the U.S. Centers for Disease Control and Prevention argued that the study was necessary. They also gained support from national medical societies. In 1972, news articles condemned the study and brought a halt to the personal and ethical tragedy. In 1974, a $10 million out-of-court settlement was reached. As we are writing this book, 12 offspring of the original participants continue to receive medical treatment as part of that settlement.

The significant human suffering and financial cost of those ethical breaches could have been avoided.

That study led to the creation of ethical guidelines and review boards to protect the rights and well-being of research participants. Still, the ethical thing to do in a specific research situation is often not obvious. Below are a few principles of ethical research that are relevant to many research situations. The Further Exploration section at the end of this chapter lists some resources for more information on research ethics.

Reading and being familiar with ethical guidelines relevant to your research focus will help you be prepared to handle ethical dilemmas that you may face.

- **Avoiding harm from research.** As with the Tuskegee Syphilis experiment, it is unethical to withhold a needed and beneficial program or service from participants for research purposes.

- **Informed consent.** The key idea for ethical research is that the subjects must be protected from harm. Part of this includes providing information to potential participants (and their parents or guardians, when applicable) about the study, its goals, and all risks and benefits that might be associated with it. Be sure the research participants know what to expect—and that they know that they can stop at any time. Their safety is more important than your research!

> **DEFINITION**
>
> **Research participants** are the people in your study. They are the people who you interview, who take part in focus groups, and who you collect other data from. They may or may not also be stakeholders.

- **Research utility.** Be sure that your research will be beneficial—the time and expertise of your participants is very valuable.

- **Cultural responsiveness.** You should always be sensitive to the cultural norms of the participants. Make sure your questions and concerns are culturally relevant to them. Use language that respects individuals and their culture. To make sure that everyone can participate, you may need to translate materials into other languages. You also may need to make materials available in formats that are accessible to people with disabilities and people with low literacy.

- **Confidentiality.** Researchers should not share data without permission from the client and the research participants who provided the data. Researchers should have access to only the data they need to conduct the study.

- **Privacy.** Another part of ethical research means protecting the privacy of the research participants. This means keeping their names and other identifying information confidential (unless they make an informed choice and give permission to share it). If someone might read your study and make a good guess as to who the participants were and/or if they might be able to attribute a particular comment to a specific individual, then you need to provide more anonymity. A common approach is to say "several people said" rather than mentioning specific interview participants. Protecting research participants' privacy also means not collecting more private information than you need to conduct your analysis. It also means protecting data about participants from being stolen or accidentally seen by others.

- **Honestly reporting research results.** Honest reporting means more than not falsifying your data. It also means reporting results for all the questions you explored and not suppressing results that are not what you expected. When results are not what you expected, that means opportunity for learning and for strengthening the program.

- **Authorship.** When reporting your research results, the authorship should accurately reflect who contributed to the study.

The American Evaluation Association provides five *Evaluators' Ethical Guiding Principles*, available on its website: https://www.eval.org/p/cm/ld/fid=51. Below is a summary; we encourage you to explore further.

1. **Systematic Inquiry:** Evaluators conduct data-based inquiries that are thorough, methodical, and contextually relevant.

2. **Competence:** Evaluators provide skilled professional services to stakeholders.

3. **Integrity:** Evaluators behave with honesty and transparency in order to ensure the integrity of the evaluation.

4. **Respect for People:** Evaluators honor the dignity, well-being, and self-worth of individuals and acknowledge the influence of culture within and across groups.

5. **Common Good and Equity:** Evaluators strive to contribute to the common good and advancement of an equitable and just society.

Institutional Review Boards

Institutional review boards (IRBs) are an important resource for protecting the rights of research participants. Many studies conducted by smaller organizations do not use IRBs. However, some grant-funded research projects require them, and they can be useful when you are dealing with studies that raise ethical challenges that require outside review.

DEFINITION

An *institutional review board* (IRB) is a formal group (generally part of a university or research organization) that sets standards and procedures for ethical research. IRBs evaluate research proposals to maintain high ethical standards for the safety of the participants.

Your institution's IRB. If you are a student or working as part of a university or large institution, you might have an IRB that sets standards and procedures for ethical research. You should contact them for more information and to see if they want to review your research project before you begin. If you (or your institution) do not have an IRB, you may be able to work with an IRB at a local college or university or a private IRB company.

Private IRBs. You can search for private IRBs at https://ohrp.cit.nih.gov/search/search.aspx?styp=bsc. The Further Exploration section at the end of this chapter provides additional resources on research ethics that can assist you whether or not you are working with an IRB.

Community IRB

A number of community–based organizations and community–academic partnerships have formed community-based research review processes (Shore et al., 2015). Some are U.S. federally recognized IRBs that approve, monitor, and review research involving human participants while others are advisory bodies. All of them routinely examine issues that institution-based IRBs typically do not, such as risks and benefits of the research for communities and cultural appropriateness of the research design.

DEFINITION

A *community IRB* is an official group that evaluates proposals for community-scale research to reduce the risk to human participants and increase the benefits to the community.

Chapter 1 Key Points

- The "wicked problems" of the world are solvable.

- Too often, applied research and program evaluation are inefficient because they are producing scraps of maps.

- New approaches to research show how we can improve the usefulness and impact of our research by evaluating (and improving) our knowledge maps on the three dimensions of meaning, data, and logic.

- Ethics comes first.

Frequently Asked Questions

Q: Why the focus on causal logic instead of Toulmin's logic of "claim, evidence, warrant, support, etc."?

A: There are many types of logic, including inductive, deductive, and (what is sometimes called) Toulminian logic (named after the person who formalized the process). While these approaches to logic seem to have worked well for advancing a revolution in the natural sciences, they have not proved useful for revolutionizing the social/behavioral sciences. So instead, this book is focused on causal logic because it is even more fundamental to scientific understanding.

(Continued)

(Continued)

Q: What if I want to do a study where the participants/subjects are unaware that they are being studied. Do I have to tell the truth if they ask me why I'm watching them?

A: For any kind of questionable research situation, the simple answer is to consult your IRB. See the following section for more resources on research ethics. You want your research to be so useful that it makes for happy headlines—not lawsuits!

Q: To narrow the gap between researchers and practitioners, could I be both?

A: Yes indeed! You should be careful, however, about potential conflicts of interest. Remember, there are benefits to having external perspectives—so we encourage collaboration because it provides different perspectives to deepen your knowledge and counter your biases.

Q: How is knowledge mapping different from concept mapping?

A: Some concept maps show how concepts are related to one another; however, they do not always show *causal* relationships. Without causal relationships, maps are not as useful for decision makers. For example, cats, mice, and wheat are concepts that are related to a greater or lesser degree. When you identify how they are causally related, you can better understand what goes on between them!

Q: How is knowledge mapping different from simulation modelling?

A: A computer simulation model is a hypothetical world reflecting (to a greater or lesser extent) a topic of study. You can adjust variables to see how those changes might lead to desired results— such as achieving program goals. While simulations provide useful insights, they also suffer from some limitations, depending on the assumptions of the programmers creating the models. They are generally limited to quantified data, while knowledge maps may include unquantified data. Knowledge maps may be used as guides for the creation of simulation models. With better maps, you could expect to create a better model.

Further Exploration

In this chapter, we've covered three basic dimensions of knowledge to help you better understand and resolve the wicked problems of the world. For those bold explorers who would like to learn more, this section provides additional information. For each section of the chapter, you will find sources on the foundational research and insights supporting this chapter. We've placed this information in this separate section for two reasons. First, so that it is here for those readers who want to explore the subject in greater depth. Second, to make other parts of the chapter easy to read.

Many of these publications are available for free online. Some may require a fee to access. If you are a student or affiliated with a university, you may be able to access these at no charge through your institution's library.

The Wicked Complexity of Problems Facing the World

The world is facing incredibly complex problems—just look at the news! For deeper understanding take a look at the following:

Camillus, J. C. (2008). Strategy as a wicked problem. *Harvard Business Review, 86*(5), 98. Retrieved from http://www.reshape.se/files/5914/2071/1790/STRATEGY_AS_A_WICKED_PROBLEM.pdf

Rittel H., & Webber M. M. (1973). Planning problems are wicked. *Polity, 4*, 155–169. Retrieved from http://www.ask-force.org/web/Discourse/Rittel-Dilemmas-General-Theory-Planning-1973.pdf

The Explosion of Information

There is an unbelievably large amount of information on the web and in our daily lives. Yet, science has not been very good about finding the "right" data or integrating the data that we do have.

Marr, B. (2018). How much data do we create every day? The mind-blowing stats everyone should read. *Forbes.* Retrieved from: https://www.forbes.com/sites/bernardmarr/2018/05/21/how-much-data-do-we-create-every-day-the-mind-blowing-stats-everyone-should-read/#b6400cc60ba9

Russom, P. (2011). Big data analytics. *TDWI best practices report, fourth quarter, 19*, 40. *TDWI Research.* Retrieved from https://vivomente.com/wp-content/uploads/2016/04/big-data-analytics-white-paper.pdf

The Disconnect Between Research and Practice

A lot of research is going on, but the results of that research too often do not provide the knowledge that decision makers need.

Carden, F. (2017). Building evaluation capacity to address problems of equity. *New Directions for Evaluation, 2017*(154), 115–125. Retrieved from http://onlinelibrary.wiley.com/doi/10.1002/ev.20245/full

Dijkers, M. (2009). When the best is the enemy of the good: The nature of research evidence used in systematic reviews and guidelines. *NCDDR Task Force on Systematic Review and Guidelines. Austin, TX: SEDL.* Retrieved from http://ktdrr.org/ktlibrary/articles_pubs/ncddrwork/tfsr_best/

Moat, K. A., Lavis, J. N., Wilson, M. G., Røttingen, J. A., & Bärnighausen, T. (2013). Twelve myths about systematic reviews for health system policymaking rebutted. *Journal of Health Services Research & Policy, 18*(1), 44–50. Retrieved from https://www.researchgate.net/profile/John_Lavis/publication/235422986_Twelve_myths_about_systematic_reviews_for_health_system_policymaking/links/54a6dd840cf257a6360aa737.pdf

Rahman, A., & Applebaum, R. (2010). What's all this about evidence-based practice? The roots, the controversies, and why it matters. *Generations, 34*(1), 6–12. Retrieved from http://www.ingentaconnect.com/content/asag/gen/2010/00000034/00000001/art00001

Schorr, L., & Gopa, S. (2016). Broadening the evidence base without "defining evidence down." *Stanford Social Innovation Review.* Retrieved from https://ssir.org/articles/entry/broadening_the_evidence_base_without_defining_evidence_down

Smyth, K. F., & Schorr, L. B. (2009). *A lot to lose: A call to rethink what constitutes "evidence" in finding social interventions that work.* Malcolm Wiener Center for Social Policy Working Paper Series. Harvard Kennedy School. Retrieved from https://www.hks.harvard.edu/research-insights/research-publications

Stern, G. E., Stame, N., Mayne, J., Forss, K., Davies, R., & Befani, B. (2012). *Broadening the range of designs and methods for impact evaluations.* Retrieved from https://www.oecd.org/derec/50399683.pdf

(Continued)

(Continued)

The Low Rates of Success in Using Data for Making Decisions

As a result of insufficient research methods, important decisions rarely lead to the desired results. National policies and organizational changes seem to succeed only about 20 percent of the time.

Dekkers, R. (2008). Adapting organizations: The instance of business process re-engineering. *Systems Research and Behavioral Science: The Official Journal of the International Federation for Systems Research, 25*(1), 45–66. Retrieved from http://onlinelibrary.wiley.com/doi/10.1002/sres.857/full

Hill, T., & Westbrook, R. (1997). SWOT analysis: It's time for a product recall. *Long Range Planning, 30*(1), 46–52. Retrieved from http://www.ftms.edu.my/images/Document/MOD001074%20-%20Strategic%20Management%20Analysis/WK6_SR_MOD001074_Hill_Westbrook_1997.pdf

Light, P. C. (2016). The 2015 John Gaus Award Lecture: Vision+ Action = Faithful Execution: Why government daydreams and how to stop the cascade of breakdowns that now haunts it. *PS: Political Science & Politics, 49*(1), 5–20. Retrieved from https://doi.org/10.1017/S1049096515001110

MacIntosh, R., & MacLean, D. (1999). Conditioned emergence: A dissipative structures approach to transformation. *Strategic Management Journal, 20*(4), 297–316. Retrieved from http://eprints.gla.ac.uk/24584/1/24584s.pdf

Smith, M. E. (2003). Changing an organisation's culture: Correlates of success and failure. *Leadership & Organization Development Journal, 24*(5), 249–261. Retrieved from http://www.emeraldinsight.com/doi/abs/10.1108/01437730310485752

Unanticipated Consequences From Policies and Programs

Duit, A., & Galaz, V. (2008). Governance and complexity—emerging issues for governance theory. *Governance, 21*(3), 311–335.

Rosegrant, M. (2000). *Transforming the rural Asian economy: The unfinished revolution* (Vol. 1). Asian Development Bank.

Schuler, S. R., Hashemi, S. M., & Badal, S. H. (1998). Men's violence against women in rural Bangladesh: Undermined or exacerbated by microcredit programmes? *Development in Practice, 8*(2), 148–157.

Human-Centered Design, Complexity, and Systems Thinking in Research and Evaluation

New ways of thinking about our world are leading to new insights into how we conduct research—and how we apply the results of that research to collaborative decision-making.

Christie, C. A., Lemire, S., & Inkelas, M. (2017). Understanding the similarities and distinctions between improvement science and evaluation. *New Directions for Evaluation, 2017*(153), 11–21. Retrieved from http://onlinelibrary.wiley.com/doi/10.1002/ev.20237/full

Lopez, A., & Lam, C. Y. (2016, February 21). Program design TIG Week: Angelina Lopez and Chi Yan Lam on the rise of design. [AEA365 blog post] Retrieved from American Evaluation Association website: http://aea365.org/blog/program-design-tig-week-angelina-lopez-and-chi-yan-lam-on-the-rise-of-design/

National Center for Biotechnology Information, https://www.ncbi.nlm.nih.gov/pmc/articles/PMC4573926/

National Implementation Research Network, https://nirn.fpg.unc.edu/learn-implementation/implementation-science-defined

National Institute of Health Fogarty International Center, https://www.fic.nih.gov/ResearchTopics/Pages/ImplementationScience.aspx

Richard, R. (2009). *The logic model and systems thinking: Can they co-exist.* PowerPoint presentation at the annual meeting of the American Evaluation Association in Orlando, FL. Retrieved from http://comm.eval.org/coffee_break_webinars/viewdocument/the-logic-model-and

Rogers, P. J. (2008). Using programme theory to evaluate complicated and complex aspects of interventions. *Evaluation, 14*(1), 29–48. Retrieved from http://journals.sagepub.com/doi/pdf/10.1177/1356389007084674

Rohanna, K. (2017). Breaking the "adopt, attack, abandon" cycle: A case for improvement science in K–12 education. *New Directions for Evaluation, 2017*(153), 65–77. Retrieved from http://onlinelibrary.wiley.com/doi/10.1002/ev.20233/full

Woolcock, M. (2013). Using case studies to explore the external validity of 'complex' development interventions. *Evaluation, 19*(3), 229–248. Retrieved from https://www.econstor.eu/bitstream/10419/93693/1/769160964.pdf

Three Dimensions of Knowledge

To understand knowledge and how to better apply it, we look at three dimensions (or "worlds") of knowledge and understanding theoretical models.

Kuhn, T. (1970). *The structure of scientific revolutions,* Chicago, IL: The University of Chicago Press. Retrieved from http://www.nemenmanlab.org/~ilya/images/c/c5/Kuhn-1970.pdf

Popper, K. (2002). *The logic of scientific discovery,* New York, NY: Routledge Classics. Retrieved from https://books.google.com/books?hl=en&lr=&id=LWSBAgAAQBAJ&oi=fnd&pg=PP1&dq=Popper+K.+(2002)+The+logic+of+scientific+discovery,+New+York:+Routledge+Classics.&ots=pzDmZ30HdL&sig=wQRUP9EJ_GazpXjHqh82wiUxdHo#v=onepage&q&f=false

Wallis, S. E. (2008). Validation of theory: Exploring and reframing Popper's worlds. *Integral Review, 4*(2), 71–91. Retrieved from http://integral-review.org/documents/Wallis,%20Validation%20of%20Theory,%20Vol.%204%20No.%202.pdf

Wallis, S. E. (2016). The science of conceptual systems: A progress report. *Foundations of Science, 21*(4), 579–602. Retrieved from https://link.springer.com/article/10.1007/s10699-015-9425-z

Wright, B., & Wallis, S. E. (2017, March 31). How good is your evidence? *Stanford Social Innovation Review (SSIR).* Retrieved from https://ssir.org/articles/entry/how_good_is_your_evidence

Techniques for and Practical Examples of Knowledge Mapping and Logic Models

Recent advances in knowledge mapping, developed by the authors of this book, have provided easier ways to make maps that are more useful to practitioners.

Fotiyeva, I., Wright, B., Lewis, L, & Wallis, S. E. (2015). *A new model for engaging under-represented high school students in STEM using popular media and technology.* Poster presented at the 2015 American Evaluation Association conference, Chicago, IL. Retrieved from http://comm.eval.org/viewdocument/a-new-model-for-enga

GAO (U.S. General Accountability Office). (2012). *Designing Evaluations.* Retrieved from https://www.gao.gov/assets/590/588146.pdf

(Continued)

(Continued)

Houston, D., & Wright, B. (2017). Re-structuring evaluation findings into useful knowledge. *Journal of MultiDisciplinary Evaluation*, 13(29). Retrieved from http://journals.sfu.ca/jmde/index.php/jmde_1/article/view/481/436

Wallis, S. E. (2013). How to choose between policy proposals: A simple tool based on systems thinking and complexity theory. *E:CO-Emergence: Complexity & Organization, 15*(3), 94–120. Retrieved from https://search.proquest.com/openview/b728a5140ab185e8533d6b88c573e7ae/1?pq-origsite=gscholar&cbl=28203

Wallis, S. E. (2014). Existing and emerging methods for integrating theories within and between disciplines. *Organisational Transformation and Social Change, 11*(1), 3–24. Retrieved from http://www.tandfonline.com/doi/abs/10.1179/1477963313Z.00000000023

Wallis, S. E., & Frese, K. (2017). *Strategic planning: A new state of the art*. [White paper] ASK MATT Solutions & TeamLMI. Retrieved from https://www.researchgate.net/publication/319220087_Strategic_Planning_A_New_State_of_the_Art

Wallis, S. E., & Wright, B. (2014). *The science of conceptual systems: Its history and usefulness for improved decision-making and organizational success*. [White paper] Retrieved from http://www.meaningfulevidence.com

Wallis, S. E., & Wright, B. (2015). *Strategic knowledge mapping: The co-creation of useful knowledge*. Paper presented at the Association for Business Simulation and Experiential Learning (ABSEL) 42nd annual conference in Las Vegas, NV. Retrieved from https://journals.tdl.org/absel/index.php/absel/article/viewFile/2899/2850

Wright, B. (2016, April 27). Getting to evidence-based policy: Three perspectives. *Stanford Social Innovation Review*. Retrieved from https://ssir.org/articles/entry/getting_to_evidence_based_policy_three_perspectives

Practical Example: After-School Programs

Brown, E. March 16, 2017. Trump budget casualty: After-school programs for 1.6 million kids. Most are poor. *The Washington Post*. http://www.washingtonpost.com/local/education/trump-budget-casualty-afterschool-programs-for-16-million-kids-most-are-poor/2017/03/16/78802430-0a6f-11e7-b77c-0047d15a24e0_story.html

Fessler, P. May 1, 2017. Trump's Budget Proposal Threatens Funding For Major After-School Program. *NPR*. http://www.npr.org/2017/05/01/526436087/trumps-budget-proposal-threatens-funding-for-major-after-school-program

Robinson, G., & Fenwick, L. (2007). *Afterschool programs as an oasis of hope for black parents in four cities*. Washington, DC: The Black Alliance for Educational Options. http://www.baeo.org/files/mottSummary.pdf

U.S. General Accountability Office (GAO). (2017, April). *Education Needs to Improve Oversight of Its 21st Century Program*. https://www.gao.gov/products/GAO-17-400

Right of Way: Research Ethics

We cannot emphasize enough the importance of maintaining high ethical standards. Here are some additional resources to help you maintain yours!

American Evaluation Association. (2004). *Guiding principles for evaluators.* Retrieved from http://www .eval.org/p/cm/ld/fid=51

Centers for Disease Control and Prevention. (2015). *U.S. Public Health Service syphilis study at Tuskegee.* (Web page). Retrieved from https://www.cdc.gov/tuskegee/index.html

The Collaborative Institutional Training Initiative (CITI Program) provides online research and ethics compliance training. Learners must affiliated with an institution that has an organizational sub-scription or pay the course fee. https://about.citiprogram.org/en/homepage/

Free Resources for Program Evaluation and Social Research Methods website. (2016). Protecting the public in research (web page). Retrieved from http://gsociology.icaap.org/methods/protect.html

Lewis, L., & Wright, B. (2014). *On the road to ethical research.* Meaningful Evidence. Retrieved from http://meaningfulevidence.com/wp-content/uploads/2014/12/On-the-Road-to-Ethical-Research -October-27-1.pdf

Resnik, D. B. (2011). What is ethics in research & why is it important. *National Institute of Environmental Health Sciences*, 1–10. Retrieved from https://www.niehs.nih.gov/research/resources/bioethics/ whatis/index.cfm?links=false

Shore, N., Ford, A., Wat, E., Brayboy, M., Isaacs, M. L., Park, A., . . . Seifer, S. D. (2015). Community-based review of research across diverse community contexts: Key characteristics, critical issues, and future directions. *American Journal of Public Health, 105*(7), 1294–1301. Retrieved from https:// www.ncbi.nlm.nih.gov/pmc/articles/PMC4463398/

Wager, E., & Kleinert, S. (2011). *Responsible research publication: International standards for authors* [A position statement developed at the 2nd World Conference on Research Integrity, Singapore, July 22–24, 2010]. In T. Mayer & N. Steneck (Eds.), *Promoting research integrity in a global environment* (Chap. 50, pp. 309–316). Singapore: Imperial College Press/World Scientific Publishing. Retrieved from http://publicationethics.org/files/International%20standards_authors_for%20website_11_ Nov_2011.pdf

Wright, B., & Lewis, L. (2014). Ethics anyone? A guide to ethics in social research. Meaningful Evidence. Retrieved from http://meaningfulevidence.com/wp-content/uploads/2014/12/Ethics-Anyone_ -October-27.pdf

MEANING

A Collaborative Mapping Approach

Photo Courtesy of Samantha Knight and NASAGA
(North American Simulation and Gaming Association).

Chapter 1 introduced three dimensions of practical knowledge maps for solving complex social issues. This chapter delves into the dimension of *meaning*. Here, we detail a collaborative technique to create meaningful maps for guiding research and action. In this chapter, you'll discover the following:

- How to work with groups to create meaningful maps

- Situations when collaborative mapping is useful

- Ways to analyze your collaborative map for planning and action

- Approaches for tracking progress and continual improvement

THE ROAD AHEAD

Collaboration is critical for effective research and for positive social change. In this chapter, we show how students, researchers, and other agents of social change can make more useful knowledge maps (KMs) for classroom learning and collaboration in the field.

DEFINITION

Collaboration is working purposefully with others toward goals that are shared (all have the same goal) and/or goals that are interrelated (different but mutually supporting).

As we introduced in Chapter 1, the three dimensions of knowledge are data, meaning, and logic. In this chapter, we will focus on meaning—specifically, how to use collaborative mapping to map out stakeholders' shared understanding of the situation at hand.

Every map-creation session starts with stakeholders choosing a *topic* for their map. That topic is what the focus of the map will be within the broader context or situation. For example, within the broader context of a community, the stakeholders might want to focus on a large construction project that has been proposed. By choosing a specific topic, stakeholders may understand it more clearly.

Stakeholders are those people with a shared interest in an activity. For example, most of your neighbors would be interested in a large construction project proposed for your neighborhood because the project will have an impact on their lives. Some might be in favor of it while others may be opposed to the project—but either way, they are stakeholders. In social programs, stakeholders include the people served, program managers, staff, volunteers, community members, funders, partnering organizations, and others. By including more stakeholders, representing more stakeholder groups, you can make maps that are more useful for guiding decision-making and action.

As discussed in Chapter 1, *concepts* are held in our minds and relate to things in the real world. For example, cars exist in the real world, but in our minds, we hold only the concept of cars.

Stakeholders use concepts to talk about and understand their situation, such as "retail shops in the neighborhood," "job opportunities," "traffic congestion," and "noise." When making a map, participants write those concepts on cards and place them on a table where everyone can see them. They also add causal arrows that connect those concepts showing how change occurs. For example, more retail shops in the neighborhood will create more job opportunities, more traffic congestion, and more noise.

By adding more concepts and causal connections to the map, the stakeholders gain a better understanding of their topic and so are able to make better decisions to reach interdependent goals. That map may be understood as a kind of logic model for program planning and program evaluation. It can also be understood as a kind of theory for research. It may also be understood as a kind of strategic plan for businesses. Collaborative knowledge mapping shows what concepts stakeholders find meaningful to the situation (Figure 2.1).

Collaboration Over Consensus

An important part of your facilitating the mapping process is to help stakeholders discover how their perspectives and interests are interconnected. In doing so, you and they will create a knowledge map that is more than the sum of its parts. It is not necessary to get everyone to agree on something. That is because each person and each group has a different part to play and a different way of understanding the world. By understanding how their activities and goals are interconnected, stakeholders learn how to help themselves and help the community as a whole.

As they create maps, each stakeholder learns to see how their part of the map is connected to others. That expanded view will help people to more easily identify opportunities

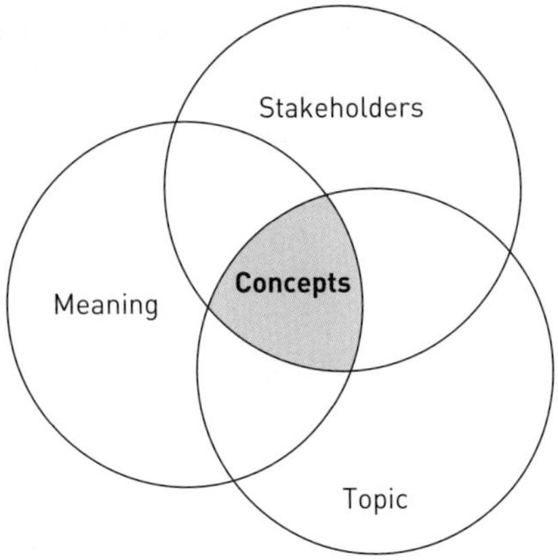

FIGURE 2.1   ●   Concepts Link Stakeholders, Meaning, and Topic

for collaboration and, by using the KM, how each person can reach their individual and collective goals.

Participants typically show a high level of agreement during these knowledge mapping sessions. They build trust between each other with each small piece that they place on the map. At the end, participants have trust in the map as a whole and in their fellow participants because they were part of the process of the map's construction.

Each participant from each stakeholder group places concepts that are meaningful to them and relevant to the topic. As more concepts are added to the map, the overall level of meaning grows for the KM as a whole.

DEFINITION

A *facilitator* is a person who guides conversations, interactions, and activities within and between groups to help them more easily reach new and useful insights and directions for action.

Relevance

Any group of stakeholders will choose a number of concepts that they decide are most relevant to the topic of their map.

For simplicity, when you facilitate the creation of a map, you will likely start with one group on one topic. Keep in mind, however, that there is a range of organizational options at this level. You might also have multiple groups, all addressing the same topic but each creating a separate map. That can be useful for comparing perspectives. You might also have multiple groups create maps with each group addressing a different topic. That approach may be useful for addressing multiple interrelated topics. Whether they are looking at the same topic or different topics, any two groups will build their maps using different concepts. However, their resulting maps will often overlap—where both groups agree that the same concepts are meaningful (Figure 2.2). That overlap may be used to help bring stakeholder groups closer together (more on that later).

FIGURE 2.2 ⬡ Concepts at the Overlap Between Stakeholder Groups

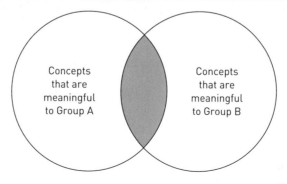

Concepts that are meaningful to Group A

Concepts that are meaningful to Group B

For example, working with a national organization for community development, one group was focused on the internal processes of the organization itself, while another delved into the broader field of community development organizations. A third group mapped interactions among neighborhood residents, while the fourth looked at processes at the neighborhood level. Each group learned from their separate map and from the maps of others. Because all of their maps included concepts that were of relevance to the other groups, it was easier to see the connections between their areas of interest.

In this chapter, we will cover how to create maps with groups of people. They may be researchers (more on that in Chapter 6), organizational leaders, community members, or others with knowledge of and interest in the topic.

Better maps include more concepts and connections that are more meaningful to the group. A better map is more useful to those groups as they plan their actions to reach their goals.

TRAVEL TIP

An important long-term goal for improving maps is to gain consensus about the usefulness and applicability of the map across the field of research and practice that is relevant to the topic. That means including more stakeholders, gaining agreements on small parts, using the maps for planning and action, and learning from the results.

USES FOR COLLABORATIVE MAPPING

Researchers and practitioners have used collaborative approaches to knowledge mapping in a wide variety of organizations for many purposes (Figure 2.3). For example, a team of policy researchers in Germany used mapping to better understand agriculture and economics in developing nations. Those maps were also useful for showing where more research is needed and enabling leaders to understand and improve the way their nations work for the betterment of all people.

TRAVEL TIP

When a person works to create something, they put something of themselves into it. A kind of bond—a sense of ownership—is created. When stakeholders create a map, that sense of ownership helps to avoid negative dynamics. The map holders are more focused on the topic, feel more hope about the future, and are more interested in changing themselves and their world. In contrast, people may be less certain when they are given a map (or sold one) that was made by others.

Leaders of various departments for a U.S. nationwide organization devoted to community development met to collaboratively map their understanding of how communities

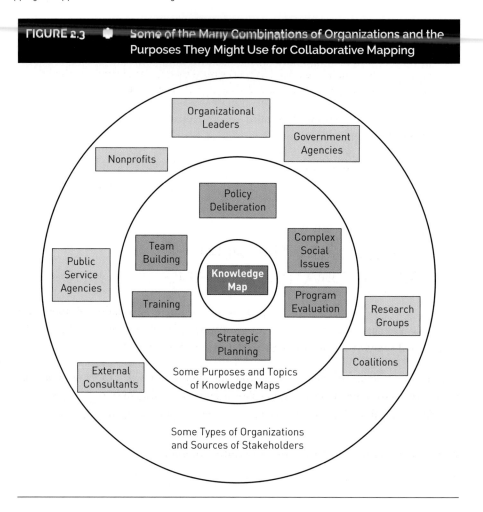

FIGURE 2.3 Some of the Many Combinations of Organizations and the Purposes They Might Use for Collaborative Mapping

change. The resulting map showed leverage points for change—helping them to improve their organizational efficiency. The board of directors for a small nonprofit in California focused on historic preservation used mapping to better understand their internal operations and how their organization interfaced with the community.

In short, collaborative KMs provide a state-of-the-art approach to planning and knowledge generation that is both fast and effective.

STOP/REFLECTION/DISCUSSION

Choose one topic/problem that is most relevant to your community, such as crime, pollution, or lack of economic growth. The problem has existed for so long that nobody knows when it started and why. Everyone is saying that someone should do something. Some people think they have a simple answer, but people have different views of what the answer is. This suggests different understandings of the causes of the problem. But despite the efforts of concerned residents and elected officials, the situation is slowly growing worse instead of better. Reflect or discuss in a small group:

- What organizations and individuals in your community might have an interest in the topic?
- Which groups and individuals would you bring together for a collaborative knowledge mapping process?
- How might they (and the community) benefit from such a process?

MILESTONES ON THE ROAD TO COLLABORATIVE MAPPING

This section provides a step-by-step guide to the collaborative creation of knowledge maps—including choosing a topic (focus), gathering stakeholder groups, facilitating the process, and applying the maps to understand and resolve real-world issues.

The process we describe here is generic. You can apply it to a wide variety of situations, such as any of the types of organizations shown above. It involves four stages: (1) preparation, (2) the collaborative mapping session, (3) from mapping to action, and (4) road trip.

Stage 1. Preparation for the Mapping Session

To prepare for a successful collaborative mapping session you will

- Choose a map topic
- Invite stakeholders
- Arrange logistics

As you can imagine, choosing a topic and inviting stakeholders are closely intertwined. Every group will want to focus on topics that are of interest to its members. Similarly, different groups will have different areas of expertise that will be more applicable for understanding different topics. Here, we will take them one at a time.

Choose a Map Topic

Before you begin a mapping project, you will need to choose a topic for your map. There are several ways to do this. If you are conducting research for a program evaluation, the topic may be assigned by your supervisor (if you are conducting an in-house evaluation) or your client (if you are an evaluation consultant). If you are facilitating or researching a community development program, your topic may be chosen by a committee and/or the consensus of community groups. Those topics might be something like "affordable housing in the community" or "building the local economy." As a professional, you might also suggest topics to stakeholders—good directions that they could explore.

Another approach is to survey stakeholder groups to find a range of possible topics. Each group will be interested in different issues. And each may benefit from a better understanding of those issues.

You might begin by surveying each department in an organization to find out what issues are important to them. One of those issues can become their topic. If your survey reveals one topic of concern to all departments, then each may create a map based on that one topic. That will reveal the perspectives of each group in a way that will likely overlap with the perspectives of the other groups (leading to new insights for collaboration). For example, consider a community health care organization such as a hospital with outlying clinics. The human resources department is struggling with hiring issues, the supply department is dealing with rising drug prices, the board of directors is concerned about expanding services to additional parts of the community, and so on. Each of these is a stakeholder group with their own specific concerns. Each group might choose a different topic based on those concerns, or they may create a map together. With a more collaborative map, new and innovative solutions may emerge by mapping the many perspectives.

In short, the topic of the map is any general area that the stakeholders are seeking to better understand.

Sometimes, choosing a topic can be confused with choosing the concepts that go on the map. For example, the topic of a map might be "economic improvement"; so people might place concepts on the map like "taxes," "jobs," "tourism," "business incubator," "investment," and so on. On the other hand, you might create a map with the topic of (for example) "business incubator," which would include topics such as "training," "expert advice," "venture capital," and so on. And there may be overlaps between the topic of economic improvement and business incubator. So, some of the best advice is to avoid over-thinking—and just invite the stakeholders to start mapping.

Invite Stakeholders

In collaboration with evaluation funders and your evaluation team, you should identify those groups who may be interested in the topic. Categories of stakeholders often include

- *People you intend to benefit.* People who you want to help, such as community members or program participants, can provide valuable insights from their first-hand experience, yet too often, they are left out of efforts to understand and act on issues that affect them.

- *People next to them.* Advocates, family members, and other representatives are often important to include because they also have experience interacting with service systems on behalf of their family members, and their lives are also impacted by your activities.

- *People near you.* Other local organizations that are addressing related issues, funders, and policymakers add useful perspectives. Their insights help explain the context of your map's topic. Plus, including them in the mapping process increases your chances for getting buy-in for carrying out then map's recommendations.

- *Your own people.* Be sure to include a variety of perspectives from people within your organization who bring experience and knowledge of the topic of the knowledge map—such as managers, staff, volunteers, board members, and consultants.

You might begin with a sponsoring organization that has an interest in addressing a specific topic. From there, other groups and/or individuals might be brought together—by direct invitation or by referral. For example, a regional nonprofit focused on energy conservation invited a range of related organizations and individuals to a mapping session. Those included other nonprofit organizations, government agencies, concerned citizens, and for-profit corporations.

For your project, you can find stakeholders in a variety of ways. Through Internet searches, contacting elected officials, or asking people you know to tell you who they know—everyone is connected with someone!

Community Meeting!

Let's learn from each other how to improve our neighborhood!

- Economic Development
- Parks and Nature
- Public Safety
- And More

Saturday—9:45 a.m. to 3:30 p.m.

Your organization may collaborate with community members to create a list of topics. Then, convene a meeting and invite members of the community—as in this sample poster.

It is worth noting that people may be more comfortable (and more willing to participate fully) when they are engaged with people of their own culture. If cultural differences are too great, they may have difficulty understanding one another (a language barrier may also be an issue). In those cases, it may be a good idea to hold separate mapping sessions for each group (you can then integrate the resulting maps, and you may be able to bring the groups together to discuss the integrated map).

Within stakeholder groups, you can consider including (and inviting) stakeholder *subgroups*. For example, if you are working on creating a map with a board of directors (representing the organization as a whole), you might also suggest creating a map with the top management team, the middle management team, supervisors, and line workers. Each of these may be seen as a stakeholder subgroup, and each level will bring in different perspectives. For another example, if you are creating a map with members of a community at the "grassroots" level, you might consider creating a map with community leaders.

The general rule here is to invite more stakeholders because mapping their diverse perspectives will lead to a more useful and comprehensive understanding of their shared situation. In order for that mapping session to be successful, it is important to consider the logistics.

Arrange Logistics

In addition to choosing the topic and stakeholders, you will need to plan the logistics for your mapping session. The logistics will depend on the number of participants. A small session might have five to eight people sitting at one table. A larger session might include a hundred people at twenty tables. Be sure to have

- Tables and chairs for everyone

- A room that is large enough for everyone and provides a comfortable working environment

- Meals—or at least snacks and beverages

- Marker pens, tape, and paper at each table

- A facilitator for each table (who is skilled in collaborative knowledge mapping techniques)

Finally, be sure you have enough material for making the maps. We suggest having at least 10 "arrows" and 10 "concept" cards per participant.

Be careful to set up the collaborative mapping session so that everyone can fully participate. Several issues are often important to consider:

- *Selecting a convenient and accessible location.* Consider the ease of attending for those traveling by public transportation and those that may be travelling by car. You may need to provide transportation or travel expense reimbursement so that all stakeholders can get to the location. Also, choose a space that is accessible for people with disabilities. If you're considering an online meeting, check that everyone has the needed technologies.

Ask participants (in advance, if possible) to find what special accommodations they may need.

- *Make mapping information accessible to all*. Make information about the mapping session and process available in a way that is clear and understandable for all stakeholders.

Just for planning purposes (we'll get into more detail later), a group will require about 90 minutes to make a very basic map. The map will be much improved with another 90 minutes of mapping. Integrating multiple maps (if applicable) will require at least 90 minutes, and action planning will be another 90 minutes. Better to allow extra time (two hours for mapping and two hours for action planning is good) if possible.

For scheduling, every situation is different. You want to take those differences into consideration, as in the following examples:

- *Working within an organization*, we suggest holding meetings of two hours each, once per day, on sequential days.

- *Working between organizations* can be more difficult, as this requires scheduling participants to get them in the same place at the same time. It might be easier to have a mapping session or two within each organization (or within each stakeholder group), then hold a shared mapping session where the groups integrate their maps.

- *For communities*, it is still more difficult to get a large number of people in one room for an extended time. Depending on what days of the week (and hours of the day) are most convenient, it might be best to have a one-day meeting with two hours in the morning for mapping, a lunch break, then two hours in the afternoon for action planning.

TRAVEL TIP

An easy way to start the mapping process is by providing a few concepts already written on cards and placed on the table (two or three concepts per table is good). Those may be chosen by a leadership team or by a survey of the participants in advance of the mapping session asking (for example) "what are the top three most important issues related to the problem of pollution in our community?" The starting concepts can also be the goals that the stakeholders are working toward. You might also get ideas for starting concepts by interviewing the person who initiated the process (manager, client, sponsor, etc.).

While it is not necessary, the process of *integrating* multiple maps (see Chapter 7) is made easier if each table receives a few of the same concepts to start with.

Activity
Ahead

CLASS ACTIVITY 2.1

Practicing Facilitation for Choosing a Topic

Working in small groups, choose one student in your group to act as facilitator.

In your group, discuss and agree on a topic for a mapping activity (you will do the actual mapping later in this chapter). The topic could be anything—from a global problem (such as wealth inequity) to a local problem (such as voter participation). You might brainstorm to come up with a wide range of possible topics. Then, categorize those possible topics and discuss why each one might be of interest.

Finally, vote on which topic will be your group's focus for creating a map. You might use "dot voting," with each person receiving three to four dots (stickers) and then placing the dots on their topics of interest. That gives each person the opportunity to express interest in a range of possible topics. The topic with the most dots wins (other topics may be mapped at a later date—or may appear during the mapping process as concepts placed by participants).

Stage 2. The Collaborative Mapping Session

After you have chosen a topic, assembled stakeholders, and arranged logistics, you are ready for creating the map. Here, we walk through the steps to facilitating a group to create a map.

Start With Introductions and Orientation

As with any meeting or workshop, particularly when the participants will be doing something new, starting with introductions for the people and the process is a good idea.

If a sponsor or manager for the project is present, he or she will likely want to talk briefly about the situation. Then, you as facilitator explain to the group that they will be pooling their expertise to generate a knowledge map (or maps) and what the map will be used for (e.g., program planning, communication, tracking and evaluation). If the group is small and if they don't know each other well, each participant might briefly introduce themselves. For larger groups, people clustered around each table can introduce themselves to others at their table.

If the collaborative mapping activity is part of a research project, explain the purpose of the research project, the voluntary nature of participation, and other information important to protecting research participants. You might also need to collect signed consent forms.

Next, we like to provide participants with the mapping metaphor. We explain that a good road map is one that shows many dots (locations such as cities or points of interest) and many roads connecting them (lines connecting dots). A better map (one with more dots and lines) will help the group make better decisions because it will show more options for how to get to desired goals.

With that, you can explain that the "dots" on their knowledge map are the concepts related to their topic and the "lines" are the causal arrows connecting them. At this point, it is useful to show what these will look like with some extra-large pieces (circles and arrows) taped to the wall. For that example, it is best to use the common or obvious concepts relating to the topic—for example, the top three concepts found in a survey. Another approach is to use your favorite presentation software and show the pieces on a projector screen.

TRAVEL TIP

Place a large sheet of paper on the wall with the collaborative mapping session's agenda. Place another large sheet of paper listing the steps that participants will follow in making their maps. Bringing handouts (that provide information such as how to do KMs, background research on the topic, and so on) is also beneficial. These provide reference points for participants so they can move forward with greater confidence.

For a smaller session, with five or six people around one table focused on one topic, you can explain the process right there at the table. For larger groups, with people seated around multiple tables, you can explain the process to the whole group and then turn the facilitation of mapping over to the individual table facilitators.

Begin Mapping

TRAVEL TIP

Use questions to help people come up with concepts. Some good questions to ask the mappers are the following:

- What is relevant to the topic?
- What is important for this problem?
- What things are changing?
- What kinds of things are staying the same?

Each answer may become a concept to be written and placed on the table—and becomes a part of the growing map. Once people have placed a few concepts, you might prompt more additions if you

- Point to one concept and ask, what would have to happen to get more of that?
- Point at two concepts and ask, does one of these cause the other to change?

To get participants started with creating their maps, walk them through the following steps—giving each person the opportunity to add something to the map.

1. Going around the table, the participants take turns placing concepts (circles) and connections (causal arrows) on the map. Everyone taking turns is important because we get a better map when we have everyone's participation and insights.

    a. The first participant places one concept that they think is relevant to the group's map (e.g., "access to healthcare," "meetings starting on time," or "grant funding").

    b. The next participant places another concept on the map.

    c. Now that two concepts are on the map, participants may place either a concept or an arrow. A connection must show a causal relationship between two concepts on the map (e.g., "grant funding" ➜ "expanding services"). Also, when placing a connection, participants should be sure to indicate whether an increase in the first concept "causes more" or "causes less" of the concept it's pointing to. That can be done by drawing a "+" or a "−" near the tip of the arrow.

2. As each object (concept or arrow) is placed on the map, the group votes on it.

    a. For each concept placed on the map, ask the group, "Is it measurable?" Encourage brief conversation if people seem unsure (but try to keep the conversation under two minutes).

    - **Yes?** If the group votes yes, the participant writes the measure for the concept on the concept card.

    - **No?** Do not write down a way to measure the concept on the card.

    - **Maybe?** If the vote does not result in a clear majority agreeing that the concept is measurable or not, write a "?" on the piece. This is an area where more work is needed "outside the room" to determine how to measure the concept.

    b. For each arrow placed on the map, ask the group, "Is it reasonable?" Encourage brief conversation (about two minutes per connection).

    A good way to test for reasonableness is to read the connection like a sentence. For example, consider three pieces: "grant funding" ➜ (helps cause more) "expanding services." You can "read" those pieces as, "The more grant funding we have, the more we will be able to expand our services."

    - **Yes?** Keep the connection on the map.

    - **No?** Remove the connection from the map.

    - **Maybe?** If the vote does not show a clear majority for or against the connection, keep it on the map and mark it with a "?" for later research and conversation outside the room.

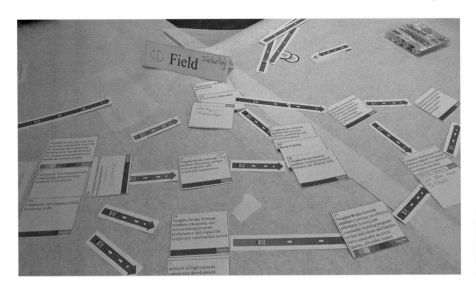

One of several collaborative knowledge maps made by stakeholder groups.

By the time every stakeholder has placed at least one piece on the table, they will probably be getting comfortable with the process. Ask if there are any questions (oh yeah, don't forget to answer their questions). Then have them continue going around the table with each person adding one piece to the map during their turn.

Encourage Transformative Concepts

After about a dozen pieces have been placed on the table, encourage participants to create "transformative" concepts. Transformative concepts are those with more than one arrow pointing directly at them. Explain that these are important because they make the map more useful for understanding, collaboration, planning, and practical implementation (more lines connecting the dots—from the road map metaphor). We like to place a "gold star" or other marker to clarify which concepts are transformative (Figure 2.5).

Encourage Loops

After more pieces have been placed and participants are increasingly comfortable with the process, encourage participants to create *loops*. A loop is four or more concepts connected by four or more causal arrows. It does not matter if the arrows indicate causes more or causes less—as long as they all point in the direction that keeps things flowing in a loop. We like to add a "blue ribbon" or other marker to indicate a loop (Figure 2.6).

Continue Mapping

Participants should continue taking turns adding concepts and arrows to the map until each person has contributed about 10 to 12 items. A general goal is to create a map in which more than half of the concepts are transformative.

FIGURE 2.5 ⬟ Transformative Structure With Star to Indicate the Transformative Concept

FIGURE 2.6 ⬟ Loop Structure With Ribbon to Remind People That It's a Loop

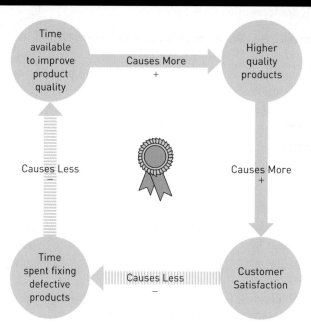

TRAVEL TIP

Collaborative mapping facilitation tips:

- The group may agree to rearrange the circles and arrows on the map. Often, rearranging the pieces can help make the map more readable.

- Grouping related concepts together is helpful for making a map easier to navigate.

- The group may change the process for creating their map with agreement of the facilitator and all participants (the rule to change the rules).

ONLINE HANDOUT: "PARTICIPANTS' GUIDE TO KNOWLEDGE MAPPING"

Download an electronic version of this handout at https://practical mapping.com

This online handout provides a guide that stakeholders can use to participate in a basic collaborative knowledge mapping session.

ONLINE HANDOUT: "TIPS FOR FACILITATING GROUPS."

Download an electronic version of this handout at https://practical mapping.com

This online handout provides advanced techniques for facilitating collaborative mapping sessions.

CLASS ACTIVITY 2.2

Collectively Creating a Map

Use the topic your student group developed in Class Activity 2.1 (along with the "Participants' Guide to Knowledge Mapping" and "Tips for Facilitating Groups" handouts provided online).

Choose one student from your group to serve as group facilitator (a different person from the person who was facilitator in Class Activity 2.1).

In your group, spend about 45 minutes collaboratively creating a map, including the perspectives of everyone in your group on your group's topic.

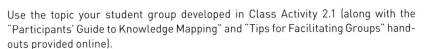

Stage 3. From Mapping to Action

In his efforts to support higher education and intellectual pursuits among the colonies, Benjamin Franklin recommended the promotion of "useful knowledge." In this section, we present a number of techniques you can use to help collaborative mapping participants apply the useful knowledge that they have created. In this stage, participants use their map as a guide for planning the paths they will take to get to desired results.

For example, the map in Figure 2.7 shows how a higher cost of fossil fuels tends to increase the amount of funding for research into alternative energies. That increase in funding into alternative energies leads to reduced costs of alternative sources of energy. So if your goal is to reduce the cost of alternative energy sources, one action that will help bring that about is to provide funding for research into alternatives.

When reading a map for action planning, we are often starting at our desired goals and working backward or "upstream" against the direction of the arrows. By "backtracking" in this way, we go from goals (which may be difficult to achieve), back to concepts, which are more easily achievable or actionable. Let's go one step more.

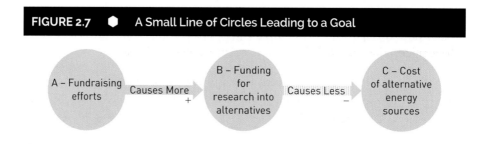

FIGURE 2.7   ●   A Small Line of Circles Leading to a Goal

What if you don't have enough cash just lying around to fund research into alternative energy? In that case, "B" is not an actionable concept for you. Then, you need to backtrack another step. Perhaps to "A" where you could engage in fundraising efforts. That seems to be more actionable than "B." However, you might ask yourself how successful you will be at fundraising. If the answer is not very positive, you may want to continue mapping— and add concepts to the left of "A" showing what will be needed for successful fundraising.

Assess Options for Action

As a facilitator, your next step is to help participants identify results they would like to see and actionable concepts where they could make changes that would make those results happen (those concepts should all be on the map!). Useful discussion questions for planning effective action include the following:

- *Learning from the mapping experience*: What did you learn from creating the map?

- *Actionable concepts*: What concepts on the map do you have the most ability to change?

- *Transformative concepts*: What are the transformative concepts on the map? Those show where actions are more likely to achieve desired results (because they show more paths to making them happen).

- *Feedback loops*: What, if any, are the feedback loops (self-reinforcing cycles)? These show where changes will build on themselves to make a bigger impact.

- *Leverage points*: What leverage points (concepts included in two or more loops) may be found? These are where the least amount of effort may promote the greatest amount of change.

Find Opportunities for Collaboration

Different stakeholder groups may use their shared map to find opportunities for collaboration. They might start by seeing that their main interest in the topic exists on different sides of the map (Figure 2.8). Next, they may find overlapping concepts of mutual interest (shown as concepts with thick borders Figure 2.8) to find potential opportunities for collaborative action that could lead to greater impact on shared goals.

Next, they may trace collaborative action paths (shown here as heavy dashed lines in Figure 2.9) that each stakeholder group can take to reach those shared actionable concepts leading to their shared goals.

Commit to Action

Looking at the map, the participants have seen where they might be able to take action to reach their desired goals and where they work with each other to reach shared goals. Now is the time for commitment to action.

Go around the table and ask each person to share their plans for moving forward, what they intend to do, and what goals they hope to reach. This will likely include a mix of some steps that can be accomplished in the short term plus bigger steps that may take many years to reach. For example, an organization's ultimate desired destination may be saving the planet from climate change. A goal for the next six months might be increasing the number of subscribers to the organization's email action list. Be sure that the short-term goals serve as stepping stones to reach the long-term goals—the big changes that the group wants to make.

Write those plans on large sheets of chart paper to serve as reminders at future meetings.

FIGURE 2.8   ●   Overlap Between Stakeholders' Perspectives

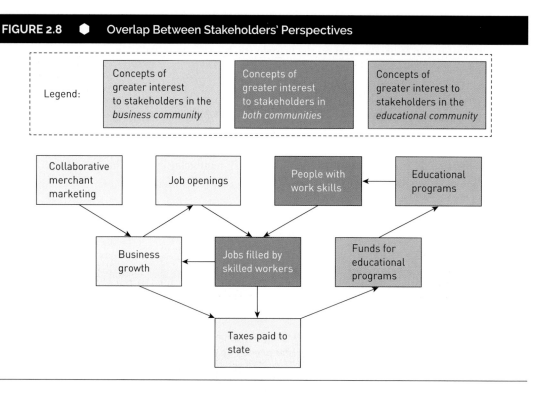

Stage 4. Road Trip

After the map has been created, action plans developed, and people have made commitments to action, the long journey to reach results begins. Because these are big knowledge maps addressing complex problems, the solution will not occur overnight.

Meet Monthly

If possible, the participants should meet about once a month. This helps them to avoid delays, interruptions, or "potholes" as they put their map into action. As facilitator, it is probably a good idea for you to run those meetings. This helps to keep some continuity of the group process. These conversations will help the group improve their understanding of the situation, obtain help when they run into unexpected problems, and coordinate their efforts as they move to reach shared and interdependent goals.

Although you may phrase them differently, the key questions you should ask to encourage conversation are the following:

- What actions did you take?

- What were the results?

FIGURE 2.9 ● Collaborative Action Paths

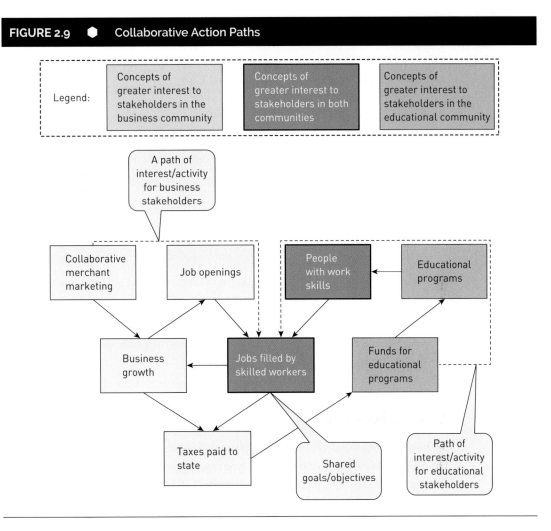

- What might you do differently between now and our next meeting?

- What additional resources, information, or collaboration might help you to better reach your goals?

Share the Results

Encourage the group to tell their stories of mapping and implementation to stakeholders, friends, and colleagues in their field, on social media, and to news organizations. That information informs and inspires others—and helps people find additional opportunities for collaboration and synergy.

You can make the collected data into a "dashboard" (available online or written on sheets of paper and posted on the office wall) that all mapping participants can see. That kind of information sharing increases transparency and trust. It can also help build enthusiasm and participation! For more on dashboards, see Chapter 7.

Revisit the Map Each Year

After 12 months, revisit the map—in depth. With the data collected over the year, the group can see what changes would improve the map. Ask participants to look at the map again with a fresh understanding. Some general questions for conversation include the following:

- *Where do you need more information?* What research might help improve the map?

- *Finding new opportunities for collaboration:* Who else would be good to collaborate with for reaching those goals who was not included in the group's original plan?

- Based on the group's measured results and experience, what changes does the group want to make to the map to guide activities going forward?

- Compare the current map with the map that they started with. What has changed, what has stayed the same, and what key things did the group learn?

- What new commitments will the group make?

Circling Back to the Leadership Team

The maps have been made, analyzed and considered, action teams have been formed and plans made. The wonderful mess of map pieces and markers has been cleaned up. Now, it's time to meet again with the sponsor (your manager, the CEO, the planning team . . . whoever worked to plan and put this all together).

The main idea here is that you should also learn from the mapping experience, and it is important for the leadership team to learn as well. This might be done after the map has been created or after the first monthly meeting. (Don't put it off too long; you want to bring up these questions while they are still fresh in peoples' minds.)

Sit down, relax, and talk. This is not about the map; rather, this is about the *process* of *creating* the map. Ask the leadership team

- What went well?

- What might we do differently next time?

- What could we do to inform the public and generate more publicity (blog posts, press releases, online dashboards, etc.)?

- Is it too early to start planning a follow-up meeting for next year?

Looking to the future, leaders may be asking, How can we improve our map so we can better plan effective action? What are the opportunities for additional mapping and action? While we will cover this in depth in Chapter 7, here are a few starting ideas:

- Form breakout groups to tease out insights from smaller clusters of concepts relevant to each breakout group's specific operations.

- Create teams interested in "drilling down" to unravel highly complex concepts to create a knowledge map focused on that topic.

- Hold meetings on a yearly basis to re-evaluate the map.

- Conduct mapping for new groups of stakeholders in other organizational divisions, other organizations, and coalitions, then integrate the existing map with those new maps.

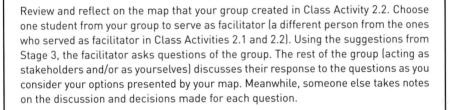

CLASS ACTIVITY 2.3

Considering Options Presented by Maps

Review and reflect on the map that your group created in Class Activity 2.2. Choose one student from your group to serve as facilitator (a different person from the ones who served as facilitator in Class Activities 2.1 and 2.2). Using the suggestions from Stage 3, the facilitator asks questions of the group. The rest of the group (acting as stakeholders and/or as yourselves) discusses their response to the questions as you consider your options presented by your map. Meanwhile, someone else takes notes on the discussion and decisions made for each question.

DEALING WITH DIFFICULT DYNAMICS

Public engagement includes a variety of processes such as "town hall" meetings, advisory groups, and crowd sourcing. These kinds of approaches are used to bring people together to share information and insights and to develop solutions to local issues.

In any mapping session, issues may arise that challenge the ability of the facilitator to move the group forward in a productive way. In this section, we will present some possible issues that you may encounter while facilitating a group and some strategies for helping participants move forward.

Gravity and Money

When creating a map, a participant might say something like, "We need the concept of 'money' in the center of the map, with arrows pointing to every other concept because nothing happens without money." This is a good time to draw a deep breath and remember that a knowledge map is not only about what is real or true—it is about what is useful. Sure, OK, perhaps what that person said was true. But is it useful? We can also say that, "Nothing happens without gravity." But is that a useful concept to include on the map? Is it worth making the map more cluttered and difficult to read? To create a more useful map, ask the person to identify the one connection that is the most important (most meaningful or relevant) to them and place the arrow on the map during the person's turn. That will help everyone in the group to focus.

Off Topic

Occasionally, a participant may create a concept that does not seem relevant to the topic. Other participants may be confused or even a little angry. This is not a cause for stress! Instead, recognize that the group does not necessarily know in advance what concepts will or won't prove useful (if they did, we probably wouldn't still be dealing with the problem). Simply leave the concept on the table and see what happens. If the concept remains unconnected at the end of the mapping session, ask the group what they would to do with it. Leave it on the map or save it for later, when it might become the topic for a new map (perhaps for another group of stakeholders or a breakout group).

"Special" Situation

If someone says something about having a "special" problem, the group might be tempted to start talking about the problem and avoid the map. In response, a facilitator should avoid asking for an explanation of the special problem. This takes the participants away from making broader progress toward understanding. Instead, ask the person to place a concept on the table to represent (and hopefully measure) the problem. Then, focusing on that, ask the participants to identify causal and resulting concepts. This will improve understanding with the most efficient use of all participants' time.

Super Talkers

Some people like to talk . . . a lot. They will go on and on (if you let them), explaining in great detail exactly how they define what their concept means and why they are placing that concept on the map. Ultimately, these long-winded explanations don't help the creation of a good map. For example, if someone places an unusual concept on the map (such as "crystal power"), don't ask them to explain what the concept "is" because that takes the participants' focus away from the map. Instead, ask participants to identify causal and resulting concepts and how they are measured. If the concept is relevant to the topic and meaningful to the people, others will connect with it. If not, it will sit off to the side, alone.

Sometimes, it's handy to use a two-minute timer with a loud alarm, giving each person two minutes per turn.

Premature Decision

A premature decision is when someone says, "It is clear we need to do 'X'—let's stop this planning and go do it!" The individual might feel confident moving forward, but without a good map, others may not. Possible responses include the following:

- If it is not there already, place the concept that the person wants to do (concept "X") on the map and ask what causes and effects may be connected with it.

- Ask participants to evaluate the map (using methods from Chapter 1 and Chapter 5). These analyses will indicate the relative quality of the map. If the levels are low, shift the conversation to talk about the quality of the map and return to mapping until the quality is much higher.

Super Connectors

Sometimes, someone will suggest that "everything is connected to everything" (so . . . their mapping work is done. Nope, they don't get off so easily.). Possible responses include the following:

- Explain that, while it may be true that everything is connected, it is also true that some things are more connected than others. For example, the walls of the building are more connected to the roof than they are connected to the map. Thus, we need to identify those things that are more closely connected because those will provide more leverage for enabling change.

- If the group agrees on something that is universally connected (for example, gravity affects all things equally), explain that it is ubiquitous and unchanging; therefore, it becomes background and so is not highly relevant.

- Take the new concept and (with the permission of the group) create a new focus for future consideration and a new mapping session.

Unstructured Conversation

Sometimes, a group won't stop to write down concepts and place them on a map. They'll want a more unstructured process of talking about many steps that are needed to reach desired goals at once. In that situation, you might want to drop the collaborative mapping session and instead use an alternative. For example, you can facilitate a group conversation and write key points (including concepts and causal connections that people mention) on a flip chart. Afterwards, you can map the results of that conversation, using the techniques for mapping from your research described in Chapter 4.

Power Dynamics

Each person attending a mapping session will have a level of "power." Power comes from a range of sources, including knowledge, wealth, charisma, and a person's position in an organization or community. Having more power means having more control. The funder has more power than the grantee, and the mayor has more power than the citizen. Also, one stakeholder group may have more power than another.

Although all stakeholders' voices are important, those power differences sometimes emerge during meetings. Those power dynamics can change the impact of some voices for the worse. Less powerful people may sit quietly—without adding suggestions or engaging in meaningful discussion. They seem to be "going along" with whatever the people with more power say.

This can be a problem because more powerful people do not have all the answers. Without the serious engagement by all, the group as a whole cannot make the best decisions to address the wicked problems they face.

We (as facilitators) must address any perceived power imbalance, so the group as a whole can make the best possible maps and so make the best possible decisions. One way to do this is to have all the participants take turns. This way, everyone gets an equal say into what is added to the map. Another approach is to have more powerful people make one map, while less powerful people make another—then merge the two maps.

Working With People
With Disabilities

When setting up a collaborative mapping session, you want to find out well in advance of the meeting who will be there and what you can provide to help make their participation meaningful. Ask people what (if any) accommodations they may need. Participants who are deaf may need sign-language interpreters. Those who are color-blind might not be able to tell the difference between red and green causal arrows. So writing "+" and "−" on the arrows to show causal directions would be helpful.

For those who are unable to attend in person, you can create maps online with screen sharing and arrange for an online facilitator to support the mapping process.

GAMIFIED APPROACH TO COLLABORATIVE MAPPING

Play is a wonderful thing. While playing, people are often more creative than when they are serious. Play also supports self-reflection, learning, problem-solving, building social relationships, taking risks, and recovering more rapidly from problems. When used to address real-world problems, we call this "serious play."

DEFINITION

Gamification is the process of taking something serious (such as knowledge mapping or strategic planning) and making it into a game or game-like process so it's a lot more fun (also leading to seriously useful insights).

"Gamification" can be used to support planning, education, and data gathering. Gamification, however, has its risks. Participants sometimes get so involved in the competition side of the game that they do not actually learn very much.

Creating a map, however, is like no other game in the world. Participants—or players—are not trying to *solve* a puzzle—they are trying to *understand* a situation. They are not trying to *test* their knowledge as they would in a trivia game—they are actually *creating new knowledge*. Nor are they exploring an online world that someone else has made as in a simulation game—they are creating a plan to change their own world.

The ASK MATT Game

Our favorite gamified process for knowledge mapping is (no surprise) the one that we developed. ASK MATT (Accessing Strategic Knowledge Meta Analytical Think Tank) is a fun and easy way to get stakeholders into a mapping process.

A wide variety of organizations have used the ASK MATT game to create collaborative maps for. Below are a few examples.

TeamLMI, in Pennsylvania, has run games for

- A law firm

- An information technology services company

- A restaurant and catering group

- The transportation industry (in conjunction with PennDOT [Pennsylvania Department of Transportation])

Photo courtesy of Pam Rich of Pam Rich Consulting

A stakeholder presenting a game-made knowledge map.

Unleashed Consulting, in California, has run games for

- A Planned Parenthood office in Texas
- Business coaching in California
- A policy, equity, and social services coalition of community leaders

ASK MATT Solutions, in California, has played the game for

- A nonprofit board
- A real estate firm
- Start-up coaching
- Theory building for a nation-wide community-development organization in Washington, DC
- Policy analysis in Germany
- A faith-based community organization in Colorado

GracefulSystems used ASK MATT to support a multi-sector energy coalition in the Pacific Northwest. StarLinks in Israel played it with a government agency providing community services.

In addition, groups have played ASK MATT in university classes for policy, management, and human resources at Michigan Technological University and at workshops for professionals, researchers, leaders, consultants, and scholars.

As you might imagine, participants have been very excited in the process and using the results. Some of their quotes include

- "It was really useful to identify options, trade-offs, and connections."
- "Helped to clarify the needs and goals [of our organization]."
- "Showed us linkages that were not apparent."
- "The best strategic planning process I've ever used."

For the most part, the ASK MATT game follows the mapping process presented in this chapter, with the addition of earning individual and group points and scorekeeping. As you work with your clients (internal and external), we hope you will add to the growing list of excited people gaining new knowledge to reach higher goals.

CASE STUDY: MAPPING A REGIONAL ENERGY COALITION

CASE STUDY ROAD

The energy sector is facing significant change as our society evolves away from fossil fuels toward renewable energy. The rapid pace of change has destabilized relationships between organizations. Suppliers, processors, distributors, and competitors face uncertainty. What changes might occur? Will they still be open for business in ten years? How can they manage the change so that everyone can work together more effectively?

Portland Energy Conservation, Inc. (PECI) is an energy consortium in the Pacific Northwest whose members include government agencies, research firms, providers of fossil fuels, providers of renewable energy, and nonprofit organizations working toward environmental and social progress. Recognizing the difficulties of understanding and managing their changing relationships, PECI hired a consultant to help consortium members better understand their situation, reach a shared understanding, and improve their shared performance.

Pamela Morgan of Graceful Systems has considerable experience in the energy sector and a deep understanding of how people and organizations can work more effectively together when they work as a system. After discussing the situation with the leadership, she considered a range of options.

They considered methods such as "Future Search," but that process requires three days of effort with leaders from each of the member organizations in one place at one time. It would be difficult or impossible to get them in the same room at the same time—let alone for such a length of time. Another option was to facilitate conversations in small groups. While this would improve some personal relationships, it would not necessarily serve as a catalyst for shared understanding by the whole consortium. After considering these and other options, Pamela settled on using the ASK MATT collaborative knowledge mapping game.

Over the course of five meetings, more than 50 people from 22 organizations gathered in groups as they were able to fit the schedule. They created five maps containing a total of over 150 concepts. Pam then integrated the maps by identifying overlaps where the same concept appeared on multiple maps (more about this in Chapter 6). She also used other techniques to reduce the complexity of the map, including categorizing/abstracting concepts and other advanced strategies for mapping that we will cover in Appendix A of this book. The final map contained over 50 concepts (Figure 2.10). Pam color-coded the concepts to reflect the topics and to support ease of reading.

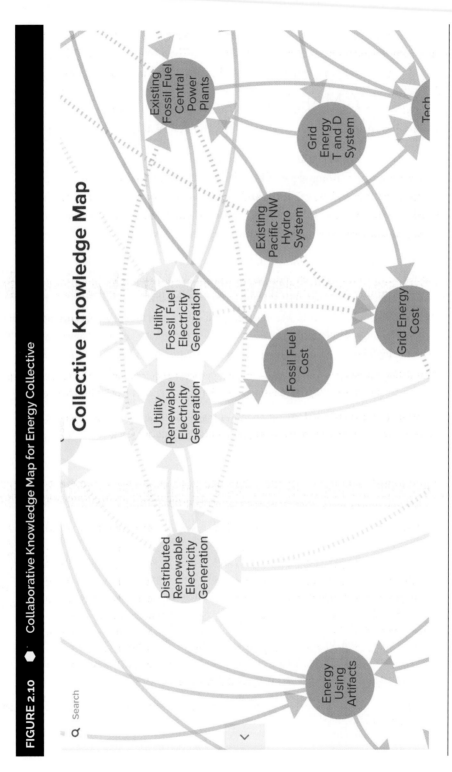

Source: Map courtesy of Pamela Morgan of Graceful Systems and PECI (Portland Energy Conservation, Inc.); and Kumu.io. For Full-Size Map, See https://peci.kumu.io/peci-generating-resilience?token=6AOHyxPW8iKsrvFk

FIGURE 2.10 ● Collaborative Knowledge Map for Energy Collective

Collective Knowledge Map

Q Search

Existing Fossil Fuel Central Power Plants

Grid Energy T and D System

Tech

Existing Pacific NW Hydro System

Utility Fossil Fuel Electricity Generation

Utility Renewable Electricity Generation

Fossil Fuel Cost

Grid Energy Cost

Distributed Renewable Electricity Generation

Energy Using Artifacts

Pam then used the integrated map to identify 10 leverage points, which the group used to make policy recommendations to its parent organization. The group also identified inter-dependencies (e.g., between the market and the technologies) and actions to improve the sustainability and resilience of the collective energy system. New insights were generated, such as the relationship between the public's demand for clean energy, advancements in technology, and major shifts in economic forces from an "extractive" economy to a "generative" one.

The process was a successful integration of knowledge. One participant, then board president of a large environmental organization, said that the process was fun, like a game. Yet, the maps led him to new insights and some "intriguing problem identifications." While we hope this case study has been interesting, the map tells its own story.

Chapter 2 Key Points

- Collaborative mapping is useful for surfacing and integrating the deep wisdom of organizations, communities, and other stakeholders for practical decision-making, tracking progress, and evaluating results.

- Conducting a productive collaborative mapping process requires careful planning and preparation to ensure a successful mapping session and to be able to deal with potential challenges.

- Knowledge maps resulting from collaborative mapping provide more useful guides for understanding and resolving the wicked problems that face our world.

Frequently Asked Questions

Q: What if one person says that (for example) A ➜ B and another person says that's not true?

A: First, deal with that quickly—we don't want to spend all day arguing one point when we could have been building an entire map! One good approach is to ask the people at the table to vote on whether or not the arrow from A to B should stay on the map. The group may decide that a majority or supermajority (more than half, such as two-thirds) rules. Another approach (if voting does not result in a clear decision) is to place a "?" on the arrow and have the parties conduct research later. Third, you can encourage participants to expand their thinking by asking guiding questions such as, "Perhaps A is a *partial cause* of B; if so, what else might be added to the map to express something that supports or works against those changes to B?"

Q: What if extensive argument arises between two groups about what concepts should or should not be on the map?

(Continued)

(Continued)

A: You can remind them that a map with more concepts will be more useful for understanding and guiding decisions to resolve complex problems. So we recommend that concepts should remain on the map. Or the two groups might want to conduct two separate mapping sessions focused on their own priorities. They might find out later that they have some connections in common.

Q: What if the group makes a map that seems too abstract?

A: Generally, this is not an issue because groups tend to work at a level of abstraction that is appropriate to their interests and activities. For example, a board of directors might talk about "fundraising," which (by itself) may be considered fairly abstract. In comparison, a fundraising committee might talk about the many concepts that are part of fundraising, such as specific venues where fundraising events will be held (less abstract). Occasionally, an individual will place a more abstract concept on the map and others will have difficulty making causal connections between that abstract concept and other concepts. In those cases, as facilitator, you might ask the participant who placed the abstract concept on the map to change it to something more concrete. You might also suggest placing the abstract concept to the side so that the group can use it as the topic for a future map.

On the other hand, pushing a little toward the abstract can help improve collaboration and reduce tension. For example, in a mapping session with many supervisors (each in charge of a single team), each might begin by creating a map that is focused on their own team without concern for the others. Instead, asking the supervisors to create a map about teams in general helps them to start thinking about what kinds of things are good for all teams—not only their own.

Q: What happens if some people will not respond to my suggestions as a facilitator?

A: Remember, you are not alone. This is an opportunity to harness the power of the group. Ask the group what they think about the situation and what might be done.

Further Exploration

In this chapter, we've focused on the collaborative creation of knowledge maps to better understand and resolve highly complex problems. For those bold explorers who would like to learn more, this section provides additional information. Here you will find sources on the foundational research supporting this chapter.

Many of these publications are available for free online. Some may require a fee to access. If you are a student or affiliated with a university, you may be able to access these at no charge through your institution's library.

Action Research

The process of creating maps to understand a situation, using those maps to make plans, taking action, learning from the results, and repeating the cycle is often referred to as "action research." Here are some resources from that perspective:

Argyris, C., & Schon, D. A. (1989). Participatory action research and action science compared. *American Behavioral Scientist, 32*(5), 612–623. Retrieved from http://journals.sagepub.com/doi/abs/10.1177/0002764289032005008?journalCode=absb

McGarvey, C. (2007). Participatory action research: Involving all the players in evaluation and change. *GrantCraft Series*. Retrieved from http://www.grantcraft.org/assets/content/resources/par.pdf

Facilitation and Change

The approaches we presented in this chapter overlap in many ways with best practices in the field of organizational development and the field of industrial/organizational psychology. Those related approaches are too many to talk about in any one book, so here are a few others:

Doyle, M., & Straus, D. (1982). *How to make meetings work.* New York, NY: Jove. Retrieved from https://www.bkconnection.com/static/How_to_Make_Collaboration_Work_EXCERPT.pdf

Dunnett, M. D. (Ed.). (1976). *Handbook of industrial and organizational psychology.* Chicago, IL: Rand McNally. Retrieved from https://books.google.com/books?id=JWYPAQAAMAAJ&q=Handbook+of+industrial+and+Organizational+Psychology&dq=Handbook+of+industrial+and+Organizational+Psychology&hl=en&sa=X&ved=0ahUKEwj6pvuwvrrZAhVK4YMKHcFuDcMQ6AEIKTAA

Goodier, C., Austin, S., Soetanto, R., & Dainty, A. (2010). Causal mapping and scenario building with multiple organisations. *Futures, 42*(3), 219–229. Retrieved from https://dspace.lboro.ac.uk/dspace-jspui/bitstream/2134/6033/1/Causal%20Mapping%20%20Scenario%20Building-%20Futures%202.pdf

Kaner, S. (2014). *Facilitator's guide to participatory decision-making.* Hoboken, NJ: John Wiley & Sons. Retrieved from https://zodml.org/sites/default/files/Facilitator%27s_Guide_to_Participatory_Decision-Making_%28Jossey-Bass_Business_%26_Management%29.pdf

Rothwell, W. J., Sullivan, R., & McLean, G. N. (Eds.). (1995). *Practicing organization development: A guide for consultants.* San Diego, CA: Pfeiffer & Company. Retrieved from https://books.google.com/books?hl=en&lr=&id=yYieWsUF-EIC&oi=fnd&pg=PR7&dq=).+Practicing+Organization+Development:+A+Guide+for+Consultants.+&ots=r9W2KN3dBv&sig=-zeTWM6tLlMKnQ1ahPFR6yTTCzg#v=onepage&q=).%20Practicing%20Organization%20Development%3A%20A%20Guide%20for%20Consultants.&f=false

Senge, P., Kleiner, K., Roberts, S., Ross, R. B., & Smith, B. J. (1994). *The fifth discipline fieldbook: Strategies and tools for building a learning organization.* New York, NY: Currency Doubleday. Retrieved from https://books.google.com/books/about/The_Fifth_Discipline_Fieldbook.html?id=thTtrQVR8EIC

Weisbord, M. R., & Janoff, S. (2000). *Future search: An action guide to finding common ground in organizations and communities* (2nd ed.). San Francisco, CA: Berrett-Koehler. Retrieved from http://futuresearch.net/about/whatis/

Importance of Involving Many Stakeholders

These resources provide guidance and tips for involving stakeholders in evaluation.

American Evaluation Association. (2018). *American Evaluation Association statement guiding principles for evaluators.* Retrieved from http://www.eval.org/p/cm/ld/fid=51

(Continued)

(Continued)

Wright, B. (2016). *Step 1 of six steps to effective program evaluation: Collaborate with stakeholders.* CharityChannel. Retrieved from https://charitychannel.com/program-evaluation-collaborate-with-stakeholders

Importance of Incorporating Many Views

These sources detail the benefits of incorporating many views.

Bolman, L. G., & Deal, T. E. (1991). *Reframing organizations: Artistry, choice, and leadership.* San Francisco, CA: Jossey-Bass.

Morgan, G. (1996). *Images of organizations.* Thousand Oaks, CA: Sage. Retrieved from http://informal coalitions.typepad.com/odin/Reflections_on_Images_of_Organization_Gareth_Morgan.pdf

Equity in Participation: Disabilities and Power

These sources provide information on how to address power dynamics, practice cultural competence, and include people of all abilities.

American Evaluation Association. (2011). *American Evaluation Association statement on cultural competence in evaluation.* Retrieved from https://www.eval.org/p/cm/ld/fid=92

Bates, K., Parker, C. S., & Ogden, C. (2018). *Power dynamics: The hidden element to effective meetings* [Blogpost of Interaction Institute for Social Change]. Retrieved from http://interactioninstitute.org/power-dynamics-the-hidden-element-to-effective-meetings/

Bernstein, D. J. (2012). *Applying universal design principles to an evaluation involving individuals with significant disabilities.* [American Evaluation Association *AEA365* blog post]. Retrieved from https://aea365.org/blog/dovp-week-david-j-bernstein-on-applying-universal-design-principles-to-an-evaluation-involving-individuals-with-significant-disabilities/

BetterEvaluation.com. (2016). *Cultural competency* [Web page]. Retrieved from https://www.better evaluation.org/en/evaluation-options/cultural_competence_evaluation

Gothberg, J. (n.d.). *Accessible evaluation techniques* [American Evaluation Association *AEA365* blog post]. Retrieved from https://aea365.org/blog/dup-week-accessible-evaluation-techniques-with-june-gothberg/

Strategic Planning for Nonprofits

These articles provide more information on knowledge mapping for strategic planning for non-profits.

Wallis, S. E., & Frese, K. E. (2017). *Strategic planning: A new state of the art* [White paper]. A. M. Solutions. Retrieved from http://askmatt.solutions/images/Strategic-Planning-white-paper-15sep17.pdf

Wallis, S., & Wright, B. (2014). Strategic planning 3.0 [White paper]. Retrieved from http://meaning fulevidence.com/wp-content/uploads/2014/12/Strategic-Planning-3.0-October-27.pdf

Strategic Planning for Businesses

While the focus of this chapter is not on business organizations, these resources in that direction may prove useful to some readers.

Håkansson, H., & Snehota, I. (1989). No business is an island: The network concept of business strategy. *Scandinavian Journal of Management, 5*(3), 187–200. Retrieved from https://www.researchgate.net/profile/Ivan_Snehota/publication/223903760_No_Business_Is_an_Island_The_Network_Concept_of_Business_Strategy/links/59f60050a6fdcc075ec5f7b7/No-Business-Is-an-Island-The-Network-Concept-of-Business-Strategy.pdf

Hubbard, D. W. (2014). *How to measure anything: Finding the value of intangibles in business.* Hoboken, NJ: John Wiley & Sons.

Teece, D. J. (2010). Business models, business strategy and innovation. *Long range planning, 43*(2), 172–194. Retrieved from http://www.bmcommunity.sitew.com/fs/Root/8jig8-businessmodelsbusinessstrategy.pdf

Serious Play

These articles provide more information on the ASK MATT collaboration knowledge mapping game and serious play.

Caldwell, C. (2003). Adult group play therapy: Passion and purpose. In C. E. Schaefer (Ed.), *Play therapy with adults* (pp. 301–316). New York, NY: Wiley. Retrieved from https://www.academia.edu/12157206/Adult_Group_Play_Therapy

Wallis, S. E., & Wright, B. (2015, March 4–6). *Strategic knowledge mapping: The co-creation of useful knowledge.* Paper presented at the Association for Business Simulation and Experiential Learning (ABSEL) 42nd annual conference, Las Vegas, NV. Retrieved from https://journals.tdl.org/absel/index.php/absel/article/view/2899/2850

DATA

Mapping From Related Research and Materials

Source: The diagram in the thought cloud is from NMAC Strong Communities Project.

n this chapter, you'll learn how to create a map using knowledge from existing research and materials. Here, we'll cover the following:

- Uses for mapping from existing research

- Steps to mapping from existing research

- Mapping from program materials

Throughout this chapter, we will refer frequently to a vignette as our primary example—NMAC's Strong Communities project. NMAC is an organization that "leads with race to urgently fight for health equity and racial justice to end the HIV epidemic in America" (NMAC, n.d.). The Strong Communities project focused on increasing racial equity in healthcare, specifically in HIV-related services in the southern United States. As part of that project, one of the authors of this book, Bernadette Wright, worked with NMAC to synthesize and map out existing knowledge on the topic.

USES FOR MAPPING FROM EXISTING RESEARCH

Mapping from related research is a way to integrate knowledge from existing studies and materials, much like conducting a literature review. When we say "related" research, we mean research that others have done that relates to what you want to know. Related research is also called "secondary research" or "existing research," to distinguish it from research based on your own collection of new data (called "primary research"). Looking at related research has many benefits for addressing complex problems:

- *Shaping effective solutions.* The experiences of past projects often reveal the lessons that the people conducting and evaluating those projects have learned and their most effective practices. This information can help leaders to strengthen existing programs and develop new programs.

- *Demonstrating value.* In many situations, existing studies can provide strong evidence to show the benefit of a program or policy, often faster than a new study and at a lower cost.

- *Planning useful research.* A review of related research shows where sufficient evidence exists and where we need more research. This lets you avoid "reinventing the wheel" (repeating previous studies to obtain the same results), so you can focus on finding new evidence. Past studies can also help you develop a strong research plan by showing what variables and relationships are important to the situation and suggesting data sources and research strategies to consider.

Creating a knowledge map can be a useful part of a review of related research in a couple of ways. First, knowledge mapping provides a systematic approach to integrating the many inter-related activities and outcomes identified in related research from across many fields of practice and academic disciplines and from many types of studies and materials. Second, knowl-edge maps can be used to make visually appealing, easy-to-digest presentations to stakeholders.

DEFINITION

Related research refers to existing publications that provide information for better understanding your topic. Examples include academic papers, organization reports, industry publications, conference presentations, and books, to name a few.

Sometimes, mapping from related research is a complete study in and of itself to understand the knowledge in the field. Other times, mapping from related research is part of a more comprehensive research process to find out what is known, then plan new research to provide additional needed information. Often, the ways in which a community sees how to address a problem may differ from suggestions provided by a literature review. As the NMAC lead on the Strong Communities project, Moisés Agosto-Rosario noted, "When you look at the knowledge from literature reviews, you see the evidence based, academic perspective" (personal communication, February 14, 2018). Talking with service providers and service participants in the community shows the same issues from a different set of eyes. So we combine existing evidence with new evidence wherever possible.

For example, after creating a literature map for the Strong Communities project, we gathered information through community interviews and integrated those perspectives into the literature map for a combined, more comprehensive map (that process will be detailed in Chapter 4). Later, NMAC presented the map findings to professionals in the field as part of a training program. When people who had been working in the field for a long time saw the map, they said "we know this." That indicated to us that the map did a good job of reflecting the realities of the situation.

In this chapter, we build on those (and related experiences) to provide a step-by-step approach that you can use to create maps from existing related research materials. Those maps, in turn, will enable you to develop a better understanding of your topic and support the effectiveness of your research.

STEPS TO MAPPING FROM EXISTING RESEARCH

Before you begin your research, you must first clarify the questions that your client needs to have answered. In Chapter 2, we talked about this in terms of the topic that

DEFINITION

Research questions (RQs) (in evaluation research, they may be called **evaluation questions**) are general and specific questions that the researcher is attempting to answer by conducting the research.

stakeholders wished to focus on and understand. That focus is also referred to as your "research question" (RQ). That question may be relatively broad, such as "What makes communities thrive?" or relatively narrow, such as "What are the effects of this professional development program for teachers on math assessment scores for fourth graders at our school?" Once you have your question(s), you can begin building your research around it.

For the NMAC Strong Communities project, those research questions were the following:

Research Question 1:

What are the relationships between racial discrimination, social drivers, and health?

Research Question 2:

What are the effective strategies to increase racial equity in healthcare, within an organization or a community?

Once you have your research question(s), write down your plan for how you'll find, select, organize, and present your findings from studies to help answer those questions (basically, that plan will look like the following five steps).

Your search plan is not written in stone. You can and should modify your search plan when needed to find useful information, as long as you document what changes you made and why. Also, as you conduct your study, remember to write down the details of what you did to conduct your review of related research. This helps others understand and interpret your results.

Creating a map from existing research in a rigorous way involves five steps:

Step 1. Searching for and choosing studies (and other related research and materials)

Step 2. Creating a table of studies

Step 3. Extracting and organizing information from studies

Step 4. Assessing research quality

Step 5. Mapping the knowledge from studies

Step 1. Searching for and Choosing Existing Studies

The first step is to search for and choose existing studies that can help answer your research questions. An important part of that step is deciding what studies you will include in your research.

Determining Your Study Inclusion Criteria

Your study inclusion criteria describe what counts as relevant knowledge that can help answer your research questions. Here are a few types of inclusion criteria that are often important.

Fit with what you want to know. You should include only those studies containing the information that will help you answer your questions. For the NMAC Strong Communities project, the reason for the study was to provide information about the connections between race, social determinants, and health strategies that could increase service providers' capacity to advance health equity. Based on that purpose, we narrowed our search to studies and materials that provided information on those topics.

Date of publication. As with every aspect of your research plan, which dates of publication you decide to include in your review depends on what you want to know. If the reason for your study is to understand the research streams on proposed changes to the Social Security Act, you will want to look for studies going back to 1935, the year the act was signed into law. For studies where we want to know the current best practices, we like to start with the most recent studies. Because the NMAC study was to surface recent insights and practices, we focused our search on studies published in the past 10 years.

Study geographic location. Which geographic areas of studies you decide to include in your review depends on what you want to know as well as what literature is available. For a study comparing health care systems across nations, we would include studies and reports from several countries as well as previous studies that compared health care systems across countries. In the case of the NMAC Strong Communities study, we wanted to find strategies that could be applied by service providers in the six Strong Communities cities in the southern United States. Therefore, we looked for studies specific to the six Strong Communities cities or specific to the South that could inform our research questions. However, we did not find any studies fitting those specific criteria, so we broadened our search to include studies relating to the United States as a whole.

Type of publication. Which types of publications to include, again, depends on what you want to know. Some studies that seek to understand public opinion on an issue analyze content of social media posts on platforms such as Facebook, blogs, and Twitter. Typically, when we review related research to inform a public policy or social program, we're interested in materials published by reliable, informed sources, such as

- Peer-reviewed journal articles

- Government reports

- Publications by leading organizations and experts, such as professional associations, university researchers, and nonprofit policy organizations that are active in the field

- Books published by leading publishers in the field

- Seminal, highly influential works

If we came across an article on our topic in a predatory journal (see Travel Tips, below) or in the personal blog by someone with no qualifications on the subject, those would not meet our inclusion criteria of publications by reliable sources. So we would not read those articles as part of our review.

A word of caution: including only studies from reliable sources is not enough to determine that the research is high quality. Articles in peer-reviewed journals, even highly cited studies, sometimes contain serious weaknesses. We'll delve further into examining research quality in Steps 2 and 4, later in this section.

Taking an inclusive approach to reviewing related research lets you detour around the "road closures" of narrow reviews (Figure 3.1).

TRAVEL TIP

Watch out for articles published in *predatory journals*, also called *"fake journals."* These are journals with names that sound like scholarly, legitimate journals, but they will publish almost anything and charge high fees to authors. For more information, see:

Kolata, G. (2017, October 30). Many academics are eager to publish in worthless journals. *New York Times*. Accessed February 16, 2018 from https://www.nytimes .com/2017/10/30/science/predatory-journals-academics.html

Deciding Where to Search

After determining your study inclusion/exclusion criteria, it's time to decide where you'll look for studies that meet those criteria. Below are eight good places that are often helpful to look. Many of these places are free or low-cost to search, although some materials may cost money to access. If you are associated with a university or college, you may be able to access these materials through your institution's library. A research librarian can help you identify appropriate databases and other related resources for your search.

FIGURE 3.1 ⬡ Detouring Around the Road Closures of "No Research Found"

ROAD CLOSED | **DETOUR**

1. No existing studies focused on your specific situation

2. Few academic, peer-reviewed studies on the topic

1. Expand your search to include studies from other similar fields that are working on the same topic. **Example**: Studies on health equity in general can be useful for a study on the specific topic of racial equity in HIV services in the southern United States.

2. Expand your search to include reliable sources outside of academia (e.g., government reports, white papers by leading organizations in the field, trade publications). **Example**: Much of the useful literature we found on health equity was from outside academic journals, such as a workbook on promoting health equity by the U.S Centers for Disease Control and Prevention (CDC) and a tool for organizations to assess their racial equity produced by the Annie E. Casey Foundation.

1. *Your own bookshelf.* You or others on your project team may already know of some useful sources that can help answer your questions. Don't overlook what might be right under your nose.

2. *The Internet.* A well-structured Internet search will often yield existing studies and materials that may be important to your study. To increase your chances of finding relevant materials, use the advanced search tools of your search engine (e.g., Google). For a more exhaustive search, repeat your search in additional search engines, such as Yahoo Search, Duck Duck Go, and Bing.

3. *Key websites.* Another technique for finding studies is to browse and search the websites of leading organizations and government agencies that are active on your issue. They will often provide relevant materials and links, such as research reports, conference presentations, and fact sheets.

4. *Scholarly literature databases.* You can find several free sources for searching for academic articles online, such as Google Scholar (https://scholar.google.com/), Academia.edu (https://www.academia.edu/), and ResearchGate (https://www.researchgate.net/). Your library may provide access to many additional databases for finding academic studies.

5. *Your sources' sources.* As you review the sources you've found, look at the sources they referenced by browsing their footnotes, references, and bibliographies. That may lead you to additional useful publications.

6. *Topic-specific repositories.* Many online repositories provide helpful tools for finding information on specific topics. A couple of examples are ERIC (http://eric.edu.gov), a collection of scholarship on education, and Health Systems Evidence (https://www .healthsystemsevidence.org/) a repository of syntheses of research on health systems.

7. *Key journals.* You can also identify key journals that cover your topic and browse the tables of contents of recent issues and search those journals.

8. *Asking researchers and experts.* After conducting your own search, you might contact study authors and other experts on the topic and ask them what additional materials they recommend that you review to find the information you need.

For the NMAC Strong Communities project, we started with a couple of highly relevant studies that the researcher remembered seeing on social media. We found more publications through advanced searches in Google and Google Scholar. We also explored the websites of national agencies and organizations involved in HIV services and health equity, such as the websites of the CDC and the Robert Wood Johnson Foundation. After selecting studies for inclusion in our review, we found additional sources by scanning the references that those sources cited.

TRAVEL TIP

Google's advanced search (https://www.google.com/advanced_search) lets you apply various filters to narrow your search, such as filters by words or phrases, language, geographic region, and last update date. To master Google search techniques, see Google's Search Tips (https://support.google.com/websearch/answer/134479?hl=en).

Google Scholar's advanced search also lets you apply various filters to refine your search. Google Scholar's search tips are available at http://scholar.google.com/intl/ en/scholar/help.html.

Check the help pages of each database and search engine you use for guidance on constructing search queries there.

Scanning Search Results and Selecting Studies

After conducting your search, it's time to choose studies that meet your inclusion criteria. This involves three steps:

1. Read the titles of articles that came up in your search and select those that are potentially relevant.

2. Read abstracts of the articles you selected and keep those that seem most relevant for your study.

3. Quickly skim the complete text of those articles and select which ones you will include in your review of related research.

As you scan each study title, abstract, and full text, ask yourself whether or not the study meets your inclusion criteria and whether or not the information in the study will be helpful for answering your research questions.

- If so, include the publication in your study.

- If not, don't include it.

- If you are unsure of whether or not a study is relevant, check with other members of your research team. Ask them to review the criteria and results, then discuss whether that study should be included in your review.

In the NMAC Strong Communities study, we ended up selecting 11 relevant publications for inclusion in our review.

Step 2. Creating a Table of Studies

Creating a table of studies is useful when you have a large number of studies and want to be able to quickly organize and describe them. In this step, we are focused on extracting the studies' bibliographic information and other details about the studies. In Step 3, we'll extract information about the study findings as they relate to our research questions.

Table 3.1 shows the table of studies we created for the NMAC Strong Communities project with bibliographic information and study details for two studies. To create your own table of studies, create a table (we use Microsoft Excel for this) with separate columns for each type of information about the studies. That structure makes it easier for you sort or filter your studies by study type and focus.

A. *Enter the bibliographic information for each of your included studies, one row per study.* Create separate columns for

- The author
- Date of publication
- Title
- Publisher and issue/pages (if applicable)
- URL

TABLE 3.1 ● Table of Studies—Including Bibliographic Information and Details for Two Studies

1	2	3	4	5	6	7	8	9	10
Study Bibliographic Information						**Study Details**			
Author(s)	**Date**	**Title**	**Publisher**	**URL**	**Topic(s)**	**Method(s)**	**Population**	**Geographic area**	**Limitations reported in study**
R. Wyatt, M. Laderman, L. Botwinic, K. Mate, & J. Whittington	2016	Achieving Health Equity: A Guide for Health Care Organizations	IHI White Paper. Cambridge, Massachusetts: Institute for Healthcare Improvement.	www.ihi.org	Increasing racial equity within your organization Partnering to improve health equity in community	Developed the framework based on the work of four Innovation Projects, which included scans of the literature on health equity, over 30 interviews with experts and patients, site visits, and learning from exemplary health care systems working to improve health equity in their communities	Health care organizations	U.S.	Did not see any reported in the paper
NPR, Robert Wood Johnson Foundation, & Harvard T. H. Chan School of Public Health	2017	Discrimination in America: Experiences and Views of Latinos	Authors.	https://www .npr.org/ documents/ 2017/oct/ discrimination-latinos-final.pdf	Latino Americans' experiences with racial discrimination	National survey about personal experiences with racial discrimination and perceptions of racial discrimination in own community	803 Latino adults	U.S.	Possible errors from non-response bias, question wording, and ordering effects

Source: NMAC Strong Communities Project.

This kind of arrangement lets you sort or filter the studies by bibliographic information. An alternative approach is to enter all bibliographic information in one column; this makes the table take up less space, which can be useful if you want to include it in a report (and want to minimize the number of pages in the report).

B. *Enter descriptive information for each study.* Following the columns with bibliographic information, create another set of columns to capture descriptive information about each study. Include the different types of study information that will be most useful for your research.

- Study topic(s). In this column, in your own words, briefly state what the study was about (e.g., "increasing racial equity in health care organizations" or "people's experiences with racial discrimination").

- The study's methods

- The study population, such as the number of study participants and their demographics

- The study's geographic location

- Reported study limitations. In this column, summarize the study limitations that the study authors reported. Frequently, you can find these in sections conveniently labeled "Methods," "Limitations," or "Discussion." All studies have methodological limitations, although they are not always reported. Entering information about the studies' limitations in one place lets you see the overall strengths and weaknesses across studies, as reported by study authors. If different studies have different limitations and they say the same thing, this gives you more confidence in the overall body of knowledge. We'll delve into how to conduct your own assessment of study strengths and limitations in Step 3.

Step 3. Extracting and Organizing Knowledge From Studies

Now that you've gathered a pile of relevant studies and organized the relevant information about those studies into a table, the next step is to make sense of it all, and, at the same time, start writing a report of your findings.

Extract Knowledge From Studies

The first step in synthesizing related studies is to identify relevant findings in the studies and record them.

Start by reading each study, looking for findings that relate to your specific questions. Often, not always, these are in the results and conclusions sections of your chosen papers.

These are the concepts and relationships that those researchers found to be relevant and that help answer your questions. Note that some materials might address more than one of your research questions. So read the studies carefully—considering your questions as you go.

As you scan and read each section of text within a study, think about whether or not that text helps answer your research questions.

- If so, summarize in your own words what the study says.

- If not, don't include that section of text.

A good way to organize those summaries is to place them in a column that you create for that purpose at the end of your table of studies (to the right of the columns shown in Table 3.1). Use one column for each of your research questions (as we did in Table 3.2). An alternative approach that we sometimes use is to start with an outline, organized by our research questions, and enter the knowledge from the studies into the outline.

Let's go through this process with one of the studies that we reviewed for the NMAC Strong Communities project, Chin and colleagues' 2012 paper, "A Roadmap and Best Practices for Organizations to Reduce Racial and Ethnic Disparities in Health Care."

Scanning the paper, we see it begins with an abstract, followed by a few introductory paragraphs describing the background and methods, then a couple of sections on general findings from the systematic reviews. While that information can be valuable, for our specific project, we were more interested in strategies for addressing disparities. So we started with the next section, which detailed the "roadmap for reducing disparities."

Here are some causal statements from that study as they relate to our research findings:

> Recognize disparities and commit to reducing them. When health care organizations and providers realize there are disparities in their own practices, they become motivated to reduce them. Therefore, the Patient Protection and Affordable Care Act of 2010 makes the collection of performance data stratified by race, ethnicity, and language (REL) a priority (Chin et al., 2012, p. 993).

That section of text mentioned collecting data by REL, so we extracted this information in our own words into the appropriate column of our table, as in Table 3.2. Because these sentences are about strategies for health care organizations to reduce disparities, we entered this information in the column for our research question of "Effective strategies to increase racial equity in healthcare."

TABLE 3.2 ●	Part of a Table Showing Study Findings (summarized in our own words). Note: See Table 3.1 for Columns 2 Through 10 (not shown here due to limits of space).	
1	**11**	**12**
Study Bibliographic Information	**Study Findings**	
Author(s)	**Effective Strategies to Increase Racial Equity in Healthcare**	**Intersections Between Racial Discrimination, Social Drivers, and Health**
M. H. Chin, A. R. Clarke, R. S. Nocon, A. A. Casey, A. P. Goddu, N. M. Keesecker, & S. C. Cook	Chin et al.'s (2012) review of research found that realizing that disparities in their practices exist motivated health care organizations and providers to reduce them. Chin et al. (2012) reported that the Patient Protection and Affordable Care Act, and initiatives of the Robert Wood Johnson Foundation, the Institute of Medicine, and others, have made collecting data by race, ethnicity, and language (REL) a priority.	

Source: NMAC Strong Communities Project.

We continued reading this paper and the other publications and extracting relevant information into our outline.

Sometimes, a paper will include a diagram of causal relationships. This will make your job easier in Step 4. So make a note of those!

Organize Study Findings

After you have described the study findings in your own words, the next step is to organize the information you have gained. With a large amount of information, breaking the question down into more specific subtopics is a good way to organize the information. Those subtopics can serve as subheadings in your outline. This helps ensure a complete and effective report for sharing the knowledge that you've gained from your research.

Our outline for reporting the results of the NMAC Strong Communities literature review ended up including six subtopics, under the two research questions:

Research Question 1:

What are the relationships between racial discrimination, social drivers, and health?

Subtopics:

1. Social drivers of health equity (including racial disparities)

2. Other forms of racism discrimination mentioned in the literature (other than those described as drivers of health)

Research Question 2:

What are the effective strategies to increase racial equity in health care, within an organization or a community?

Subtopics:

1. Effective practices for addressing racial equity and health equity in organizations

2. Effective practices for initiatives to address equity

3. Strategies for organizations to impact social drivers

4. Strategies for impacting health equity in communities

Let's go through an example using the Chin et al. (2012) study findings from Table 3.2. These findings focused on collecting data by race, ethnicity, and language (so that organizations and providers will realize that disparities exist and be motivated to take action). We therefore created a subsection of our outline on Collecting and Analyzing Data by Race, Ethnicity, and Language, within the section on Effective Practices for Addressing Equity in Your Organization, and grouped those findings with other findings on that topic in that subsection.

Once you have organized the findings from your research into topics and subtopics, read through your findings and reflect on what you are learning. Reorganize your outline and edit your writing as needed. Continue re-reading and editing until you have no further improvements to make. You will now have written a well-organized description of your research findings. This will make your job easier when you are writing a report of your research findings (for a sample report, see Appendix B) and when you are creating a map of your findings (Step 5). Working from your organized outline is an easier way to create a map that integrates similar causal statements across studies because your organized outline groups together all the studies that provided similar causal statements. In addition, your headings and subheadings from your outline can provide a framework for organizing a large map.

Step 4. Assessing Research Quality

Making decisions and taking action based on limited knowledge always involves some risk. To reduce that risk, you may be tempted to avoid action until you have the studies of the highest possible quality. However, when we are willing to consider *only* the highest quality studies, we end up considering fewer studies and so we risk doing nothing about the problem. To reduce the risks associated with limited knowledge while also reducing the risk of doing nothing, we need to glean all the knowledge we can from the available studies, even though those studies may have imperfections.

In Step 1, we discussed the importance (in most situations) of selecting studies from reliable, trustworthy sources. While that gives some assurance of reasonable quality, all studies have limitations, and sometimes peer-reviewed studies by well-qualified researchers contain serious weaknesses.

A more advanced and rigorous approach is to also conduct your own assessment of the quality of each study that you review. This may be especially important in situations where few studies exist or where one study is highly influential (with serious ramifications for public policy and for funding). In such situations, legislators and nonprofit policy organizations may ask you to conduct a more in-depth analysis of the strengths and weaknesses of that study.

Study Appraisal Checklist

Chapter 1 introduced the knowledge appraisal matrix as a tool for assessing the quality of a knowledge map. Table 3.3 provides a similar tool that you can use to assess the quality of evidence from each study in your review of related research. Then you can summarize the information across those studies to assess the overall strengths and limitations of knowledge in the field. If different studies have different limitations and they are reaching the same conclusions/results, you can be more confident in the overall body of studies. It also shows how much confidence to put in the information from the studies and what new research may be needed to strengthen the body of evidence.

The assessment of the *quality* of the available studies in Table 3.3 is separate from but could be combined with an assessment of the *magnitude of effect* across studies, as in a quantitative meta-analysis (see Appendix C).

Most studies cannot fully meet all criteria. Sometimes, when you are conducting practical research, you need to make trade-offs between the criteria. For example, in the NMAC study we conducted several interviews and focus groups in six cities, synthesized information from 11 existing publications, and conducted a survey of key informants. We could improve the quality of our data by interviewing and surveying more people, incorporating more existing literature, or having another researcher re-analyze the data. While that would provide greater confidence in the findings, there are trade-offs. Such a study would increase research costs and require more participant time. Also, the research would take longer to complete and so delay decisions and successful action based on those research results.

TABLE 3.3 ⬢ Study Appraisal Checklist	
Criteria	**Study meets criteria?** **(Yes/No and why)**
MEANING	
Meaning to researchers • You, as a knowledgeable researcher reading the article, have confidence in the findings. • Study author(s) has the necessary qualifications to conduct the study. (And presumably they agree with the article or they wouldn't have written it.) • Study was peer-reviewed or published by a leading organization in the field. • Study has shown meaning to broader community of researchers (e.g., award-winning, highly cited, or highly influential/seminal study).	
Meaning to the study's stakeholders • Stakeholders participated in study design/planning, interpretation of results, and development of recommendations. Research questions and measures of success reflect stakeholders' perspectives. Research is ethical. • Consensus agreement with the study has been reached among stakeholders in the field.	
DATA	
Study is based on data. Researcher discloses potential conflict of interest. Study is not influenced by bias. Data support the study's conclusions.	
Data fit the purpose. The research focus, design, and methods fit the specific situation. Data collection instruments are culturally appropriate. Research implementation adapts to fit the purpose. The data meet the research objectives.	
Data are properly collected and analyzed. Researchers clearly explain what they did to collect and analyze the data and the study limitations. Researchers follow proper procedures for the designs and methods used.	
Data are consistent and repeatable. More than one researcher analyzed the data and obtained similar results. Researchers repeated data collection and got similar results.	
Data from real-world application confirm study predictions. Study findings have been applied and made measurable contributions to decision-making and change.	
Findings are generalizable to other situations outside of the study.	
LOGIC	
Structured understanding of the situation. Researcher explicitly states understanding of the context. Researcher provides a clear explanation of hypotheses or expected outcomes and how they are expected to be achieved.	

Criteria	Study meets criteria? (Yes/No and why)
Structured understanding of existing knowledge. Researcher demonstrates understanding of the related literature across disciplines. Researcher describes how the study fits in with models, frameworks, and theories from the literature.	
Structured understanding of the data. Analysis reflects systems thinking. Examines alternative explanations.	

Note: We developed this tool from several frameworks for assessing study quality in the research literature (Stern et al., 2012; Belcher et al., 2016; Lynn & Preskill, 2016) and from our own experience. Each of the criteria that these frameworks mention can be thought of as part of the three dimensions of knowledge. We encourage you to read the sources listed in the Further Exploration section for more information.

Step 5. Mapping the Knowledge From Studies

The final step in mapping related studies is to actually create your map(s). You will want to go back to your synthesis of study findings (from Step 3) to focus on causal statements along with any causal diagrams that the study authors may have included (remember, you made notes of them in Step 3).

In the Strong Communities project, Treatment Division Director Moisés Agosto-Rosario wanted to include a knowledge map as part of the project because, for a long time, program people had tended to address each social driver, such as housing, food, and transportation, "in a vacuum." The map shows that social determinants "don't happen in a silo," that a social determinant is connected with other social determinants. The map will also help constituents to see how the field can tackle issues of race at the same time as it tackles the social drivers of HIV.

Mapping Propositions in Studies

From your synthesized study findings (your organized description of findings across studies, which you created from your extracted findings from each study, back in Step 3), identify the causal propositions. As you do, circle the concepts and draw arrows to clarify their causal relationships. You might do this in the margins of your document or other paper because (for many) drawing the maps by hand helps you to identify and understand the causal relationships you've found in your research.

> **DEFINITION**
>
> *Coding* in qualitative research is the process of assigning words or short phrases (codes) to chunks of text (words, sentences, parts of sentences, paragraphs, etc.) from some source of data (academic paper, interview transcript, industry publication, etc.). Researchers do this to organize and simplify large quantities of data (which helps you and others to make sense of it all).

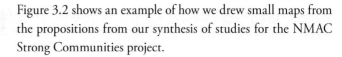

Figure 3.2 shows an example of how we drew small maps from the propositions from our synthesis of studies for the NMAC Strong Communities project.

Note here that the extracted information includes information about the source of each causal proposition and a brief description of the source study. This provides you with a "paper trail" to follow. If anyone has a question about your report or presentation (and they probably will), you can easily show them the details of the literature behind your circles and arrows.

When doing this process of mapping from written documents, we are essentially *coding* (see definition box). Each circle includes a specific *code* relating to a common theme among many concepts within the text (e.g., "getting sick less often," "feeling better," and "improved blood pressure" may all be included under the overarching code [circle] of "improved health and well-being"). We are also taking the added step of noting the causal relationships between those concepts. Thus, we call this type of coding *causal coding*.

DEFINITION

Causal coding is a type of coding that, in addition to the usual coding process of organizing data by specific concepts and overarching concepts, also takes the added step of organizing data by causal relationships. This process gives us concepts in circles (circles may also be organized by overarching codes for a common theme or a collection of concepts) and arrows between the circles.

TRAVEL TIP

Try the following tips to maximize the accuracy of your mapping of the extracted information from the studies:

- *Review your mapping.* After finding and mapping the propositions in your studies, review how you mapped the study information to check that your maps still make sense.

- *Have another member of your research team review your mapping* by going back to the original article. Then the two of you can discuss your understandings of what the original author meant to say to resolve your differences.

- *Have another researcher independently code the materials, then compare and discuss your results.* As in any qualitative coding, a good way to increase the validity of your results is to have two people each map the same study and compare their results and discuss any differences between their maps. We have done this and found that our maps are mostly similar.

FIGURE 3.2 ● Moving From Extracted Study Information to Maps

5. Conducting systems analysis of root causes of inequities
The Anne E. Casey Foundation (2014)'s Action Guide includes as the fourth step to advancing race equity within your organization, conducting a systems analysis of the root causes of racial inequities. The guide states a systems analysis is designed to do three things: 1) identify root causes and contributing factors, 2) surface possible strategies and solutions to address problems, and 3) help choose strategies that can make systemic change.

6. Demonstrating commitment to equity
One of the five components of the IHI (2016) framework for health care organizations to achieve health equity is making health equity a strategic priority for the organization. This includes demonstrating commitment to improving equity at the organization. An example is Robert Wood Johnson University Hospital, which build health equity into the executive compensation plan. Another example is HealthPartners in Minnesota, with a business plan that involved partnerships in the community to address the non-medical social determinants of health.

[Handwritten margin notes:] health equity/ race equity in organization; systems analysis → identify root causes; surface solutions; choose strategies; Demonstrating commitment to equity; Building equity into compensation Plan; Including equity in business plan

Source: NMAC Strong Communities Project.

Integrating Multiple Maps

Now that you've made one small map for each relevant proposition stated in your source articles, the next step is to integrate those maps into a larger map. Figure 3.3 shows the integrated map made from smaller maps diagrammed in Figure 3.2.

CLASS ACTIVITY 3.1

Creating Maps From Related Studies

Review the example excerpted study information from the NMAC Strong Communities project, in the handout for Class Activity 3.1.

Working in teams of two to three students, identify concepts and circle them. Identify causal relationships between the concepts and draw arrows to indicate the causal relationships. Draw small maps of each circle and arrows in the page margin to the right of the study information (as we did in Figure 3.2).

Discuss the following in your group:

- What questions did you have about what concepts and relationships to include on the map? How did you resolve those questions?

(Continued)

(Continued)

- Do you see any logical gaps (places where additional circles and arrows might exist but are not explicitly stated in the study information) that might need more conversations and/or more research?

HANDOUT FOR CLASS ACTIVITY 3.1. CREATING MAPS FROM TEXT—EXCERPT FROM NMAC STRONG COMMUNITIES PROJECT

Excerpt of Study Findings	Small Maps
Effective Practices for Addressing Racial Equity and Health Equity in Your Organization from The Annie E. Casey Foundation's (2014) Action Guide. 1. **Shared understanding and conversations about race** The first of seven steps to advancing race equity within your organization is to "establish an understanding of race equity and inclusion principles." Race-focused conversations often derail because people use the same terms in different ways. Also, a clear understanding and vision of racial equity and a shared language makes it easier to communicate and act to advance racial equity. A challenge in communicating effectively about race is moving people from a focus on individual racism to a more systemic awareness, by "name it, frame it, and explain it." To make it easier to have conversations about race, focus the conversation on causes, effects, systems, and solutions. To help create shared understanding, use personal stories and project widely shared values, such as fairness, equity, inclusion, unity, and dignity.	

Download an electronic version of this handout at https://practicalmapping.com

FIGURE 3.3 ⬢ Example Excerpt of Integrated Map From Related Research

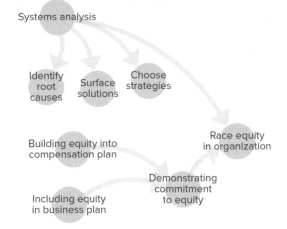

Source: NMAC Strong Communities Project.

MAPPING FROM PROGRAM MATERIALS

Similar to mapping causal statements from the related literature, we can also map causal statements from program-specific materials. Those are materials written to communicate information about a program. Examples include strategic plans, business plans, project plans from grant proposals, and promotional materials (such as a program brochures and web-pages). Creating a knowledge map from a strategic plan or other program materials provides important benefits for evaluation planning and for action for reasons including the following:

- *Guides data tracking and program evaluation*, by providing a framework that you can use to align your data collection and analysis with how the program was expected to work (see Chapter 4, Mapping from Your Own Research).

- *Makes the strategic plan amenable to structural analysis*, using techniques such as the Integrative Propositional Analysis approach presented in Chapter 5. That type of analysis helps organization leaders to improve the structure of their strategies and hence increase their likelihood of success.

- *Clarifies areas for collaborative research* by graphically presenting the different subtopics where you might bring in experts from other fields (Chapter 6).

- *Supports collaboration and communication*, by clearly showing staff, coalition members, and other stakeholders the connections between each step leading to desired results (see Chapter 7, Communication, Collaboration, and Action).

CASE STUDY ROAD

CASE STUDY: MAPPING FROM PROGRAM MATERIALS

Our case study for mapping from program materials is a knowledge map that one of the authors of this book, Steven Wallis, created from an academic research institution's written strategic plan. That work was based on Wallis's participation in a Fulbright Specialist Project with an academic research center, the Leibniz Institute of Agricultural Development in Transition Economies (IAMO), in Germany. This case study draws from and quotes the following:

> Wallis, S. (2019). Integrative Propositional Analysis for Developing Capacity in an Academic Research Institution by Improving Strategic Planning. *Systems Research and Behavioral Science*, (in press).

Creating an Initial Knowledge Map From Program Materials

In advance of meeting with the department director, Wallis created a knowledge map of IAMO's strategic plan (*Leitbild* in German), as presented on its website (Leibniz Institute for Agricultural Development in Transition Economics, n.d.). The process is similar to how we create a map from related research. We read the strategic plan and identified concepts and causal relationships to map. Below are a few examples of statements from the strategic plan text and concepts we identified (in bold).

> The first sentence states, "The Leibniz Institute of Agricultural Development in Transition Economies (IAMO) **performs basic and applied research in the agricultural and food sector as well as rural areas of the formerly centrally planned economies of Europe and Asia against the context of international developments**." We mapped this as concept #32 (in Figure 3.4), "Performing basic and applied research in the agricultural and food sector and in rural areas of the former planned economies of Europe and Asia in the context of international developments."

> The next sentence said, "**This research approach is unique worldwide**." From this sentence, we identified one concept to add to the program map, concept #1, "This research approach is unique worldwide."

> The third sentence stated, "The institute makes a **significant contribution to describing and improving the living conditions of the people and the economic development** of these regions." From this sentence, we identified another concept for the map, concept #7, "Significant contribution to describing and improving living conditions and economic development." We also added a causal arrow from concept #32 (representing the institute's activities) to concept #7 to reflect the causal relationship expressed in the sentence.

We continued mapping the complete plan. Figure 3.4 shows the complete knowledge map developed from IAMO's full strategic plan.

FIGURE 3.4 ● Example Knowledge Map From a Strategic Plan (Shaded boxes indicate "transformative" concepts—that is, concepts that have more than one arrow pointing to them.)

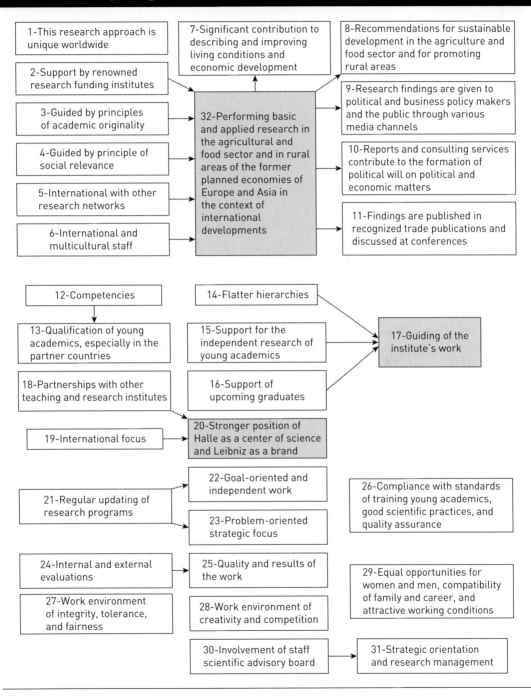

FIGURE 3.5 ◆ Example Knowledge Map of a Strategic Plan From Additional Conversations (Solid arrows indicate positive causal influences, dashed lines indicate feedback loops, and shaded boxes indicate key leverage points.)

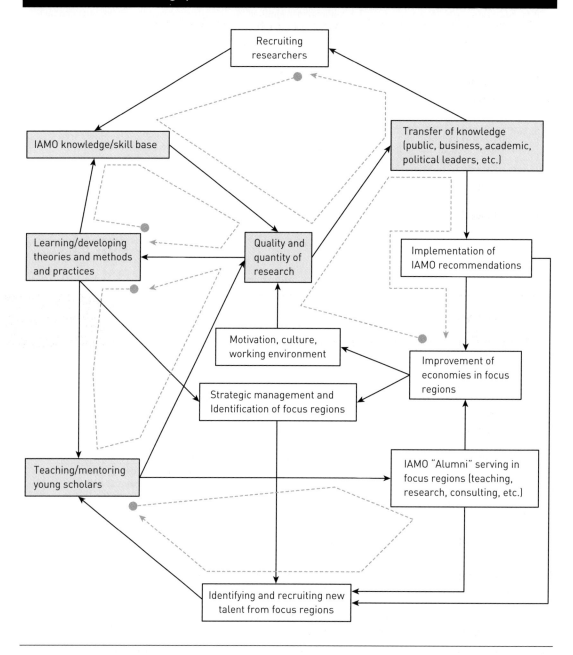

Clarifying and Refining a
Map From Program Materials

After developing the initial map from the written strategic plan, conversations with an IAMO director and close staff led us to connect the dots and show additional understandings that were not part of the written document. The director expressed appreciation for the systems-based analysis and insights into restructuring and improving IAMO's plan, reporting "This information will prove very useful for preparing for our upcoming evaluation and for improving our operations in the future" (Prof. Dr. Alfons Balmann, personal communication, July 7, 2015).

Whereas the initial knowledge map from the written strategic plan showed some logical gaps, the refined knowledge map from conversations had a more interconnected structure. As it provided better logical structure, the new map will provide greater usefulness for finding synergies to strengthen the capacity of IAMO.

Figure 3.5 shows the knowledge map of the strategic plan from additional conversations.

CLASS ACTIVITY 3.2

Mapping From Program Materials

Review the project description in the Handout for Activity 3.2. This was part of a grant proposal for the Howard University *PAC-Involved: Engaging Students in PAC (Physics, Astronomy, Cosmology) Learning Through Repurposing of Popular Media* pilot project (we'll return to this project in Chapter 4).

Working in teams of two or three students, identify concepts in the project description and circle them. Identify causal relationships between the concepts and draw arrows to indicate the causal relationships. Draw small maps of each circle and arrows in the page margin to the right of the study information (as we did in Figure 3.2).

Discuss the following in your group:

- What questions did we have about what concepts and relationships to include on the map? How did we resolve those questions?

- Where are the spots in the map where you have questions or need more information, from conversations with your team?

HANDOUT FOR CLASS ACTIVITY 3.2. PART OF A GRANT PROPOSAL

Example Excerpt From Project Description	Small Maps
The goal of this pilot project is to plan, design, implement, and test a new model of learning environment that increases student interest and achievement in high school science.	

This goal focuses on addressing the following challenges:

- How can students be presented the opportunity to learn significant STEM content in context of informal science?

- How can we engage the learners and provide high quality STEM education for students?

- How can we create new learning environments by infusing cutting-edge technologies that enhance learning experiences for a diverse student body?

- How can we create the strong and engaging content with interdisciplinary links?

The PAC-Involved pilot project will introduce and teach selected high school physics and astronomy topics in an engaging and novel way through the vehicle of repurposing popular sci-fi movies and TV shows to focus on science content.

The PAC-Involved pilot project seeks to meet students' needs in traditionally underserved and underrepresented schools where there is a lack of quality educational options. High school students from public high schools in an urban area (Washington Metropolitan Area Public School Systems) will be immersed in an innovative learning environment that PAC-Involved will create, which allows students to learn physics, astronomy, and cosmology in an investigative way, connect students with STEM professionals, and provide them with rich, hands-on experiences related to science, while at the same time utilizing the full potential that modern technology can offer.

Source: Howard University PAC-Involved Project.

Download an electronic version of this handout at https://practicalmapping.com

Chapter 3 Key Points

- Integrating related research is important for designing and implementing effective solutions, demonstrating the value of your activities, and planning effective new research. Mapping provides a systematic way to integrate knowledge from related research.

- Creating a practical map from existing research involves five steps: (1) searching for and choosing studies, (2) creating a table of study information, (3) synthesizing study findings, (4) assessing research quality, and (5) mapping the knowledge from studies.

- In the same way that you map findings from related research, you can map understandings from program materials, such as strategic plans and grant proposals. A map from program materials is useful for guiding program evaluation, making the strategic plan amenable to structural analysis, and supporting collaboration and communication.

Frequently Asked Questions

Q: How does a map show the difference between one study reporting something that only a few interview participants mentioned compared with another study reporting something that a lot of people mentioned?

A: You can approach this in different ways, depending on what works best for your situation. Here are a few possible approaches:

- The quickest approach—and what we did in the NMAC Strong Communities project—is to start by mapping the circles and arrows. Then, add a note about the details of the study findings for each circle and arrow. That way, when a map user wants to know the magnitude of agreement studies found for a particular arrow, they can look at the details of that arrow to see that information.

- If all studies measured something in the same quantified way (e.g., the amount of increase in student scores on a standardized test attributed to various causes), you might calculate an average or median magnitude of change for each causal relationship across studies and write that number on the appropriate arrow. Your map would then make it easy to see how much effect each arrow pointing to that result showed.

- If the studies used qualitative methods, you might devise your own system for comparing the magnitude of effect across studies, such as whether the studies said that something was had an effect for "many people" or for "few people," and note that on the map's arrows.

Q: How would you handle a situation in which one study says that A caused more B and another study says no effect was found between A and B?

A: Your literature map shows the knowledge from the whole body of literature that you found. So review and consider the quantity and quality of evidence for that arrow from all the studies:

(Continued)

(Continued)

- *Does the evidence support that the arrow is true*? That is, do the studies generally support that more A causes more B? If so, keep the arrow on your map.

- *Does the evidence indicate no relationship between A and B*? If so, do not include that arrow on your map.

- *Is the evidence for that arrow mixed or uncertain*? If so, add a question mark or other symbol to the arrow to show that the causal relationship is uncertain. This is also an opportunity for more research.

- Look at the studies in greater depth. Look to see whether you can find some difference in the measures used or the situation of the studies that might explain why one study found an effect and the other study did not and what that might mean for your map. For example, what you initially thought was one concept might really be two separate concepts if the studies measured it in different ways.

Q: I came across a study in which participants noted that "attending to urgent, including housing" was a barrier to engaging in care. How do you map "urgent daily problems including housing"? Are "urgent daily problems" and "housing" two separate circles or one circle?

A: The best way to map any concept depends on your research questions. Consider whether "urgent daily problems" and "housing" are both important to what you want to know. If so, include them both on the map. If you don't need that much detail, create one circle for "urgent daily problems" and mention that these problems include housing in the details for that circle. For more on this kind of difference, see "scale of abstraction" in Appendix A.

Q: One study said, "A related barrier to engagement in care was housing services policies that require a health decline before people can obtain housing." Does this mean that having a health decline causes more obtaining housing?

A: We only map what the studies explicitly say, not what they may imply (because different people may see different implications). The study you mention is talking about a barrier to care: housing service policies that require a health decline. So I would map this as "housing policies that require health decline" cause less (are a barrier to) "engagement in care."

Q: Is conducting an in-depth appraisal of the quality of each study a necessary step?

A: When you're doing practical research and program evaluation, every step that you take should be driven by what you want to know. In our experience, conducting an in-depth appraisal of the quality of a study is useful in situations when a particular study is likely to be highly influential in public conversations and in public policy and program funding decisions.

Q: What is the difference between a "research purpose" and a "research question"?

A: In research lingo, your research purpose is your reason for doing the study. Your research questions are the specific questions that your study will explore. In practice, we have found that these terms overlap, as a specific research purpose can often be re-worded as a set of questions, and a question can often be re-worded as a purpose.

Further Exploration

Below are references for further reading on topics covered in this chapter.

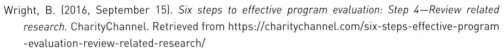

Techniques for Reviewing Related Research

BetterEvaluation.org. (n.d.). *Synthesize data across evaluations.* Retrieved from http://betterevaluation.org/en/plan/synthesize_value/synthesize_ across_evaluations

U.S. General Accounting Office. (GAO, now U.S. Government Accountability Office). (1990). *Prospective Evaluation Methods: The Prospective Evaluation Synthesis.* Retrieved from https://www.gao.gov/products/PEMD-10.1.10

U.S. Government Accountability Office, Program Evaluation and Methodology Division. (1992.) *The Evaluation Synthesis* (GAO/PEMD-10.1.2). Retrieved from http://www.gao.gov/special.pubs/pemd1012.pdf

Wright, B. (2016, September 15). *Six steps to effective program evaluation: Step 4—Review related research.* CharityChannel. Retrieved from https://charitychannel.com/six-steps-effective-program -evaluation-review-related-research/

Wright, B. & Lewis, L. (2016, October). *Reviewing related research (R3) workbook.* Meaningful Evidence. Retrieved from http://meaningfulevidence.com/download-r3-workbook

Issues to Consider in Reviewing Related Research

Berk, R. (2011). Evidence-based versus junk-based evaluation research: Some lessons from 35 years of the *Evaluation Review. Evaluation Review, 35*(191). Retrieved from https://journals.sagepub.com/doi/ abs/10.1177/0193841x11419281

Dijkers, M. P. J. M. for the NCDDR Task Force on Systematic Review and Guidelines. (2009). *When the best is the enemy of the good: The nature of research evidence used in systematic reviews and guidelines.* Austin, TX: SEDL. Retrieved from http://www.ncddr.org/kt/products/tfpapers/tfsr_best/

Gough, D., Oliver, S., & Thomas, J. (2012). Introducing systematic reviews. In D. Gough, S. Oliver, & J. Thomas (Eds.), *An introduction to systematic reviews* (pp. 1–16). Retrieved from http://www.uk .sagepub.com/upm-data/46999_Gough_Chapter_1.pdf

Johnston, M. V., Vanderheiden, G. C., Farkas, M. D., Rogers, E. S., Summers, J. A., & Westbrook, J. D., for the NCDDR Task Force on Standards of Evidence and Methods. (2009). *The challenge of evidence in disability and rehabilitation research and practice: A position paper.* Austin, TX: SEDL. Retrieved from www.ncddr.org/kt/products/tfpapers/tfse_challenge/

Kolata, G. (2017, October 30). Many academics are eager to publish in worthless journals. *New York Times.* Retrieved from https://www.nytimes.com/2017/10/30/science/predatory-journals-academics.html

Moat, K. A., Lavis, J. N., Wilson, M. G., Rettingen, J., & Bärnighausen, T. (2013, January). Twelve myths about systematic reviews for health system policymaking rebutted. *J Health Serv Res Policy, 18*(1), 44–50. Retrieved from http://hsr.sagepub.com/content/18/1/44.abstract

Guidelines for Reporting and Conducting Reviews of Related Research

Liberati, A., Altman, D. G., Tetzlaff, J., Mulrow, C., Gøtzsche, P. C., Ioannidis, J. P. A., . . . Moher, D. (2009). The PRISMA statement for reporting systematic reviews and meta-analyses of studies that evaluate

(Continued)

(Continued)

health care interventions: Explanation and elaboration. *PLoS Med, 6*(7), e1000100. doi:10.1371/journal .pmed.1000100. http://www.plosmedicine.org/article/info%3Adoi%2F10.1371%2Fjournal.pmed.1000100

Task Force on Systematic Review and Guidelines. (2011). *Guidelines for assessing the quality and applicability of systematic reviews*. Austin, TX: SEDL, National Center for the Dissemination of Disability Research. Retrieved from http://www.ncddr.org/guidelines

Assessing the Quality of Evidence From Related Research

Belcher, B. M., Rasmussen, K. E., Kemshaw, M. R., & Zornes, D. A. (2016). Defining and assessing research quality in a transdisciplinary context. *Research Evaluation, 25*, 1–17. Retrieved from http://rev.oxfordjournals.org/content/25/1/1.full

IDRC. (2017, December). The Research Quality Plus (RQ+) Assessment Instrument. Retrieved from https:// www.idrc.ca/en/research-in-action/new-evaluation-tool-now-available-assess-research-quality

Lynn, J., & Preskill, H. (2016, January). *Rethinking rigor: Increasing credibility and use*. Retrieved from http://fsg.org/tools-and-resources/rethinking-rigor

Roller, M. (2017, December 8). *Qualitative research: What is the total quality framework*. Retrieved from https://www.slideshare.net/MargaretRoller/qualitative-research-what-is-the-total-quality -framework. This was adapted from Roller M. R., & Lavrakas, P. J. (2015). *Applied qualitative research design: A total quality framework approach*. New York, NY: Guilford Press.

Stern, E., Stame, N., Mayne, J., Forss, K., Davies, R., & Befani, B. (2012). *Broadening the range of designs and methods for impact evaluations* (DFID working paper 38). Retrieved from http://r4d.dfid.gov.uk/ Output/189575/Default.aspx

Walser, T. M. (n.d.). *Trust and applicability of research findings: An organizing structure* [Blog post]. Retrieved from Route One Evaluation website.

Wright, B., & Lewis, L. (2016). *Reviewing related research (R3) workbook* (pp. 26–27). Meaningful Evidence. Retrieved from http://meaningfulevidence.com/download-r3-workbook

Wright, B., & Wallis, S. E. (2017, March 31). How good is your evidence? *Stanford Social Innovation Review (SSIR)*. Retrieved from https://ssir.org/articles/entry/how_good_is_your_evidence

Yarbrough, D. B., Shulha, L. M., Hopson, R. K., & Caruthers, F. A. (2011). *The program evaluation standards: A guide for evaluators and evaluation users* (3rd ed.). Thousand Oaks, CA: Sage. Retrieved from http://www.jcsee.org/program-evaluation-standards-statements

Techniques for Mapping From Related Research

Wright, B. (2016, February, 17). *Bernadette Wright on "Little is known?" Better using background research*. American Evaluation Association AEA 365 [Blog post]. Retrieved from http://aea365.org/blog/ bernadette-wright-on-little-is-known-better-using-background-research/

Wright, B. (2016, April 27). Getting to evidence-based policy: Three perspectives. *Stanford Social Innovation Review (SSIR)*. Retrieved from https://ssir.org/articles/entry/getting_to_evidence_based_ policy_three_perspectives

Case Study: NMAC Strong Communities Project

Annie E. Casey Foundation, The. (2014). *Race equity and inclusion action guide. Embracing equity: &
steps to advance and embed race equity and inclusion within your organization.* Retrieved from
http://www.aecf.org/resources/race-equity-and-inclusion-action-guide/

Brennan Ramirez, L. K., Baker, E. A., & Metzler, M. (2008). *Promoting health equity: A resource to help
communities address social determinants of health.* Atlanta, GA: U.S. Department of Health and
Human Services, Centers for Disease Control and Prevention. Retrieved from https://www.cdc.gov/
nccdphp/dch/programs/healthycommunitiesprogram/tools/pdf/SDOH-workbook.pdf

Chin, M. H., Clarke, A. R., Nocon, R. S., Casey, A. A., Goddu, A. P., Keesecker, N. M., & Cook, S. C. (2012).
A roadmap and best practices for organizations to reduce racial and ethnic disparities in health
care. *J. Gen. Intern. Med., 27*(8), 992–1000.

Houston, D., Wright, B., & Wallis, S. E. (2017, September). Re-structuring evaluation Findings into
useful knowledge. *Journal of MultiDisciplinary Evaluation (JMDE).* Retrieved from http://journals
.sfu.ca/jmde/index.php/jmde_1/article/view/481 (Note: This article is based on Phase 1 of the Strong
Communities article; the examples in this chapter are from Phase 2 of the project.)

NMAC. (n.d.). NMAC mission statement. Retrieved from http://www.nmac.org/

Case Study: Map of an Academic Research Institution's Strategic Plan

Leibniz Institute for Agricultural Development in Transition Economics. (n.d.). IAMO mission statement.
Retrieved from https://www.iamo.de/en/institute/mission-statement/

Wallis, S. E. (n.d.). *Integrative propositional analysis for developing capacity in an academic research
institution by improving strategic plans.* Manuscript submitted for publication. Retrieved from
https://www.academia.edu/26140848/Integrative_Propositional_Analysis_for_Developing_
Capacity_in_an_Academic_Research_Institution_by_improving_Strategic_Plans

Example of Mapping From Related Research

Panetti, E., Parmentola, A, Wallis, S. E., & Ferretti, M. (2018). What drives technology transitions?
An integration of different approaches within transition studies. *Technology Analysis & Strategic
Management.* Retrieved from https://doi.org/10.1080/09537325.2018.1433295

4

MAPPING FROM YOUR OWN RESEARCH

istock.com/electravk

This chapter covers the following:

- Developing questions to guide research and evaluations

- Choosing research methods to answer those questions

- Conducting interviews to find data

- Organizing your findings

- Mapping your results

- Using maps to visualize data

THE ROAD AHEAD

In terms of the three dimensions presented in Chapter 1, this chapter focuses on the dimension of data. Specifically, this chapter focuses on collecting and mapping data from research that you conduct, such as a program evaluation. Creating knowledge maps from your research helps you

- Integrate your new research map with other maps, such as a collaborative map (Chapter 2), to create a better map

- Integrate your new research map with other maps you create from related research (Chapter 3) to create a better map and show how your research findings add knowledge to the field

Throughout this chapter, we draw on examples from a project at Howard University called *PAC-Involved: Engaging Students in PAC (Physics, Astronomy, Cosmology) Learning through Repurposing of Popular Media*. Funded by a National Science Foundation grant, "PAC-Involved" (for short) developed and tested an innovative learning model to engage under-represented high school students in science, technology, engineering, and math (STEM), using popular media. The Further Exploration section, at the end of this chapter, provides links to more information about that study. For clarity, we made small edits/clarifications to the original PAC-Involved logic model for use in this book.

DEVELOPING RESEARCH QUESTIONS FOR BETTER MAPS

Practitioners need useful knowledge if they are to make effective decisions for successful action. They need a better understanding of how their organizations and programs are working and what they might do to improve them. Our job as evaluators and researchers is to provide that knowledge.

The questions that practitioners need answered may be general (What is happening with our program?) or more specific (In what ways has our program improved student performance?). Those kinds of questions provide a good start. However, to have focused and effective research we want to have formal "research questions" (RQ, in program evaluations, also called "evaluation questions," EQ). Those questions are key because we use them as a guide for choosing our evaluation methods, which ultimately shapes the outcome of the research.

Part of developing effective RQ is understanding what goals are important to stakeholders and how they expect their programs to function. So we start by clarifying our understanding of the program or situation that is being studied.

A typical approach to clarification involves creating a *logic model* (Figure 4.1).

For the PAC-Involved evaluation, we began by creating that kind of logic model. A logic model is one of many approaches to developing a diagram showing how a program functions. Other approaches include theory of change, results chain, and many others (see the Further Exploration section for resources with information on these approaches). We read the grant proposal for the project and conducted interviews with the Howard University project team and the participating high school teachers. That let us uncover both the formally stated goals of the program (from the proposal) and what stakeholders wanted to see the program accomplish.

- The first column in Figure 4.1 shows concepts related to the program *context and resources* (Howard University, interdisciplinary project team, web designer, etc.).

- The second column shows concepts related to *activities and strategies*, grouped together by when the activities are taking place (fall 2013 to summer 2014, fall 2014, and spring 2015).

- The third column shows *two-year/pilot project goals*. These were the goals that the project expected to achieve within the two years of the pilot project and the evaluation.

- The fourth column shows the *long-term/expanded project goals*. These were the hoped-for goals for beyond the two years of the pilot project and the evaluation.

DEFINITION

A *logic model* shows an understanding of how a policy, program, or other action functions (or will function, if it is still in the planning stages) to achieve results. May be represented in many forms, including as a causal knowledge map or a table.

Logic models of this kind do not always have arrows between the specific concepts. Sometimes, they may include arrows indicating that everything in one column will lead to everything in the next column to the right. Often, it is simply assumed that each column leads to the next. To clarify this relationship, we included arrows at the top of the table (similar to the way we've been using arrows for knowledge mapping throughout this book).

In short, the arrows show our understanding of how using resources in this context will enable activities that will lead to successfully reaching short-term and long-term goals.

FIGURE 4.1   PAC-Involved Logic Model

Causal Connections (often tacitly understood)

Causes or Leads to: Causes or Leads to: Causes or Leads to:

Context and Resources	Activities and Strategies	Two-Year/ Pilot Project Goals	Long-Term/Expanded Project Goals
Howard University	**Fall 2013–Summer 2014**	Students' interest and engagement in PAC-Involved and students seeing the relevance of physics and the relevance of STEM to their everyday lives	Students enrolling and succeeding in college level STEM courses and STEM careers
Interdisciplinary project team	Interdisciplinary team developing modules and materials		Refining the PAC-Involved model and expanding it to a larger group of students, for the entire school year
Web designer	Amount of time for hands-on activities		
Vendors for student lunches	Selecting movie scenes	Interest and motivation toward studying STEM/physics and considering STEM careers	
Supplies for labs	Creating website (http://pacinvolved.com/), populating it, and search engine optimizing it		Incorporating Saturday content into everyday class assignments
Computers and $300 stipends for students	Recruiting high schools and high school physics teachers	Math skills and knowledge of physics/STEM	Sharing findings with the larger field, including high school and college instructors and researchers
	Developing student recruitment/parent outreach plan and materials	College exposure	
	Teachers recruiting/selecting students to participate	Exposure to and understanding of realities of being a scientist	Extending to more themes beyond the two themes of the pilot
	Fall 2014		
	Delivering the new learning model with 30 students	Students' research and problem-solving skills	Involving more teachers and adding workshops for teachers
	Updating website and adding new content (text, video, and interactive)		
	Spring 2015		
	Open online learning environment to all Washington, DC, public schools' students and teachers		
	Virtual with teachers		
	Virtual self-learning		

Source: Howard University PAC-Involved Project.

Whether you start with a large and detailed causal knowledge map or a traditional logic model, having a map or model helps you to choose the specific questions that your study will explore. These will be your RQs or EQs. Just to clarify, all evaluation is research (specifically practical research for planning, enhancing, and assessing social programs and other efforts to create change), but not all research is evaluation. Although, research that is not evaluation may also contribute to the development of policies and/or programs. In addition, program evaluations may contribute knowledge to academic fields. So there is a lot of overlap between the two terms. Here, we will mostly refer to these as EQs because our main example is a program evaluation.

TRAVEL TIP

When you're doing research for solving complex problems, your EQs should be developed in collaboration with evaluation clients and other stakeholders. Your EQs should focus on what evaluation audiences (practitioners, stakeholders, decision makers, etc.) need to know for effective decision-making and action. You can also use a causal knowledge map to identify more specific questions that your study might usefully explore. (See Appendix A, "Looking for Sub-Structures.")

Generally, there are two types of EQs:

- *Questions for measuring concepts and connections on your map.* Does our logic model or map work as we expect (are we doing what we planned, is our program achieving the results we expected)?

- *Questions for building a better map.* What happened that we did not anticipate (or what might we do differently)?

Let's explore each of those.

Research Questions for Measuring Concepts and Connections on Your Map

Within those two general categories of questions, managers often have more focused questions. Within the question of "What worked as we expected, and what didn't?" (measuring concepts and connections on your map), specific questions may include the following:

- Were our strategies carried out as planned?

- Did our project have the effects we expected?

- Which program components are most useful, and which are less useful?

- How are outcomes similar or different for each group of participants?

- How long do program effects last?

Answers to these questions are important for holding individuals and organizations accountable. Funders, donors, and board members want to know that a project is performing as promised. Program managers want to know which of their existing program components to keep, which could be dropped, and which to expand, to maximize the success of their activities.

For a more concrete example, in conducting the PAC-Involved evaluation, our evaluation team collaborated with the principal investigator and project team from Howard University to develop a set of EQs to guide the evaluation. These included questions focused on measuring circles and arrows in the initial logic model/map representing the program activities and their effects on the short-term goals achieved during the two-year project, such as the following:

EQ 1: How to structure the sessions (e.g., how much time for hands-on activities)?

EQ 2: What impacts did PAC-Involved have on its goals?

EQ 2a: What impact did it have on the goals of (1) peaking and maintaining students' interest and engagement in PAC-Involved, (2) seeing the relevance of physics, and (3) the relevance of STEM to their everyday lives?

EQ 2b: What impact did it have on the goal of increasing interest and motivation toward studying STEM/physics and considering STEM careers?

EQ 2c: What impact did it have on the goal of enhancing math skills and knowledge of physics/STEM?

Answering the first question was important for helping the principal investigator (PI) and project team to decide whether to increase, decrease, or keep the same the amount of time spent on hands-on activities in the future. Question 2, and sub-questions 2a to 2c, explored the impact of the whole program on its goals. That was important to demonstrate the results of the grant project to funders.

> **DEFINITION**
>
> *Principal investigator* (PI) is the person who leads and manages a whole research project.

In Figure 4.2, we've added circles and arrows to the logic model to graphically indicate the concepts and causal relationships between what will be investigated in our research project. Those arrows are also labeled according to their respective EQs (EQ1, EQ2, etc.).

Research Questions for Expanding Maps

It is important to measure the concepts and connections that exist on your model to show whether that map is working as they expected it to in the real world. However, managers should also address questions of what lies beyond the

FIGURE 4.2 ● Example PAC-Involved Evaluation Questions Linked to Specific Elements Within the Logic Model

Context and Resources	Activities and Strategies	Two-Year/Pilot Project Goals
Howard University	Fall 2013–Summer 2014	a. Students' interest and engagement in PAC-Involved and students seeing the relevance of physics and relevance of STEM to their everyday lives
Interdisciplinary project team	Interdisciplinary te... ...veloping modules and materials	
Web designer	• Amount of time for hands... ...ctivities	
Vendors for student lunches	• Selecting movie scenes	b. Interest and motivation toward studying STEM/physics and considering STEM careers
Supplies for labs	Creating website (http://pacinvolved.co... populating it, and search engine optimizing	
Computers and $300 stipends for students	Recruiting high schools and high school physics teachers	c. Enhancing math skills and knowledge of physics/STEM
	Washington, D.C., public schools and project team developing student recruitment/parent outreach plan and materials	d. College exposure
	Teachers recruiting/selecting students to participate	

Source: Howard University PAC-Involved Project.

bounds of the existing map. Only there can they discover new circles and arrows that they may add to the map to gain a more useful understanding of their situation.

That exploration calls for a different kind of RQ (EQ). Some generic examples of EQs for expanding your map include the following:

- What effects did the program have, including anticipated and unanticipated positive and negative effects?

- What were the challenges in implementation?

- What were the effective strategies?

- What are peoples' new ideas for enhancing the program?

Answers to these questions (and more like them) help managers to improve upon past successes, respond to changing circumstances, and avoid unexpected roadblocks. This information also helps with planning new research by finding new concepts and causal relationships that may be important.

TRAVEL TIP

In this chapter and throughout this book, we detail a process for designing a plan to bring about change (creating a map), putting a map into action, tracking progress with data, and using results for improvement. Some people might call this process a kind of "implementation science" or "improvement science." For more on those, see these resources:

Christie, C. A., Lemire, S., & Inkelas, M. (2017). Understanding the similarities and distinctions between improvement science and evaluation. *Improvement Science in Evaluation: Methods and Uses, 2017*(153), 11–21. https://onlinelibrary.wiley .com/doi/10.1002/ev.20237

Lemire, S., Christie, C. A., & Inkelas, M. (2017). The methods and tools of improvement science. *Improvement Science in Evaluation: Methods and Uses, 2017*(153), 23–33. https://onlinelibrary.wiley.com/doi/full/10.1002/ev.20235

In addition to the EQs for measuring the concepts on the map (EQs 1 and 2), we talked with the PI and project team to develop questions that would help to expand the map. The PAC-Involved evaluation also included the following:

EQ 3: What were the challenges and effective strategies in implementing PAC-Involved?

EQ 4: What difference did PAC-Involve make, including any unanticipated effects?

EQs 3 and 4 are shown graphically on the logic model in Figure 4.3. These encourage us to explore—to find what new circles and arrows will fill the blank spots on the map.

TRAVEL TIP

For research with the purpose of speeding progress in solving complex problems, studies may need to focus questions less on understanding problems and more on identifying solutions and how to put them into action (see Fazey et al., 2018).

Together, all four EQs set the focus for the study. That is, the directions we will explore to collect, analyze, and report the results. To answer those questions, we must choose specific approaches or research methods.

SPECIFYING METHODS TO ANSWER YOUR RESEARCH QUESTIONS

There are a wide variety of research methods you might choose to answer your questions (interviews, surveys, etc.—see Appendix C). For your research and evaluation projects, you will want to consider carefully which combination of methods you might use.

FIGURE 4.3 ● Exploring New Circles and Arrows to Expand and Improve a Knowledge Map

Context and Resources	Activities and Strategies	Two-Year/Pilot Project Goals
Howard University	**Fall 2013–Summer 2014**	Students' interest and engagement in PAC-Involved and students seeing the relevance of physics and the relevance of STEM to their everyday lives
Interdisciplinary project team	Interdisciplinary team developing modules and materials	
Web designer	• Amount of time for hands-on activities	
Vendors for student lunches	• Selecting movie scenes	Interest and motivation toward studying STEM/physics and considering STEM careers
Supplies for labs	Creating website (http://pacinvolved.com/), populating it, and search engine optimizing it	Math skills and knowledge of physics/STEM
Computers and $300 stipends for students	Recruiting high schools and high school physics teachers	College exposure
	Washington, DC, public schools and project team developing student recruitment/parent outreach plan and materials	Exposure to, understanding of realities of being a scientist
	Teachers recruiting/selecting students to participate	Students' research and problem-solving skills

The figure shows circles labeled "Q3 – What challenges impacted implementation?" and "Q4 – what unanticipated effects occurred?" with arrows pointing to "Activities and Strategies."

Source: Howard University PAC-Involved Project.

To answer these four EQs, our evaluation of the PAC-Involved project incorporated a mix of five methods. We decided to use these five methods because of the following:

- Each of the methods was able to provide data to answer one or more questions.
  - The interviews, open-ended survey questions, focus group, and narrative documents (in the form of students' journals) provided data from the perspectives of stakeholders.
  - The closed-ended survey questions and qualitative observation provided another perspective.
- The methods were doable within the evaluation timeframe and budget.
- The narrative documents (in the form of students' journals) let us take advantage of data that had already been collected, thus providing a cost-effective additional data source.

Using multiple methods for each question gives us more confidence that our results will effectively answer that question.

The methods we used for this evaluation were the following:

1. *Before and after surveys of participating and non-participating students*

   The survey included closed-ended questions to assess change in students' attitudes toward STEM and STEM careers and knowledge of physics concepts (Q2c).

   We also included an open-ended question to find out what interested students most about their initial interest in PAC-Involved. This question helped to answer Q3, to find the most effective strategies for recruiting students.

2. *Focus group of students participating in PAC-Involved*

   The purpose of the student focus group was to examine in greater depth students' perspectives of the program and their perceptions of how it affected them. The focus group questions included questions to ask students about the following:

   - What students liked best and least and their reasons for coming to PAC-Involved, to find out what strategies worked well for recruiting and engaging students (Q3)
   - What difference participating in the program made for them (Q4)
   - Whether they planned to pursue a career in science or math or take more science or math courses (Q2b)

3. *Qualitative observation of two PAC-Involved sessions*

   The observation was an important part of the evaluation because we can learn a lot more about the project by seeing it in action. During the observation, the evaluator took notes to answer questions related to the following:

   - Whether students appeared to be learning science and math concepts (Q2c)
   - Whether they appeared to be engaged and interested (Q2a)
   - Factors that appeared to be causing students to be learning and engaged or not (Q1, Q3)

4. *Interviews with project team members* (PI, instructors of the PAC-Involved course, and high school teachers)

   The conversations with project team members provided another source of information to address EQs, from the perspective of those involved in developing and implementing the program. The project team interviews were a useful method for exploring many EQs at once:

   - What goals project team members expected PAC-Involved to achieve (Q4)
   - What the program would do or was doing to achieve those goals (Q3)

- Their perceptions of whether students were gaining knowledge of physics and STEM (Q2c)

- What they saw as the biggest impact of the program (Q4)

- Whether they noticed any change in students' interest in studying STEM and STEM careers (2b)

- What they would do differently in structuring the sessions (Q1)

- Their thoughts on the approach of using popular media to show students the relevance of physics and the relevance of STEM to their everyday lives (Q2a)

See the next section of this chapter for more information about the interviews.

5. *Review of narrative documents* in the form of students' reflective journal entries after the first and last PAC-Involved sessions provided a readily available source of information on the following:

- Students' perceptions of how the program affected them (Q4)

- Their comments on the session structure, such as the amount of time spent in hands-on activities (Q1)

- Their comments suggesting challenges and effective strategies for the PAC-Involved sessions (Q3)

Table 4.1 summarizes the methods we used and the EQs that each method was able to help answer.

Creating a table showing your evaluation methods and the questions that each method will answer, such as Table 4.1, helps you to plan your evaluation research to focus on providing the needed information. And after your study has been completed, it helps you show others what you did—so they can have more confidence in your results (see for example our sample report in Appendix B).

CLASS ACTIVITY 4.1

Thinking About Multiple Methods

1. Working as individuals (or in small groups), imagine a problem that you would like to help solve (in your community, school, work, etc.).

2. Consider the research methods listed above and choose one or more that you might use for answering your EQs.

(Continued)

Activity Ahead

(Continued)

3. Consider what each method might see in that situation, and what it might miss.

4. Present your results to the class for conversations and alternative suggestions.

5. For "bonus points," explain how each method you chose might build on another method or fill in the gaps left by another method.

6. For "double bonus points," consider the additional research methods in Appendix C and discuss whether any of those methods could be useful for answering your EQs.

TABLE 4.1 ● Methods for Answering Example EQs, Howard University PAC-Involved Project					
Evaluation Questions	Student Surveys	Student Focus Group	Observation	Project Team Interviews	Review of Student Journals
Q1: How to structure the sessions (e.g., How much time for hands-on activities?)?			✓	✓	✓
Q2: What impacts did the PAC-Involved have on its goals?					
Q2a: What impact did it have on the goal of peaking and maintaining students' interest and engagement in PAC-Involved and in students seeing the relevance of physics and the relevance of STEM to their everyday lives?			✓	✓	
Q2b: What impact did it have on the goal of increasing interest and motivation toward studying STEM/physics and considering STEM careers?		✓		✓	
Q2c: What impact did it have on the goal of enhancing math skills and knowledge of physics/STEM?			✓	✓	
Q3: What were the challenges and effective strategies in implementing the program?	✓	✓	✓	✓	✓
Q4: What difference did PAC-Involve make, including any unanticipated effects?		✓		✓	✓

Source: Howard University PAC-Involved Project.

FOCUS ON CONDUCTING INTERVIEWS

Due to the limitations of space in this book, we will focus on interviewing as one of the most versatile, effective, and commonly used of all the research methods. Conducting interviews scientifically differs from getting feedback through casual conversations. Unlike a casual conversation, good interview research follows a documented process to accurately capture needed data, minimize bias, and clearly explain how the interviews were done.

Interviews can be used to gather perspectives on whether the processes, outcomes, and causal relationships on your initial map are happening as planned. Interviews can also reveal additional strategies, outcomes, and considerations for building a better map for guiding new research and program planning.

DEFINITION

An *interview* is a systematic process of asking questions of an individual or a group to surface their knowledge, experiences, opinions, and/or beliefs as they relate to the RQs.

Interviews may be conducted one-on-one, between the researcher and a participant, or in a group (focus group), with one or more researchers working with many participants at the same time.

Like any method, interviews have limitations, such as the following:

- People may not know or may not remember important details.

- People are not always comfortable sharing their candid opinions.

- Participants in focus groups may be influenced to go along with what others have said.

- Interview participants' views may not reflect views of nonparticipants.

To produce useful and reliable interview results, you need to start with an interview plan detailing how you'll conduct the interviews and analyze the results. While creating a plan, you will want to consider the following:

- What groups you will want to interview

- How you'll get those people to participate (how you will recruit interview participants)

- Logistics, such as dates, times, location, recording interview duration, and who will conduct the interviews

istock.com/fstop123

Focus group interview.

- Interview discussion guides (script for establishing rapport and what questions to ask)
- Ethical issues (see Chapter 1)

Who to Interview

Similar to collaborative mapping (Chapter 2), interviews are a great way to get in-depth understanding of a topic from the perspective of knowledgeable stakeholders. You will want to interview people who have knowledge and experience related to your RQs. Examples include the following:

- People served by the particular program or project that you are evaluating
- Community members
- Program staff/project team
- Representatives of partnering organizations
- Elected officials
- Experts

In some situations, you may be able to interview everyone in a stakeholder group—the whole "population" (such as interviewing every manager and worker in an organization). Other times, based on the evaluation budget and group size, you may need to select smaller samples of people to interview from each stakeholder group (such as interviewing only 20% of the students and teachers at a school). The key to selecting your sample is to create a sampling strategy that fits your specific situation and to be able to explain why you selected those interview participants when you report your evaluation results. This will help others to understand your research project and your findings. Table 4.2 shows some example strategies for selecting samples of interview participants, according to the purpose of the research.

STOP/REFLECTION/DISCUSSION

On your own or in small groups, think about an improvement that you'd like to see in your community. You might choose to use the same situation that you discussed in Class Activity 4.1.

Brainstorm a list of organizations and/or groups who might be interested (either for or against) that change.

Next, consider which individuals within those organizations might be best to interview. That is, identify who would be able to provide valuable information, experiences, and opinions to better understand and plan how to make the change (or if it should be made at all).

Hint—you can often find lists of people on the websites of organizations that are active on the issue.

TABLE 4.2 ⬡ Some Strategies for Selecting Samples of Interview Participants, by Research Purpose	
Sampling Strategy	**Purpose**
Key persons	Understanding an issue from the perspective of the most knowledgeable persons, such as the stakeholders listed above
People from most successful/least successful situations	To identify effective practices and conditions associated with success
People representing maximum variation in context, such as urban, suburban, and rural locations, or large and small organizations	To identify what's similar and what's different across different conditions
Random sample/stratified random sample of people	To describe how often something occurs and generalize your results to the entire population
Least likely person	To use a single case to show that if something happens in the least likely case, then it probably also happens in other cases
Convenience sample	Often used in exploratory studies and for testing data collection instruments, to quickly get feedback from a small, readily available group, so you can use that feedback to plan a larger study

For the interviews with PAC-Involved project team members—because there were only eight—we decided to interview all of them. That is, we decided to interview the entire population of PAC-Involved project team members rather than selecting a sample of them to interview as in Table 4.2.

Participant Recruitment and Logistics

The next part of an interview plan is to detail how you will recruit individual participants from one or more stakeholder groups and other relevant logistics.

Strategies for Recruiting Interview Participants

After you've identified the general populations (one or more groups) of people you want to interview, the next step is to recruit the individual participants from those groups. Write an invitation to send via email, mail, or phone (whichever is the best way to reach them). To maximize the number of positive responses, write follow-up messages for people who don't respond to your first message within a few days.

Not everyone jumps at the chance to be interviewed. Another way to encourage a positive response is to send the invitation from a source that potential interview participants know and respect. That might be you, the PI, their manager, or some other person (whoever is most likely to inspire a response).

For the PAC-Involved evaluation, we collaborated with the Howard University PI to write outreach messages. These were sent to project team members, informing them about the evaluation and requesting their participation in a telephone interview. An example is in the box titled, "Example interview participant recruitment message."

Example interview participant recruitment message

Subject: Could we plan a call re PAC-Involved?

Hi [NAME],

We are conducting the evaluation of the PAC-Involved project. As part of this research, we would very much like to talk with you about your experiences as a [PROJECT ROLE]. Dr. Fotiyeva gave us your email address.

Our goal is to better understand what PAC-Involved is doing, so that we can design the evaluation to get useful and relevant results.

Should you choose to participate, Dr. Ladel Lewis and I will interview you by phone at a time that is convenient for you. This call will take about 20 to 30 minutes.

Your participation is voluntary and confidential.

Let me know when during these days and times would work for you to schedule a call.

* Friday, May 9, 9:30 a.m.–5 p.m.

* Monday, May 12, 10 a.m.–3 p.m.

* Tuesday, May 13, 9:30 a.m.–5 p.m.

* Wednesday, May 14, 9:30 a.m.–5 p.m.

* Thursday, May 15, noon–4 p.m.

Email or call me if you have any questions. We greatly appreciate your interest and help in this research.

Bernadette Wright, PhD

[EMAIL SIGNATURE]

Consider also what the challenges may be to participation in the interviews and how you can "detour around" those challenges to enable and encourage more people to participate.

Detouring around the road closures to engage more stakeholders in interviews

ROAD CLOSED	DETOUR
1. **No transportation**. People who you want to interview don't have transportation to get to the interview site.	1. **Provide transportation**, such as van rides to and from meetings, or transportation reimbursement.
2. **Don't know you**. People who you want to interview may be less likely to respond because they don't know you.	2. **Work with trusted individuals/organizations** that have relationships with the people who you want to interview to let them know about the interviews and encourage participation.
3. **Unmotivated**. People are unmotivated to take the time to participate in an interview.	3. **Provide incentives**. Many incentives can motivate people to participate in research, such as providing meals at focus groups, offering respondents the opportunity to receive a copy of the research results, monetary incentives, and the opportunity to help improve a program and benefit others.
4. **Too busy**. People who you want to interview are too busy, or their schedules are too unpredictable, to schedule an in-person or phone interview.	4. **Be flexible**. For example, you could offer the option to respond to interview questions by email instead of in-person or by phone, if respondents prefer.
5. **No communication**. People speak a different language than you.	5. **Get help**. Bring on translators and/or researchers who speak the local language.
6. **Culture gap**. Communities may have different traditions from yours.	6. **Collaborate**. Work with community members as you develop your research plan to account for cultural differences (to avoid confusion and misunderstanding).
7. **Disabilities**. People may have disabilities such as deafness, blindness, or an intellectual disability.	7. **Support**. Ask research participants what accommodations would be useful for them and provide them with needed accommodations.

For the interviews with the Howard University PAC-Involved project staff, we planned to interview the following individuals:

- Four Howard University project team members (the PI and the other three Howard University professors who were involved in designing and implementing the program)

- Two physics teachers from the participating high school

istock.com/sturti

Phone interviews are often more convenient for the interviewer and the interview participant but are less effective for building rapport or for seeing facial expressions or body language, which help with understanding the meaning behind what the person is saying.

- The graduate assistant

- The technology consultant

Interview Format and Location

Researchers conduct interviews in a variety of formats (with individuals or in groups) and with a variety of technologies (in-person, by phone, or via video conferencing).

Each format and technology for conducting interviews has advantages and disadvantages. Face-to-face and online/video interviews let you see the expressions and body language of the person being interviewed. This enables the researcher to better understand the meaning behind what the person is saying. Face-to-face interviews also provide a good opportunity for building rapport so that interview participants will feel comfortable providing candid answers to your interview questions. Phone interviews are often (but not always) more convenient for both the interviewer and the person being interviewed. They are also faster and less expensive.

You will also want to consider how much time will be needed for each interview. One hour is a common length, and so is half an hour. The time may vary, however, depending on the complexity of the questions. Much over 60 minutes and your participants may become fatigued.

For the PAC-Involved evaluation, we conducted individual interviews with project team members by phone, for convenience and to save time and money.

Interview Timing

Consider when would be the best time(s) to conduct the interviews relative to the program operation. Data may be collected at the start of a project, at the end, and/or anywhere along the way (whatever is needed to answer the review questions).

For the PAC-Involved study, we conducted three rounds of interviews with the project staff:

- At the beginning of the planning process, to learn about the program context and staff's perceptions of program goals and how those goals would be accomplished

- Before the project started, to find out about their readiness to begin the project and also to find if any changes had been made since the first round of interviews

- At the end of the project, to find out their perceptions of the program's impact, what worked, and what they would change

We also communicated with the principal investigator throughout the project by email and by phone. Those communications provided opportunity for us to

- Update the PI about evaluation work completed, discuss next steps, stay apprised of what was happening in the program, and collaborate on shaping data collection plans, to ensure that the evaluation stayed focused on what was relevant and useful

- Share preliminary findings so that the project team could use that knowledge gained to strengthen the program

- Coordinate data collection to encourage and make it easier for people to participate in the research

Interviewers

One interviewer will generally suffice for one-on-one conversations. For focus group interviews, having two or three facilitators is often useful, depending on the size of the participant group (for example, one facilitator can focus on engaging the group while another takes notes).

For the phone interviews with PAC-Involved project team members, one researcher led the conversation, while another researcher took notes.

Techniques for Capturing Interview Data

To ensure that you capture as much data as possible, it's a good idea to record the interview conversations (by using an audio-recording device) and then transcribe the recordings or obtain the assistance of a skilled notetaker. Both help you capture quotes, which you can include in your presentation and report.

"Quotes are like rubies."

Saul Eisen, PhD (Personal communication, 1997)

TRAVEL TIP

We've found that the recording mode on smartphones works well for recording phone interviews and in-person interviews with individuals and small groups. They don't work so well if you are interviewing many people who are seated throughout a large room. In large-room interviews, you might need a good notetaker or more advanced recording equipment.

On many smartphones, putting your phone in "airplane mode" prevents any incoming calls from disrupting your recording.

Also, many video conferencing platforms include a recording function.

Procedures for Protecting Research Participants

Always remember to consider ethical issues, such as ensuring informed consent of interview participants and protecting their privacy. (See Chapter 1 for more information on research ethics.)

For the interviews with PAC-Involved project team members, we provided that informed consent and privacy information in the email invitation and again by phone at the start of the interview sessions.

Because the students were under 18 years of age, there were special considerations for the student focus group and for other data collection from students. Details of the evaluation methods involving students were reviewed and approved by the Howard University IRB. Parents and students both signed consent forms to participate in the project.

Your Interview Discussion Guide

Basically, there are three kinds of interviews—structured, semi-structured, and unstructured. In a structured interview, we always ask the same questions in the same way. We are generally looking for straight-forward answers (like yes/no) to simple questions (like, "How many times does your boss give you positive feedback in a typical week?"). In contrast, an unstructured interview is like a casual conversation ("Hi, what's happening here?)". It doesn't follow a script of specific interview questions, but it does focus on a particular topic.

For creating and improving knowledge maps (and logic models), we find that semi-structured interviews are often the most useful. This approach is more like a friendly, thoughtful conversation. You develop and follow a list of interview questions, but you may make small changes to the question wording or the order of the questions to allow for natural conversation flow. You may also ask new questions to follow-up on new things that participants mention.

In any type of interview research, a discussion guide helps you keep conversations focused on collecting relevant information. Generally, a discussion guide consists of three parts.

> *First, the welcome and introductions/warm-up.* Here, you might have a detailed script or a short set of notes on what to say as you introduce yourself and explain the purpose of the interview. You also provide the participant with information about confidentiality, ask permission to record the conversation if applicable, and answer any questions that the interview participant may have.

TRAVEL TIP

Using existing interview guides and other existing data collection instruments can make your life easier, but proceed with caution. Interview guides from past studies may contain questions that you could incorporate or adapt for your own interview research. However, "off-the-shelf" guides may not work for your study because you are collecting data from a different group of people in a different place and time. Existing guides are particularly useful when data collection tools are available that would let you compare your results with the results from other organizations that are collecting the same data (using the same guides).

For the Howard University PAC-Involved project, we explored existing materials and found that none of those existing tools would be suitable for use in our evaluation. For example, one survey tool that we found would take 45 minutes for students to complete, and it only measured *one* of the outcomes that we wanted to measure. We wanted to keep the student survey to no more than 10 minutes, so that teachers would be willing to administer the survey to students and students would have time to answer all the questions.

However, we found several existing guides that contained some useful questions that we were able to use and adapt. For example, we used some parts of a focus group guide developed for use in a study with under-represented students in the Operation SMART Eureka! Program. We found that focus group guide on a website that provides a repository of education-related evaluation instruments (OERL: Instruments: Under-Represented Populations website: http://oerl.sri.com/instruments/up/studfocus/instr119.html).

We also developed new questions to include in our student focus group guide to collect information specific to the PAC-Involved evaluation, such as "What was the main reason you decided to be in PAC-Involved?"

The second part of the discussion guide contains the interview questions. Your interview questions are tied to your EQs (RQs). For building better maps, ask questions about causes and effects as they relate to your RQs. Include open-ended questions such as "What would you say has been the biggest effect of the program?" Also, for each question, you might ask "probing" questions or follow-up questions, such as the following:

a. "Could you give an example of that?"

b. "You mentioned X. Tell me more that."

c. "Was there any other reason?"

d. "Do you have any other thoughts about that?"

You might also ask clarifying questions such as, "You said X and Y—did you mean that X causes Y, Y causes X, or something else?"

TRAVEL TIP

Help jog interview participants' memories. When you are making your list of interview questions, pay attention to how they are organized—it can make a difference. You can help interview participants remember things if you lead their thinking toward what you want them to remember, one step at a time.

Let's say you are conducting an evaluation of an agency that provides programs to support education. Part of that evaluation is to ask the program staff for their suggestions on improving the agency's education programming. You can help participants to remember (and provide more helpful comments) if you ask them questions in a chronological order that follows their personal experiences. For example, start by asking when they joined the agency. Then, ask what kinds of good work they've done. Next, ask what problems they've encountered along the way, what has been done in the past to solve those problems, and so on. Notice here that you are helping bring the past to life for them—bringing those old buried thoughts into their minds. Give participants helpful questions so that they can refresh their own memories.

If, instead, you start by asking (something like) "What should your agency do differently?" they might respond by making a suggestion about whatever is on their minds at the moment. It might be a good answer, but it might not be as informative an answer as you would get if you ask a series of questions that helps them to recall their experiences.

Make interview questions bite sized. Participants may have difficulty answering a big question like, "What are all the problems and opportunities facing your agency today?" You can help them by breaking a big question up into bite-sized chunks. For example, you might ask about problems facing each individual department or section. Then, ask about the opportunities for each. After a few of those questions, the participant's mind will be full of memories and ideas. *Then*, you might be able to ask a complex question such as, "What might your agency do that will improve the situation for all departments?"

Avoid letting your personal views bias interview participants into providing the answers that you expect. For example, avoid saying things such as "I think that X is important; don't you agree that X is important?" Also, avoid arguing with or attempting to persuade the people you are interviewing. Stay focused on your purpose of gathering information.

TRAVEL TIP

Nothing ever goes as planned. To make sure that your interviews go as smoothly as possible, try a practice run. Starting with the draft interview discussion guide you created, interview a few people to see how it goes. Their responses might suggest ways you can improve your questions. For example, a question that you think is clear may actually be confusing to others.

The third and final part of your interview discussion guide is the wrap-up. Ask the interview participant, "Do you have anything else you would like to add?" Give them time to think about their answer. Then, thank the person for their time, participation, and contribution to the research project.

TRAVEL TIP

As you are interviewing someone, ask questions to clarify how they see causal connections that they mention, such as the following:

- Are you saying that A causes B?
- You mentioned A. What causes A? What can be done to address A?

Table 4.3 shows an example interview discussion guide used in one of the rounds of project team interviews.

HANDOUT: INTERVIEW PLANNING CHECKLIST

Use this checklist for developing your interview plan. Spelling out these details will help ensure that your interviews are conducted in a systematic way so that you get convincing, practical, and useful results.

- ☐ *Who to interview.* Decide which stakeholder groups should be included, how many people you'll interview from each group, and how you'll select prospective interview participants.
- ☐ *Participant recruitment and logistics.*
  - ☐ *Strategies for recruiting interview participants.* What you will do to reach out to and follow up with prospective interview participants to maximize response
  - ☐ *Interview format and location.* Interview format (phone, in person, or video; individual or group interviews), how much time will be required for each interview, and locations for in-person interviews (if applicable)
  - ☐ *Interview timing.* When the interviews will be done
  - ☐ *Interviewers.* How many people and who will conduct the interviews
  - ☐ *Techniques for capturing interview data.* Whether you record and transcribe the conversations, use a skilled note-taker, or both
- ☐ *Procedures for protecting participants.* How you will ensure informed consent and protect participants' privacy.
- ☐ *Interview discussion guide.* Prepare your script for guiding the conversation, from establishing rapport, to asking questions, to wrapping up.

Download an electronic version of this handout at https://practicalmapping.com

TABLE 4.3 ⬡ Discussion Guide, Howard University PAC-Involved Evaluation, Round I Project Team Interviews

Project: PAC-Involved: Engaging Students in PAC (Physics, Astronomy, Cosmology) Learning Through Repurposing of Popular Media

Funding Source: National Science Foundation (NSF) Innovative Technology Experience for Students and Teachers (ITEST) award number 1311427

Principal Investigator: Izolda Fotiyeva, PhD, Howard University

Co-Principal Investigators: Marcus Alfred, PhD, Marilyn Irving, PhD, & Prabhakar Misra, PhD, Howard University

Evaluators: Bernadette Wright, PhD, & Ladel Lewis, PhD, Meaningful Evidence, LLC

Discussion Guide for Round One Project Team Interviews

Project Team Members	Things to Cover and Questions to Ask
All	**Welcome & Introductions** Welcome and warm-up conversation. Introduce self and explain purpose of interview. Ask permission to record the conversation so that we don't miss anything they say. Do you have any questions?
PI and Co-PI: School of Education	**PAC-Involved Goals & Activities** What do you see as the overall goals that the PAC-Involved pilot project will accomplish? In other words, what would you consider success? • Anything else? • What would you say are the *longer-term* goals that PAC-Involved will achieve beyond this 2-year pilot? In your view, how will PAC-Involved accomplish these goals? That is, what specific strategies will it use, or could it use, to accomplish these goals? Describe how you recruited and selected high schools and teachers to participate. So far, has PAC-Involved been developing as you expected? What have been the accomplishments and progress in developing the model to date? • What resources or strategies would you say have helped the most to effectively develop the PAC-Involved pilot? What would have helped things go better?

Project Team Members	Things to Cover and Questions to Ask
Co-PIs: Physics Faculty	Describe the process of how you're selecting popular media and developing materials for PAC-Involved. • What challenges have you had in this process? What has been helpful for you? • What are the learning objectives for your lesson? • Any other outcomes you expect for participating students, teachers, or schools?
High School Teachers	We're trying to know more about what's going on in schools, so that we can understand how to better serve the schools. • What led you to teaching physics at DC Public Schools? Did you previously teach anywhere else? • We understand that the students in PAC-Involved will be from your "concepts of physics" or "principles of physics" class—is that right? Is this class mandatory for DC Public School high school students? • What other physics classes are available at the school where you teach? • Are students interested in physics? If not, why not? • Are there enough physics teachers and classes for students who would like to take physics, or do you think your school needs to hire more physics teachers? Why would you say that is? Tell us about your process for recruiting and selecting students to participate in PAC-Involved. • What selection criteria are you using? How did you decide those selection criteria? • Tell me about your process for involving parents in PAC-Involved? • What difficulties or challenges have you had in recruiting students and involving parents? • What has been helpful? • What effects do you hope to see for students, yourself, or your school as a result of being part of PAC-Involved? Anything else?
All	**Evaluation Questions** Are there any questions or topics that you think are particularly important to consider in the evaluation of PAC-Involved? What do you see as the planned uses for the findings from this project? **Wrap-Up** Do you have anything else you would like to add? Thank participant.

CLASS ACTIVITY 4.2

Interview Practice

1. Working individually, think of something you would like to learn from your classmates.

2. Again individually, create a list of three to four open-ended questions to ask your classmates to help you learn about that topic.

3. Work in groups of three—with one person asking questions, the second person responding, and the third person observing. After about 10 minutes of interviewing, conduct a debriefing with all three, talking about what went well in the interview and what the interviewer might do better next time.

4. Rotate roles and repeat.

TRAVEL TIP

Researcher bias is important because every researcher comes to their research with some existing opinions, experiences, and beliefs—their own maps in their minds.

In our view, some types of researcher bias are OK. One kind of bias is toward high-quality research—to working on research projects that will be more beneficial to society as a whole.

We want to avoid bias that interferes with high-quality research results. For example, a researcher with a gender bias might interpret results differently from male and female interview subjects (even if they give the same answers). Another kind of bias is seen when the researcher believes that he or she knows "the answer" before the research begins. This can lead to big problems if the researcher tries to push that answer onto the stakeholders instead of relying on the research.

It's an interesting and useful exercise to take some time and consider what YOUR biases are. If you think you have none . . . ask someone else. After all, everyone has them. It takes some effort to avoid them, but this effort improves the quality and impact of your research.

By incorporating multiple stakeholders' perspectives, materials, and existing data as you develop your map, then using multiple methods and data sources to test and improve your map, you can reduce your bias. Assessing your map's structure (Chapter 5), collaborating with other researchers to integrate maps across disciplines (Chapter 6), and sharing and getting feedback on your map from stakeholders (Chapter 7) also reduces the influence of researcher bias on the map structure and data emerging from your research.

Finally, don't forget that the interview plan is only part of the research project. You will also want to detail how you will analyze and present your results. For interview research, this means detailing how you will code, synthesize, and present the interview results.

ORGANIZING YOUR RESEARCH FINDINGS

Now that you've conducted all your research, it's time to organize your findings for presentation. Those findings may include notes and results of interviews (and/or any other research strategies, see Appendix C), including all your data and descriptions of what you did to collect and analyze the data. If you made recordings, you should transcribe them (or have them transcribed or listen to them and take notes). Then, gather your transcripts and notes, so you can have all the information easily accessible.

If you like mapping, you may be tempted to create a map immediately after each interview or other data collection. We suggest instead that you collect all your data, then consolidate the data, *and then* map it, just like you organized propositions from existing studies and then mapped them in Chapter 3. Otherwise, you might find yourself with a lot of maps and a confusing range of concepts in the circles. We have found that organizing your data first makes the mapping process more manageable. So let's start with organizing your data, then move to mapping (although, it's certainly possible to do it the other way around).

This approach is much like Chapter 3, Step 3, in which you extracted the knowledge from written reports and organized your findings. Here, instead, you will be extracting knowledge from the notes and transcripts you made from interviews. This means you will have a large amount of data to organize.

As in Chapter 3, you start by causally coding your data (here, from interview transcripts). Carefully read through the transcripts to identify concepts and causal relationships and assign codes (circles and arrows) to them. Remember that you will be reading through transcripts multiple times as you create and revise your codes.

TRAVEL TIP

Analyzing interview data for improving knowledge maps. As you are reading your interview transcripts or notes, think about what concepts and causal relationships people are describing, as they relate to your RQs. This makes creating a knowledge map from the findings easier.

By the end of this process, you should have a large amount of coded data. From this, summarize the data in a series of propositions, much as in Figure 3.2 (in Chapter 3). Be sure to keep notes showing how each of your propositions relates to the coded data. Now, your research results are concise and organized according to your RQ and sources.

REPORTING AND PRESENTING YOUR RESEARCH

Your report is whatever presentation, article, or other format you use for communicating your research results. Typically, there will be two levels to your report. A *detailed findings* section captures many or all of the propositions that you found in your research, such as interviews. A report with more detail equips decision makers and other researchers with a more complete understanding of the options and issues to consider. However, you may end up with hundreds of propositions—leading to a very large report. To make the report more accessible for decision makers, you can also make a more focused version.

A *key findings* report shows the parts of your research that are most relevant to the RQs and the decision makers. Those key findings may be a completely separate document from your report or may be included in a section of your report, as in a report summary or executive summary. This should also be accompanied by a smaller map illustrating these key findings from your research.

The main idea here is to present your findings (as we did in Appendix B), explaining the results you found (propositions), how frequently they were found, and the sources of the propositions (which stakeholder groups). Importantly, you should explain how these findings are connected to the RQs.

Finding and Mapping Propositions of Your Research Findings

From your report, first identify the chunks of text (report sections, paragraphs, or sentences) in which you state your findings. Although your report may include background about the program, description of your methods, and other information, for knowledge mapping we are focused on your findings. Then, circle or highlight the propositions in those chunks of text (as in Chapter 3). We also like to draw arrows on the page for causal connections between the concepts.

Below are some examples of propositions we found and **bolded** in the PAC-Involved evaluation report. Note how each paragraph provides one or more key propositions (here in bold) as well as which data sources supported each proposition.

> Project team members interviewed frequently mentioned **college exposure** as what they hoped students would get out of the project. PAC-Involved students who completed the pre-survey most frequently mentioned the **college campus experience/Howard University** as what **interested them the most about the project** (7 students).

> In the student focus group, when asked if they would recommend the program for other students, one student said they would recommend it because "**for friends who are not going to college, this trip to Howard University may change their minds.**"

As we reviewed the propositions we initially found, we made changes to better organize the concepts for mapping. For example, we noticed that the concepts "college exposure" and "Howard University setting" were very similar. We therefore combined these into

---

FIGURE 4.4 ● **Mapping Propositions in Our Research Findings**

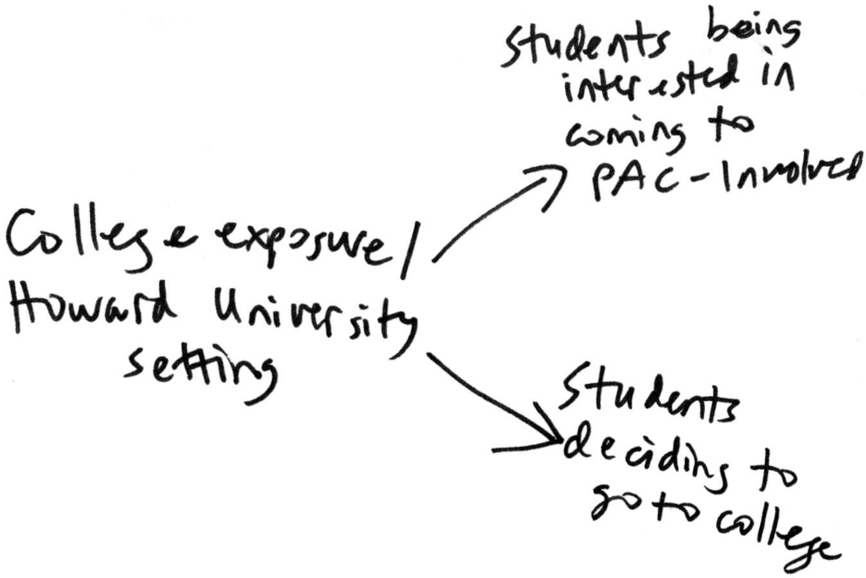

Source: Howard University PAC-Involved Project.

one concept for "college exposure/Howard University setting." This experience highlights the importance of going back and forth with your data. Because, as you do, you become more familiar with it, and new insights emerge that may be useful for organizing your data and providing explanations to your clients.

As in previous chapters, here you identify concepts and causal connections to create a map. Figure 4.4 shows the map we created from the text above.

Next, create a more formal map of those propositions, one circle for each concept and arrows to show where more of one thing causes more (or less) of something else. You can do this on a blank piece of paper or use 3 × 5 cards (makes it easier to move things around). As you do, it may be helpful to think those relationships to yourself (or say them out loud)—to say what you see on the map. For example, "More X causes more Y."

This process helps you to think about what causal propositions your research found and how those propositions fit together to form a cohesive understanding (knowledge map). As you go through your research findings and find propositions, occasionally go back and review your work. Ask yourself these questions:

- *Did I miss any propositions that are important to mention?* If you see any important propositions that are not highlighted (or bolded), highlight (or bold) them.

- *Do I have two or more concepts (circles) that mean the same thing?* If so, combine them into one concept (e.g., "students" and "learners").

- *Do any concepts need to be split up?* If you see a broad concept that is really talking about two or more separate things, it may make sense to split it up.

- *Do the diagrams fit the data?* As you are finding propositions, also make note of what data (interviews, surveys, etc.) support each proposition. After you have found propositions, review the propositions you've found and make sure that they fit what the data actually show (rather than your speculations or assumptions).

Figure 4.5 shows the final map that we created from the PAC-Involved evaluation findings. Although the text of the figure is too small to read in this book, the figure is useful for giving you an idea of the number of concepts and causal relationships emerging from the study. In Chapter 7, we'll cover how to present large maps such as this in a way that is useful for information sharing and planning.

This new causal knowledge map provides a far more systemic structure than the initial map with a typical logic model structure (Figure 4.1). That more systemic mapped understanding represents greater ability to navigate the program to success (more about structure in Chapter 5).

FIGURE 4.5 ⬡ Causal Knowledge Map From PAC-Involved Evaluation Findings

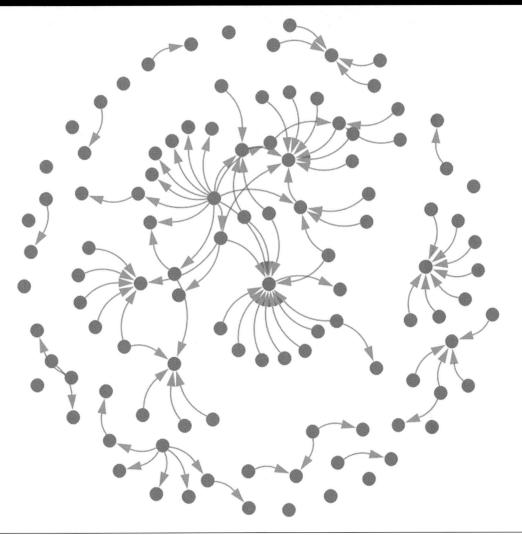

Source: Howard University PAC-Involved Project.

TRAVEL TIP

As when you are finding propositions in existing studies, a way to help make sure that your diagrams fit what the data are saying is to have two (or more) researchers each independently code the material as circles and arrows, just like you did in Chapter 3, then discuss and resolve any differences. If possible, the two researchers could consult a third researcher to resolve any remaining uncertainties.

HANDOUT: TIPS FOR CREATING CAUSAL KNOWLEDGE MAPS FROM YOUR RESEARCH FINDINGS

1. *Phrase concepts as nouns or gerunds* ("-ing" words used as nouns), such as "job growth," "collaboration," or "protecting the environment."

2. *Don't diagram "no relationship,"* such as "money does not cause happiness."

3. *Place a question mark on arrows to show uncertain relationships* and areas where people disagree about whether one thing causes more (or less) of another thing or not.

4. *"Merge" concepts that are saying the same thing,* such as when you're creating a map from statements by many people who used different words to mean the same thing, such as "evaluation" and "assessment."

5. *"More A causes less B = More 'opposite of A' causes more B."* When you have two causal relationships such as "more education causes better job opportunities" and "lack of education is a barrier to job opportunities," these can be combined into one concept, because they are stating the same causal relationship in different ways.

6. *Diagram only what the data show.* Don't map connections that are based on "reading between the lines." You can add your interpretations later as "recommendations for future research."

7. *Use their wording.* Label the circles on your map using wording that is close to what your research participants said. This makes it easier to show what data support the concepts and causal relationships on your map. Some amount of wordsmithing is acceptable, such as rephrasing concepts as nouns (tip #1) or making them less wordy (tip #8).

8. *Keep concepts succinct.* You can add details in explanatory text that goes with your map.

Note: this handout was originally prepared as a handout for the authors' workshop at the American Evaluation Association Summer Evaluation Institute in Atlanta, Georgia, June 2018.

Download an electronic version of this handout at https://practicalmapping.com

CLASS ACTIVITY 4.3

Mapping From Research Findings

Instructions: Working in small groups, identify and map propositions (circles and arrows) from the research summary below (also available online).

First, read the summary. Then collaborate with others in your group to identify and map concepts and causal relationships that you see. You can write in the margins of the page. Use an extra piece of paper if you need it.

Then discuss the following among yourselves in your small group and as a class:

- Were there any concepts or relationships that your group was unsure of how to map or that they had different opinions about how to map? If so, how did you handle those areas of uncertainty?

- Did everyone in your group generally agree about how to map everything?

HANDOUT FOR CLASS ACTIVITY 4.3. MAPPING FROM RESEARCH FINDINGS

Excerpt of a Research Summary	Small Maps
This evaluation provides information about effective strategies and opportunities for positive change, to help plan future projects to improve and expand the Howard University PAC-Involved model. Key recommendations include the following: • *Spend more time on more interactive activities, less time on lectures.* While students liked exposure to movies/TV shows, they were more engaged when this was combined with "hands-on" components. • *Expand opportunities for students to be exposed to college,* such as participants attending lectures with college students, so they can see how college students behave during class. Although not a goal of the program, several students shared that they appreciated exposure to college life, which gave them a better idea of what to expect. A related idea is to use a lecture hall for lectures and the lab for lab work, consistent with standard university practice; this could increase students' attentiveness and comfort. • *Increase collaboration and communication with high school teachers,* to better benefit from their experience and to improve coordination. • *Continue to include a young graduate student* in the sessions with students as a classroom assistant. Students related to the graduate assistant more than the professors because he was closer to their age. Increasing stipends will make it easier to recruit qualified graduate assistants.	

(Continued)

(Continued)

Excerpt of a Research Summary	Small Maps
• *Consider creating a future program that lasts longer than one semester.* Some students were reluctant at first, saying they came only to receive the incentive stipend. However, as they became more involved, several students expressed verbally and in writing that their interest increased, and some said they were sorry the program ended after one semester. A potential downside of lengthening the program could be fewer students participating, so care would need to be taken to ensure that students were interested in a longer session.	

Download an electronic version of this handout at https://practicalmapping.com

Visualizing Data on Your Map

Overall, the quality of your research is assessed on the three dimensions (Chapter 1) of relevance (Chapter 2), data (Chapter 3), and structure (Chapter 5). Here, we show some additional techniques for visualizing what parts of your map have more data and where more data may be needed to improve its overall quality.

We have more confidence in causal links when they are supported by more data and when that data come from a wider variety of sources and methods. Visualizing the data on your map clarifies how each causal link is supported.

Comparing Figures 4.6 and 4.7 helps you see the difference between one relationship (supported by many sources of evaluation data), compared with a relationship that has only one data source. Figure 4.6 has data from only one source—student focus groups. In contrast, in Figure 4.7, all five evaluation data sources—the project team interviews, student focus group, review of student reflective journals, observation, and student surveys—provided evidence that more experiments/demos/hands-on activities caused students to be more engaged in PAC-Involved.

FIGURE 4.6 ● Causal Relationship With Less Evidence (One Focus Group)

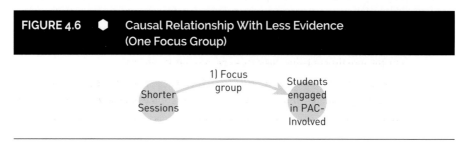

Source: Howard University PAC-Involved Project.

FIGURE 4.7 ● Causal Relationship With More Evidence (Multiple Sources)

Experiments/demos/
hands-on activities

1) Focus groups 2) Surveys
3) Interviews 4) Journals
5) Observation

Students engaged in
PAC-Involved

Source: Howard University PAC-Involved Project.

As you create your maps, you can use this approach to show the strength of your data—how each link is supported by one or more sources of data. That way, looking at the map, your audience (stakeholders, decision makers, etc.) can easily see which parts of the map are more reliable (according to the data) and the parts that might be improved with more research.

Chapter 4 Key Points

- Two types of EQs are often important for providing the information needed for planning and decision-making: Does our logic model or map work as we expect? and, What are the effective strategies, challenges, and positive and negative outcomes that we did not anticipate?

- Conducting interviews (with individuals and/or with groups) is often your best path for surfacing the data needed to improve our collective understanding of and ability to solve complex issues.

- After conducting your research, you can create a new map from your research results. This map provides greater understanding and is more useful for navigating to desired goals than your initial map.

- You can use your mapped research findings to visualize which propositions have more data to support them and where more research may be needed.

Frequently Asked Questions

Q: I'm conducting a focus group with students as part of a program evaluation. I've assured the group that the conversation is confidential and made sure that no professors who are teaching the program are in the room. Yet they are all giving similar answers. I wonder if they might be giving answers that they think people want to hear. I'm not sure they're telling their true opinions. What can I do?

A: This is a common challenge with interview research called "social desirability responding." One tip for dealing with this is to make the interviews confidential and remind participants that their responses will be confidential. You can also ask "What

(Continued)

(Continued)

else?" questions. In the Howard University PAC-Involved student focus group, when we asked students to go around the room and each give their reason for coming to PAC-Involved, the students talked about how they liked science or thought it would help their grades or career. We then we asked them to each say *why else* they were in the program. Students then gave several additional reasons, most frequently mentioning the free laptop and/or monetary incentive provided at the end of the program.

Q: I am interviewing staff at several service organizations for a study on health care in their city. I just completed interviews with staff and clients of one organization. I was chatting with the director of another organization in the community. She had heard about my research and was curious. She asked me what interesting things the people who I interviewed at the other organization had said. Would it be OK for me to tell her?

A: It depends on your specific situation. The important thing is that, as you share your interview findings—whether in casual conversations or in your report of research results—you honor any and all confidentiality agreements promised to participants. For example, if you promised the interview participants that the name of their organization would not be reported, then you need to keep that information confidential. In that case, tell the person that you cannot talk about that. If the interview participants agreed that the name of their organization would be attached to their comments in the report of research results, which would be made available to the public, then it may be OK to share that information.

Q: I'm conducting a focus group. Two of the participants are getting into a long discussion between themselves, arguing over their different opinions. I don't want to be rude and interrupt, but I want to leave time for others to talk and to cover all the questions. What can I do?

A: Some talk between participants can be good—when it's on topic and contributing new ideas. But private conversations and arguments aren't helpful. You might ask people at the beginning of the focus group to avoid private conversations and apologize in advance that you might have to interrupt them. When people get into side conversations, politely interrupt and ask them to let you move on to the next question, or ask who else would like to share their impressions.

Further Exploration

Additional research strategies for improving your map and for collecting data are provided in Appendix C.

Developing Useful Research Questions

Fazey, J., Schäpkeb, N., Caniglia, G., Pattersond, J., Hultmane, J., van Mierlo, B., . . . Wyborn, C. (2018). Ten essentials for action-oriented and second order energy transitions, transformations and climate change research. *Energy Research & Social Science, 40* (54–70). Retrieved from https://www.sciencedirect.com/science/article/pii/S2214629617304413

Wright, B. (2016). *Six steps to effective program evaluation (Part 3): Ask useful questions.* CharityChannel. Retrieved from https://charitychannel.com/six-steps-to-effective-program-evaluation-ask-useful-questions/

Wright, B., & Lewis, L. (2014, July 23). *Asking useful evaluation questions* (Tip sheet). Meaningful Evidence. Retrieved from http://meaningfulevidence.com/wp-content/uploads/2014/12/Asking-Useful-Evaluation-Questions-October-27.pdf

Interview and Focus Group Methods

BetterEvaluation.com. (n.d.). Interviews [webpage]. Retrieved May 29, 2018 from https://www.betterevaluation.org/en/evaluation-options/interviews

Krueger, R. A. (2002). *Designing and conducting focus group interviews.* Retrieved from http://www.eiu.edu/ihec/Krueger-FocusGroupInterviews.pdf

Shackman, G. (n.d.). Methods—Qualitative. (Free resources for program evaluation and social research methods, includes a section on interviewing). Retrieved from http://gsociology.icaap.org/methods/qual.htm

Williams, R. (2018). *Creating great focus groups.* American Evaluation Association Coffee Break Demonstration [Webinar #314]. Retrieved from http://comm.eval.org/coffee_break_webinars/coffeebreak/coffeebreak

Sampling

BetterEvaluation.org. (n.d.). *Sample.* Retrieved March 26, 2018. from http://www.betterevaluation.org/en/plan/describe/sample

Flyvbjerg. B. (2006, April). Five misunderstandings about case-study research. *Qualitative Inquiry, 12*(2), 219–245. Retrieved from https://journals.sagepub.com/doi/abs/10.1177/1077800405284363

Saunders, B., Sim, J., Kingstone, T., Baker, S., Waterfield, J., Bartlam, B., Burroughs, H., & Jinks, C. (2018). Saturation in qualitative research: Exploring its conceptualization and operationalization. *Qual Quant, 52*, 1893–1907. Retrieved from https://doi.org/10.1007/s11135-017-0574-8

Knowledge Mapping From Interviews

Houston D., Wright B., & Wallis S. E. (2017). Re-structuring evaluation findings into useful knowledge. *Journal of Multi-Disciplinary Evaluation, 30*(29). Retrieved from http://journals.sfu.ca/jmde/index.php/jmde_1/article/view/481/436

Wright, B. (2017, March 23). *Using KUMU for visualizing interview data* [American Evaluation Association *AEA365* blog post]. Retrieved from http://aea365.org/blog/using-kumu-for-visualizing-interview-data-by-bernadette-wright/

Case Study: Howard University PAC-Involved Evaluation

Fotiyeva, I., Wright, B., Lewis, L., & Wallis, S. E. (2015, November 9–14). *A new model for engaging under-represented high school students in STEM using popular media and technology: Lessons from the PAC-Involved evaluation.* Poster presentation at American Evaluation Association conference, Chicago, IL. Retrieved from http://comm.eval.org/communities/community-home/library documents/viewdocument?DocumentKey=8601c7b6-9bad-46a1-80b3-f6e5f8e54a6c

(Continued)

(Continued)

Fotiyeva, I., Wright, B., Lewis, L., & Wallis, S. E. (2015, November 9–14). *Theory visualization: Integrating findings from the PAC-Involved evaluation into a strategic knowledge map*. Poster presentation at the American Evaluation Association annual conference, Chicago, IL. Retrieved from http://comm.eval .org/communities/community-home/librarydocuments/viewdocument?DocumentKey=36dcff45-7f 70-431e-a3ca-c855e7a3975d&tab=librarydocuments.

Wright, B. (2016, January 6). *Strategic knowledge mapping: A new tool for visualizing and using evaluation findings in STEM*. [*EvaluATE* blog]. Retrieved from http://www.evalu-ate.org/blog/ wright-jan2016/

Wright, B., Lewis, L., Wallis, S. E., & Fotiyeva, I. (2015, November 9–14). *A two-phase, mixed methods approach to evaluating and improving an innovative program model: The PAC-Involved evaluation*. Ignite Presentation at the American Evaluation Association annual conference, Chicago, IL. Retrieved from http://comm.eval.org/viewdocument/a-two-phase-mixed-methods -approach

Approaches to Logic Models, Theories of Change, and so Forth

Better Evaluation. (n.d.). *Develop programme theory/theory of change*. Retrieved from https://www .betterevaluation.org/en/rainbow_framework/define/develop_programme_theory

Margoluis, R., Stem, C., Swaminathan, V., Brown, M., Johnson, A., Placci, G., . . . , I. (2013). Results chains: A tool for conservation action design, management, and evaluation. *Ecology and Society* 18(3), 22. Retrieved from http://dx.doi.org/10.5751/ES-05610-180322

Morell, J. A. (2011, November 2–5). *Logic models—Beyond the traditional view: Metrics, methods, expected and unexpected change*. Workshop at American Evaluation Association annual meeting, Anaheim, CA. Retrieved from http://www.jamorell.com/documents/LM%20Workshop%20AEA%202011%20 10_27_2011.pdf

Roberts, D., & Khattri, N. (2012). Independent Evaluation Group/The World Bank. (2012). *Designing a results framework for achieving results: A how-to guide*. Washington, DC: World Bank. Retrieved from http://siteresources.worldbank.org/EXTEVACAPDEV/Resources/designing_results_framework.pdf

Rogers, P. (2000). Causal models in program theory evaluation. *New Directions for Evaluation, 87*. Retrieved from https://onlinelibrary.wiley.com/doi/epdf/10.1002/ev.1181

Rogers, P. J. (2008). Using programme theory to evaluate complicated and complex aspects of interventions. *Evaluation*. Retrieved from https://doi.org/10.1177%2F1356389007084674

Smith, C. (2011, December 13). WMU Week: Corey Smith on alternative .logic models [American Evaluation Association AEA365 blog]. Retrieved from http://aea365.org/blog/?p=5245

Smith, V., & Metzner, C. (2012, February 22). *DVR week: Veronica Smith and Chris Metzner on creating a fuzzy logic model on a budget* [American Evaluation Association AEA365 blog]. Retrieved from http://aea365.org/blog/?p=5667

W. K. Kellogg Foundation. (2006). *Logic model development guide*. Retrieved from https://www.wkkf .org/resource-directory/resource/2006/02/wk-kellogg-foundation-logic-model-development-guide

LOGIC

Evaluating the Structure of Maps

istock.com/PeopleImages

In this chapter you will learn the following:

- The importance of structure for knowledge and navigation

- Methods for evaluating the logic structure of knowledge maps

- Deeper insights into structure

THE WELL-BUILT ROAD

In this chapter, we'll focus on the "logic structure" of knowledge maps. This is an important topic because a map with more structure is more useful for sharing information and making decisions to reach goals. By learning to create, analyze, and improve the structure of our knowledge maps, we boost our ability to evaluate and improve programs and policies for solving the wicked problems of the world.

We will assume, for the focus and purpose of this chapter, that the logical relationships presented here are based on meaningful concepts (Chapter 2) and supported by data from good studies (Chapters 3 and 4).

OUR EVOLVING UNDERSTANDING OF KNOWLEDGE MAPS

When it comes to knowledge, researchers are increasingly using visuals to make their results understandable and engaging to a broad variety of audiences. Sometimes, however, those graphics or diagrams are not used to their full potential. A poorly made graphic might be interpreted to mean different things by different people—leading to confusion instead of collaboration.

istock.com/sergeynivens

Graphic recording is one person using a whole wall to take picture-based notes for a meeting.

In this section, we provide a very brief history of knowledge mapping. Then, we'll focus on the key elements of knowledge mapping that will enable you to easily create, evaluate, and improve knowledge maps that will be useful for evaluating programs and supporting decision-making.

While charts and graphs have been around for a few hundred years, there was a dramatic increase in their popularity (and many new types of charts emerged) in the first half of the 20th century as people tried to make sense of increasingly complex organizations.

One common example is the *organizational chart* (a diagram of the organization's social network), showing the boss at the top, managers in the middle, and workers at the bottom (Figure 5.1). *Venn diagrams* with two or more overlapping circles show overlapping relationships (Figure 5.2). *Flowcharts* are used to show organizational operations and to clarify decision-making processes (Figure 5.3). *Concept charts* are used to

FIGURE 5.1 ● An Organizational Chart Showing Authority and Reporting Relationships

istock.com/spxChrome

FIGURE 5.2 ● A Venn Diagram Shows Where Interests Overlap and Where They Are Separate

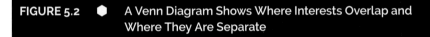

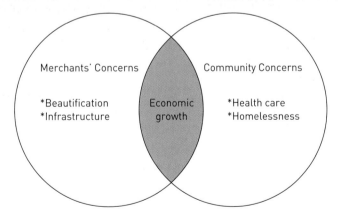

show the similarities (and other relationships) between various concepts. While these diagrams and charts all have their place and purpose, they have not proved highly useful for solving large complex problems (because that was not their intended purpose). Metaphorically, they provide a bike trail, where a deeper understanding requires a six-lane highway.

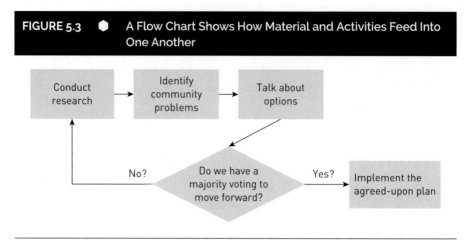

FIGURE 5.3 ● A Flow Chart Shows How Material and Activities Feed Into One Another

STOP/REFLECTION/DISCUSSION

Look at the four diagrams (graphic recording, organizational chart, Venn, and flowchart). Notice how each has a different structure—a different way of presenting the concepts and the relationships between them. What is similar and what is different between the four? How might each be interpreted in a way that supports decision-making?

In general, diagrams are useful because they can be used to present data in a way that viewers can make sense of very easily. While those kinds of diagrams can help, their low level of structure means they will be more useful for understanding and communicating relatively simple relationships. They are less likely to be useful for navigating an organization through highly complex situations.

Consider, for example, an *abnormal* map of your home state. Instead of showing cities (as dots) connected by roads (as lines), the map shows many dots in one corner of the page and many lines (not connected to the dots) in another corner. A third corner might contain the labels for those dots and lines, while the fourth corner contains additional icons representing natural elements such as mountains, rivers, forests, and such. That map would have all the data of a *normal* map. However, because the *relationships* are not accurately represented, the map is useless—its *structure* does not make it useful for navigation.

Our collective understanding took a big step forward with Robert Axelrod's work on the structure of decisions in the 1970s, which popularized the idea that using *causal* connections between concepts provided a more useful map.

TRAVEL TIP

When we talk about causation, we are talking about how we believe things happen in the world—how one thing leads to another. It is important, however, that we do not confuse correlation with causation. For example, consider the hard-working entrepreneur who sets her alarm for 4:30 a.m.—so she can get to work before the sun rises. Every day, the alarm goes off, then the sun rises. But that doesn't mean that the alarm causes the sun to rise!

The cure to that kind of confusion is to expand the map—to identify more causal connections. If you were to explore that strange phenomena (of the alarm clock going off being followed by the sun rising), you would create a map showing that the entrepreneur has an expectation that the sun will rise (and that the business day will start). Based on that expectation, she sets her alarm. That would show how the rising of the sun (indirectly) causes the setting of the alarm clock—which makes more sense than the other way around.

From Inference to Structure

Those historical methods of making diagrams to represent our social world (including maps made for programs and policies) have shared a critical limitation. They do not have a rigorous or reasonably objective way to evaluate the structure of the map itself to determine its potential usefulness for understanding situations and supporting effective decision-making.

istock.com/NoppolMahawanjam

Leaping the inferential gap between data and action.

This has been a problem throughout history, particularly in the practice and study of communication. In receiving any information, the individual is faced with an "inferential leap"—a gap between information, understanding, and action.

When maps have a *lower* level of structure, the leap is *larger* and we are more likely to stumble and fall. We are less able to use the data to help us make decisions to reach goals. For example, a phone book contains a list of addresses that may be seen as a large list of facts. But because they are organized alphabetically instead of geographically, all that data is useless for navigation from one address to another. A road map, by comparison, contains less data, but what is there is well connected—well structured. The inferential leap is larger for the phone book than for the map, so using the phone book would make you more likely to get lost.

For understanding our world, to make better decisions, and to take effective action, our maps must have a more useful structure.

Early Techniques for Understanding Structure for Knowledge

When concepts are arranged on a map, we say that they have structure because of the way they relate to each other. Of course, some kinds of structure are better than others. We can look at a pile of bricks and say that they are structured in the shape of a pile. However, stacking them to make walls (and a house) provides more structure.

Knowledge maps with better structure are more useful for communication and decision-making in much the same way that stacked bricks have more structure and so provide better shelter. Similarly, when writing has more structure, it is more useful for communication (see Figure 5.4).

One stream of research (integrative complexity—more about this in the Further Exploration section of this chapter) has been investigating the structure of knowledge since the 1970s. That research shows that individuals and teams holding more structured knowledge are better able to understand situations, make effective decisions, and reach goals. A higher score indicates that the minds hold more concepts and the possibilities of how those concepts might be interrelated. Research in this area shows that individuals and teams with more structured knowledge are indeed more successful. Politicians had longer careers, managers made more money for their firms, and students received higher test scores.

Evaluators are increasingly interested in maps with more structure. In that field, a growing number of evaluators, such as Dr. Patricia Rogers (2008), have seen that evaluators

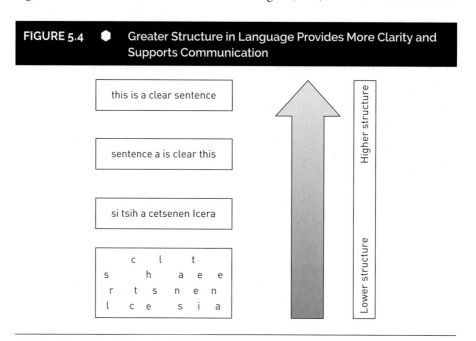

FIGURE 5.4 ● Greater Structure in Language Provides More Clarity and Supports Communication

STOP/REFLECTION/DISCUSSION

What diagrams or knowledge maps have you seen or used at work or in school? What did they look like? Were they useful, and if so, how? What kinds of problems or limitations did you have with those diagrams or maps (if any)?

have been using very simple logic models. Those basic maps show simple one-way relationships. Instead, these evaluators have realized that evaluations would benefit from using maps that include more concepts (not limited to one page), complex causal relationships, and reinforcing loops. This is an important perspective because the better our understanding, the better we can engage and enact change in the world.

CLASS ACTIVITY 5.1

Choosing a Topic

Choose a topic from a previous chapter or pick a new topic (related to the focus of your class) that you would like to better understand—homelessness, poverty, neighborhood revitalization, international health . . . whatever works for you and your class. You will construct maps on this topic later in this chapter.

Summing it up, to create a well-structured house, you use bricks and mortar. To create a well-structured knowledge map, you use circles and arrows. Recent developments in the fields of integrative complexity and program evaluation have focused on the structure of knowledge maps. In the next section, we present a tool for evaluating the structure of knowledge maps, integrative propositional analysis (IPA).

MEASURING THE STRUCTURE OF MAPS

IPA is a method for evaluating the *structure* of maps. IPA lets you quantitatively compare knowledge maps. Importantly, IPA provides a set of rules for indicating objective directions for improving knowledge maps, such as theories and models.

In this section, you will learn the following:

- The basics of how to use IPA for analyzing knowledge maps (e.g., theories and policy models)

- Some uses and benefits of IPA for improving knowledge maps for practical application

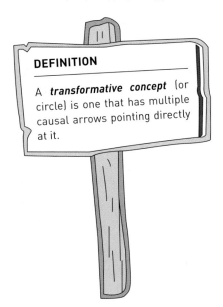

DEFINITION

A *transformative concept* (or circle) is one that has multiple causal arrows pointing directly at it.

Evaluating the Structure of Knowledge Maps

IPA is a two-phase process. In creating a knowledge map, you've already completed the first phase (identifying propositions from research and diagramming them as circles and arrows). The second phase includes three steps for measuring the structure of your map.

1. Identify the **total number** of concepts (circles) to find the breadth.

2. Identify **transformative** concepts (circles with more than one arrow pointing towards them).

3. **Divide** the number of transformative concepts by the total number of concepts in the model (to find the depth).

Test-Drive

Let's work through a simple example one step at a time, starting with a simple map (Figure 5.5).

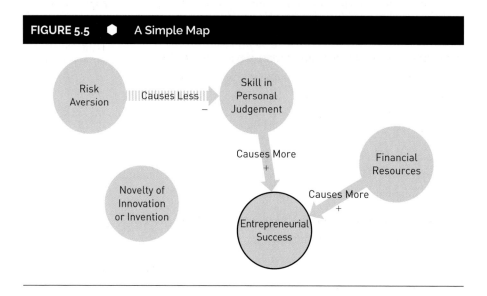

FIGURE 5.5 ● A Simple Map

Step 1. Identify the **total number** of concepts (to find the breadth)

From Figure 5.5, each concept is in one circle, and there are five circles. So the breadth of the model is B = 5.

Breadth is a "soft" or secondary measure of structure—like knowing how many bricks there are (even if they are only in a pile). Metaphorically, improving the breadth is like drawing a road map with more cities. The more the better! However, a map with many points and few or no connecting roads can also lead to confusion and arguments about which way to go.

Generally, breadth is an important measure because it represents the range of concepts you are consciously taking into consideration. It is easier to reach your destination when that destination is actually on the map!

Step 2. Identify **transformative** concepts

A transformative concept is one that has more than one causal arrow pointing toward it.

In Figure 5.5, there is one *transformative* concept (entrepreneurial success).

Transformative concepts are important because they represent something that is relatively well understood. Using map 5.5 as an example, we can see two paths for creating (or improving the chances for) entrepreneurial success. Indeed, we could not be successful with only one of these. In contrast, there are no paths to novelty of innovation, so (according to the map) we don't really know how to create a novel innovation.

Step 3. Divide the number of transformative concepts by the total number of concepts in the model (to find the depth)

Because there is one transformative concept divided by five total concepts, the depth of the map is 20% (one divided by five).

Depth is the "key" or primary measure of the map's structure and provides a strong indicator for the potential usefulness of the map as a whole in practical application.

DEFINITION

Breadth is an IPA measure of the number of concepts on a knowledge map or the range of conceptual territory covered by the map. Sometimes called "complexity." With more breadth, a map is more likely to be relevant or applicable in more situations.

DEFINITION

Depth is an IPA measure of a map's potential for useful application based on its systemic structure. More depth means decisions made with the map are more likely to lead to successful results.

CLASS ACTIVITY 5.2

Evaluating the Structure of a Map

Using a map you made in a previous chapter, evaluate its logic structure and write the results on the handout, *Worksheet for Making a Basic Knowledge Map and Measuring the Breadth and Depth of a Knowledge Map.*

- Identify breadth
- Identify transformative concepts
- Calculate the depth

Present the results to the class and discuss. What maps have greater breadth and depth?

Where are the best/easiest opportunities to improve the structure of the maps?

Using IPA to evaluate your knowledge maps is one way to predict how useful each map will be in practical application for supporting collaboration and decision-making to resolve wicked complex problems. Good decision-making is also supported by having more stakeholder groups involved (Chapter 2) and having more supporting evidence (Chapters 3 and 4).

COMPARING AND IMPROVING MAPS

By now, through your class exercises, you have identified a topic, created a map, and measured the breadth and depth of the map.

Basically, those numbers allow you to evaluate and to compare maps with some level of objectivity, to support choosing effective maps and showing how your knowledge map improves upon existing maps. The ability to make objective comparisons is critically important to improving your maps—a necessary process if we are to solve the problems of the world. You can improve the structure of your map by improving its breadth and depth.

As a numerical indicator, the breadth shows the range of ideas that might be represented by the map. A map with more concepts will usually be a better guide than a map with fewer concepts.

For example, you might be striving to better understand entrepreneurship. Perhaps you want to be a better entrepreneur, conduct research on entrepreneurship, teach

HANDOUT 5.1—WORKSHEET FOR MAKING A BASIC KNOWLEDGE MAP AND MEASURING THE BREADTH AND DEPTH OF A KNOWLEDGE MAP

STEPS	RESULTS
Phase 1: Create Map	
1. **Identify propositions** from one or more texts.	Identified (e.g., underlined, circled, or bolded) words and phrases (as in Chapter 3).
2. **Diagram** those propositions with one circle for each concept and arrows indicating directions of *causal* effects.	Creation of a drawing (as in Chapter 3).
3. **Find overlaps** where the same concept is found in different circles to eliminate redundancies and link concepts within and between maps.	Where the concepts are the same, put them in the same circle.
Phase 2: Evaluate Map	
4. Identify the **total number** of circles (to find the breadth).	Number of circles:
5. Identify **transformative** concepts (circles with more than one arrow pointing towards them).	Number of transformative circles:
6. **Divide** the number of transformative concepts by the total number of concepts in the model (to find the depth).	Depth:

Download an electronic version of this handout at https://practicalmapping.com

entrepreneurship, or support more entrepreneurship in your community. You can do all of those things better when you are using a map with greater breadth.

The depth of the map shows the strength or effectiveness of your understanding. If your depth is closer to 100%, your map reflects a more effective understanding. If your depth is closer to 0%—watch out. Your map doesn't reflect a very good understanding at all.

Four Quadrants

You can plot the breadth and depth on a chart to more easily present and compare the structure of your maps. We like to think of that chart as having four quadrants. In this section, we will talk about the strengths and limitations of each quadrant, using real-world examples.

With measures of breadth and depth, we can easily compare the logical structure of maps (as visual representations of theories and models). Depending on those measures, we can "place" that theory on a chart such as Figure 5.6. Let's take a closer look at each of those quadrants.

The "social science quadrant" is where you are likely to find most theories and models published in the academic literature. Also in that quadrant, you are likely to find most strategic plans.

For one example, Figure 5.7 shows a theory of entrepreneurship with a breadth = 4 and a depth = 25%.

While their relative simplicity makes these theories easier to understand, their low level of breadth and depth means that they will not be very useful for understanding and resolving wicked complex problems.

The "destination quadrant" is where we want our maps to be. This is where we find maps of greatest depth and breadth—those that will be most reliably useful for understanding and resolving highly complex problems.

FIGURE 5.6 ⬢ Four General Areas—For Comparing Four General Categories of Maps

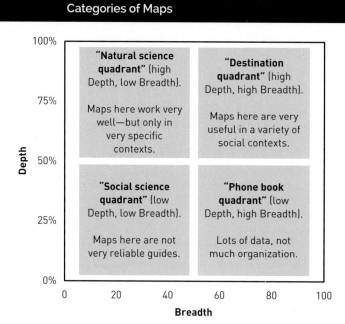

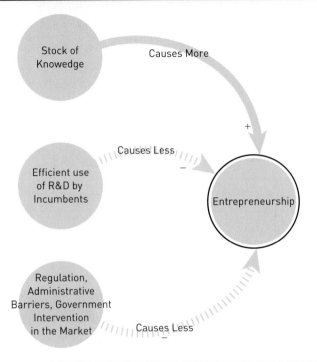

FIGURE 5.7 ● Simple Version of Entrepreneurship Theory (Authors' Partial Map of Propositions From Hypotheses in the "Knowledge Spillover Theory of Entrepreneurship," Acs, Braunerhjelm, Audretsch, & Carlsson, 2009)

Increasingly, organizations are gaining the expertise for creating and using destination quadrant (high depth, high breadth) maps. One entrepreneurial business used this process to create a map with breadth = 26 and a depth = 54% (Figure 5.8). Their mapping process was followed by (at least) two record-breaking quarters of income!

TRAVEL TIP

While a larger, more complex knowledge map will help you understand your situation better, a more complex situation will require more resources for making things happen at each area (represented by a concept). Also, more resources will be needed for tracking data for the evaluation and continued improvement of the map.

The "natural science quadrant" is where we find the knowledge maps that work very well in practical application, such as engineering formulae and laws of physics. One example is Ohm's Law. When measuring an electrical circuit, Ohm's Law is used to calculate one

FIGURE 5.8   ●   Map for a More Successful Organization

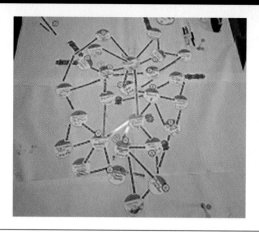

Note: Overview of map to give you a sense of its structure. Text not readable due to size constraints.

Source: Photo Courtesy of Kent Frese of Team LMI.

unknown variable when the other two are known. As text, it may be written as follows: Volts is equal to amps multiplied by resistance. It is mapped out in Figure 5.9.

FIGURE 5.9   ●   Map of Ohm's Law of Electricity

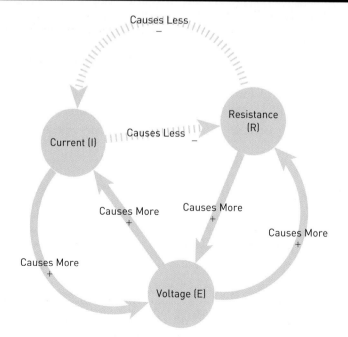

However, those theories contain relatively few concepts—enough to handle the relatively simple problems of physics (problems that can be reduced to an equation containing few concepts) but not enough breadth to overcome the very complex problems of society.

Finally, the "phone book quadrant" (the lower right) is where you will find collections of facts. For example, a phone book has a great deal of information—all the phone numbers and all the addresses in the city. However, it does not say how those addresses are connected, so it does not serve as a good map.

While theories in this quadrant contain many concepts, they may also be quite confusing because they lack the causal relationships that provide a useful guide.

Now, Moving On

You can use this kind of four-quadrant diagram to compare two or more theories and also to show the progress you've made in moving theories from the lower-left quadrant (where most theories in the social sciences start) to the upper right (more on this in Chapter 6). Those improvements support better understanding, communication, collaboration, and decision-making (Chapter 7).

STOP/REFLECTION/DISCUSSION

For each of the quadrants of breadth and depth, describe a real or hypothetical situation where a map in that quadrant might be useful. Look at the maps you created in previous chapters and see which quadrant from Figure 5.6 that they fit. Discuss general and specific ways you might improve your map in a way that shifts it to a better quadrant (more breadth and depth).

CASE STUDY: EVALUATING THE STRUCTURE OF ENTREPRENEURSHIP THEORIES

In this case study, we show how a set of theories may be evaluated. This kind of analysis may be useful for a literature review to show how your efforts at integration are improving the theory. This case study draws from and quotes the following:

Wright, B., & Wallis, S. E. (2015, July–September). Using integrative propositional analysis (IPA) for evaluating entrepreneurship theories. *SAGE Open*, 1–9. Retrieved from http://journals.sagepub.com/doi/pdf/10.1177/2158244015604190

Introduction and Problem Statement

Entrepreneurship theory is important because the study and teaching of entrepreneurship is vital to the nation's economic growth and stability as well as individual income and a personal sense of fulfilment.

Teachers should provide entrepreneurs with the knowledge they need to succeed. However, the number of theories found in research studies and textbooks on entrepreneurship is rapidly growing, with little agreement about which theory (or theories) might best represent our shared understanding of entrepreneurship. This situation makes it difficult to find the best theory for application in teaching, practice, and research. It also piqued our interest as researchers and practitioners. To better understand the situation from a metatheoretical (theory about theory) perspective and to help impel the field toward improvement in theory and practice, we decided to conduct a systematic analysis comparing a sample of theories of entrepreneurship from the research literature.

Method and Sample

We chose IPA as the preferred method for analysis for two reasons:

- Because of IPA's unique ability to evaluate and improve the logic structure of theories

- Because IPA provides a more objective approach to integrating theories in a literature review than other methods for integrating studies across disciplines. With IPA, we can reduce the number of "judgement calls" and so improve the overall rigor and quality of our research.

We chose a small number of theories, drawing on a convenience sample of academic papers known to the authors. From that collection, we purposefully selected nine papers to represent diverse subdisciplines, use of diverse methods to develop and test the theories, and diverse definitions of entrepreneurship. That approach let us maximize the variation of cases and explore the potential importance of theory variations.

While using IPA to identify and map propositions in the theories in those papers, we avoided speculating on what we thought the authors "meant to say," always striving to use the original authors' wording. Some propositions identified something as true or important but did not specify any causal relationships. We diagrammed each of those concepts as a stand-alone circle (no arrows leading to or away from it).

Some propositions contained multiple causal relationships. For example, Holmes and Schmitz's (1990) theory of entrepreneurship that they applied to business transfers included the statement, "Numerous studies have shown that entrepreneurial ability can be enhanced through experience, training, schooling, and improvements in health." We diagrammed this as shown in Figure 5.10.

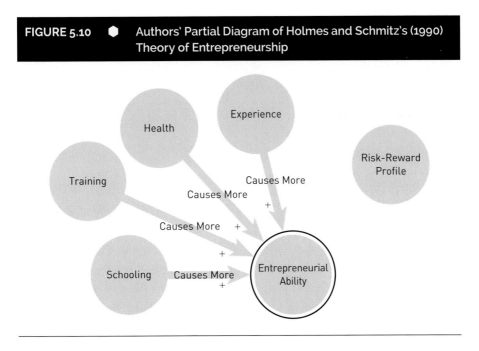

FIGURE 5.10 ● Authors' Partial Diagram of Holmes and Schmitz's (1990) Theory of Entrepreneurship

Figure 5.10 serves as an example of some propositions from one theory. Complete diagrams for all of the theories are not shown due to space constraint.

Results and Insights

The results of those analyses are shown in Table 5.1 and Figure 5.11.

TABLE 5.1 ● IPA Results for Nine Theories of Entrepreneurship

Study	Data Used to Develop/Test Theory	Breadth (B)	Depth (D)
1	Literature on country and individual level entrepreneurship from multiple fields, employment data for 23 OECD countries	B = 15	D = 40%
2	Economic and managerial literature on entrepreneurship	B = 26	D = 38%
3	Regression analysis, employment data from 19 OECD countries	B = 4	D = 25%
4	Schultz and other theories; model using data on U.S. business transfers in 1940s and 1950s	B = 13	D = 23%
5	Resource-based theory, other literature	B = 48	D = 25%
6	Covin and Slevin model, other literature	B = 5	D = 20%

(Continued)

TABLE 5.1 ● (Continued)			
Study	Data Used to Develop/Test Theory	Breadth (B)	Depth (D)
7	Schumpeter, Kirzner theories, epic poem	B = 7	D = 14%
8	Classic and recent literature, case study of an entrepreneur awards contest	B = 10	D = 10%
9	Literature on social responsibility and social entrepreneurship	B = 9	D = 0%

The results of this exploratory study provided insights for teaching, practice, and research.

For professors, the general idea is (or should be) to teach their students about those theories with greater depth (because they will be more useful). However, the results in this study suggest that teachers might find it difficult or impossible to find theories of great depth, as we found depth scores between 0% and 40% for the nine theories that we examined. So as a fall-back position, professors should teach multiple theories of entrepreneurship and encourage their students to integrate and improve the theories.

Practitioners (including managers, entrepreneurs, and public services agencies) should recognize the limits of existing theories. Results of our analysis found that all nine theories that we examined were in the low-depth, low-breadth quadrant. That in turn suggests that practitioners should follow a strategy of experimentation—to apply the best available theory and then modify the theory according to the results.

FIGURE 5.11 ● IPA Results for Nine Theories of Entrepreneurship

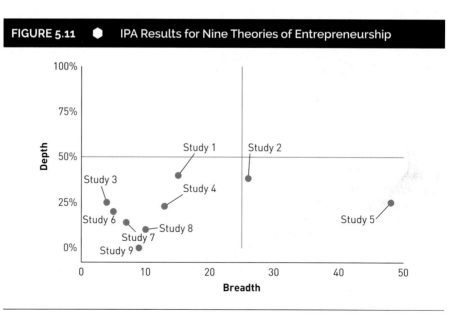

For researchers, the maps developed in this project will be useful for identifying opporutnities to accelerate the advancement of the field. For example, in the above Figure 5.10, there are no causal links between the concepts of training, schooling, and experience. These are "causal orphans" (there are no arrows pointing toward them) waiting to be connected with other concepts.

istock.com/Six_Characters

With structure, you have strength.

On the academic side, it was interesting to note that the more frequently cited papers were those that synthesized multiple theories and had the greatest level of depth. The papers with less depth were less cited. While this is only a small sample, the results suggests a potential benefit to scholars striving to advance their careers by increasing the number of citations as an area for further investigation.

Limitations and Conclusions

Because this study contained only nine theories, all from papers in academic journals, it should be thought of as an exploratory study. Future studies should use more theories and include more sources (including entrepreneurship textbooks, business plan contests, venture magazines, conference proceedings, government reports, and learning from practicing entrepreneurs).

More generally, this kind of IPA research for evaluating, integrating, and improving the logic structure of theories may be expected to support improved practice for building businesses and communities. These benefits could be enhanced by encouraging collaboration between the worlds of academia, business, and community service. Together with new tools we can advance the field more quickly for the benefit of our communities.

MORE VIEWS OF STRUCTURE

Here are some additional approaches to understanding the structure of your knowledge maps. For additional in-depth approaches to understanding the structure of maps, see Appendix A: Advanced Strategies for Making Maps More Useful.

Loops

When four (or more) circles are connected with all the causal arrows following one another, as in Figure 5.12, we call it a loop. Loops are important because they show how action in one area can circle back, reinforce, and build on itself. A loop may indicate growth or sustainability.

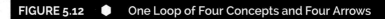

FIGURE 5.12   ●   One Loop of Four Concepts and Four Arrows

The reason we ask for four (or more) concepts in the loop is to help people expand their thinking. For many, the tendency is to identify two circles and say that there is a loop between them. Unfortunately, that tends to limit our thinking and causes us to become trapped in our assumptions! For example, if you assume that productivity causes motivation and motivation causes productivity, you miss out on other important concepts, such as skills and other kinds of motivation. So while loops of two or three concepts may show many interesting things, we anticipate needing loops with four or more concepts to understand and solve the wicked problems of the world.

You can leverage one idea to change the world.

You will notice in Figure 5.12 that a loop can include causal arrows that are "causes more" and "causes less." The important thing is that they are all pointing in the same direction.

Leverage Points

A leverage point is any concept that is shared between two or more loops. Leverage points are important because they show where action in one place (that concept) can start a cascading and mutually reinforcing effect through multiple loops.

FIGURE 5.13 ● At the Intersection of Two Loops, "C" Is the Leverage Point

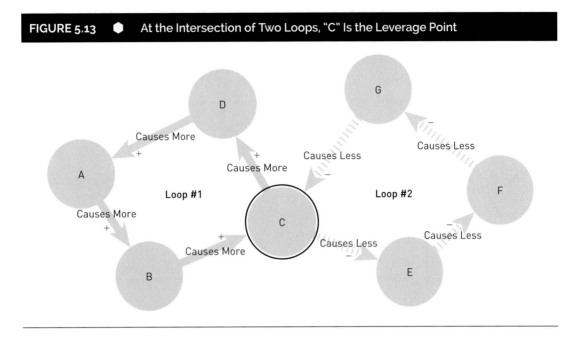

Leverage points are where you can intervene in a system to get the greatest results with the least effort. In the abstract example shown in Figure 5.13, "C" is the leverage point.

How many concepts can be shared between two loops? This is a good question! If there is more than one, you could ask the team if the two paths are redundant (see Appendix A). Or there may simply be multiple leverage points between the two loops.

Clustering

Clustering is the art of placing circles closer together when they are somehow related. Clustering often occurs naturally—as similar concepts are placed near each other. There are times, however, when people at different sides of the table have a similar idea and/or are not able to take in the map as a whole. Or you may be mapping data from two publications that discuss similar concepts and those concepts don't end up next to each other on your map.

In Figure 5.14, Concepts H, I, and J are more clustered than Concepts L and M.

Are there too many concepts on the map? You can use clustering to make the map easier to read. You can also create different views of the map (each focusing on different parts of the map). We'll show how to do that in Chapter 7.

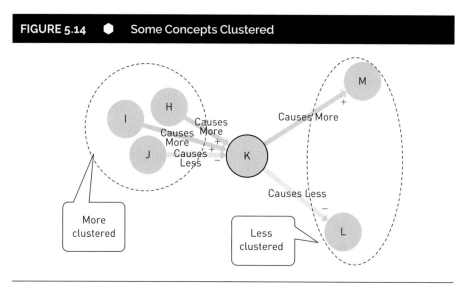

FIGURE 5.14   ●   Some Concepts Clustered

CLASS ACTIVITY 5.3

Clustering and Categorizing

- Consider the topic selected in Activity 5.1.

- Working individually or in small groups, spend a few minutes brainstorming concepts related to your topic.

- Write each concept in a separate circle (card or sticky note).

- Arrange circles so that similar concepts are clustered closer together.

- Discuss the similarities and differences between the concepts: Do some circles contain concepts that overlap with others? If so, talk about how they might (or might not!) be categorized to make the map easier to read and more focused on the topic (see abstraction/categorization, below).

Abstraction/Categorization

To further improve the readability of your map, you might start with a number of clustered concepts and categorize or abstract them into fewer circles. For example, you might have three circles: "income from web-based sales," "income from store-based sales," and "income from catalog sales" and combine them into a single concept of "sales." In a sense, you might also think of this process as one of merging codes (circles) from your research data (see Chapter 3).

Deconstruction

When a map has more circles, we can say it has more structure (although that is a weak form of structure, like bricks that are loosely piled). The structure of the map, however, should not be confused with the structure "inside" the circle. For example, the concept of GDP (gross domestic product) of a nation is a very complicated thing (including the market value of every object made and every service provided in the entire nation). Yet all of that complexity may be summed up in a simple number.

A complex concept could also be "deconstructed" into multiple concepts, such as "objects made" and "services provided," or further deconstructed into services provided in different industries (banking, consulting, etc.), depending on how abstract or concrete you want the concept to be. Deconstruction can be a useful technique if stakeholders are confused or arguing about a concept; then, dividing one complex concept into two or more simpler concepts may help to resolve the confusion or disagreement. This can also be useful for adjusting the level of abstraction for the map as a whole (see Appendix A "Scale of Abstraction").

Simplicity

Like having a pile of bricks, having a map with disconnected circles gives us the lowest level of logical structure. We think of these as *isolated or atomistic* concepts or/and beliefs.

TRAVEL TIP

You should not be distracted (or attracted) by simple maps (or a puzzle having only a few pieces). We do not live in a simple world and do not travel on an easy road. Yet there are some people who think that the best maps are those that are the simplest. Research in the field of decision-making, however, tells a different story. I mean really, how does anyone find their way through a complex world using only a simple map? We now know that the best maps for navigation are those with many locations and many connections. Once you have a complex map, you can more easily choose a simple route to a simple destination . . . if you like.

For many, simplicity may seem attractive. However, it is important to note that the atomistic structure of disconnected concepts provides a map that is of very limited usefulness. Notice in Figure 5.15 that concepts include, "Market opportunity," "Entrepreneurial ability," and "Videos of adorable cats." Those concepts appear as isolated circles—no arrows connect them. While these simple statements may be good for communicating your values or inciting emotion, they are not good for communicating logical understanding. When you see one of these maps, you should start thinking about adding more concepts and especially looking for more connections! For more on structure, see Appendix A.

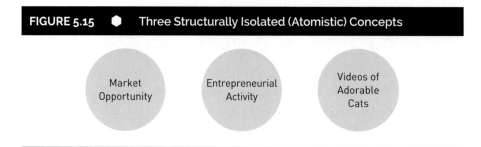

FIGURE 5.15   ⬡   Three Structurally Isolated (Atomistic) Concepts

What? Not!

Eliminating relationships that don't exist makes our maps easier to read. It is not useful to map "negative statements," such as, "Having a lucky rabbit's foot does *not* help you be a more successful entrepreneur." Imagine, just for a moment, how crazy a map would be if it showed everything that did not exist and everything that was not connected! You could still use such a text to identify circles (one for rabbit's feet and one for entrepreneurial success), but there would be *no* connecting arrow. While such connections should be left off the map, the concepts should remain if they are meaningful to the stakeholders.

Another thing that does not work is to include "singular" things on your map—for example, starting with the text, "The planet Earth is the *only* place to open a barbershop because that's where all the people are." This text won't help because a map is only useful if the concepts are variables. If there is only "one" thing or place, then we can't manipulate or change it. A proposition that would be more useful would be, "The more people walking by your barbershop (foot traffic), the more successful it will be."

Show the Invisible

We can also use our understanding of structure to help us visualize where something is missing. This is a kind of "gap analysis" that helps us to "see the invisible." If a circle does not have arrows pointing to it, we know that there is "something" that should be added to the map.

When something is missing, it suggests the opportunity for more research to see if something can fill those "blank spots on the map" (and improve the structure of the map).

For example, Figure 5.16 shows the simple map from Figure 5.5, along with arrows and circles marked with a "?" to highlight blank spaces.

FIGURE 5.16 ⬡ Circles and Arrows With "?" Show Some of the Blank Spaces Where We Need More Information

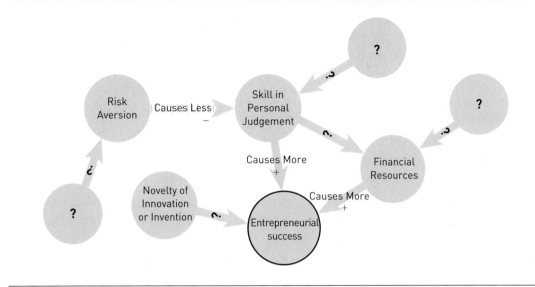

Because there are no causal arrows between some concepts (only "?" arrows and "?" circles), we might wonder whether "novelty of invention" causes an increase in "entrepreneurial success." This could be a topic for future exploration. Future studies might also add new concepts (where the "?" circles are). This might help answer a research question, such as "What else causes skill in personal judgment?"

CLASS ACTIVITY 5.4

Gap Analysis

Students work in small groups using the circles (concepts) created in the previous activity (written on 3 × 5 cards or sticky notes) connected with arrows to create a knowledge map. You may also use the maps that you developed in previous chapters.

Working in small groups, identify *blank* spaces on your map. Talk about what circles and arrows might be added to improve the structure of the map. For bonus points, talk about your options for research (Chapter 3, Chapter 4, Appendix C).

Chapter 5 Key Points

In this chapter, we've shown how to understand and evaluate maps from a structural perspective. This perspective supports researchers, such as yourself, who are striving to understand and resolve the wicked problems of the world by creating maps with better structure because maps with better structure are more useful/effective for communication, teaching, learning, planning, and making decisions to reach individual and organizational goals.

- To understand a situation (especially one that is complex) you need knowledge with more structure. With more structured knowledge, you can make better choices or decisions; ones that will lead you closer to the results you want.

- Integrative propositional analysis is a tool for quantitatively evaluating the logic structure of your maps—the breadth and depth of knowledge represented by the research.

- Maps with higher breadth and greater depth are more likely to be very useful in a variety of contexts. You are likely to find low breadth and depth for most theories and models published in the social science literature.

- In addition to IPA, other approaches to understanding the structure of your knowledge maps include loops, leverage points, and abstraction.

Frequently Asked Questions

Q: Are all kinds of mapping equally useful or effective?

A: The type of mapping (causal, relational, concept, etc.) that will work best depends on the situation you are striving to understand and your goals for using the map. Most types of mapping (for example, concept and relational) simply show a number of things and how they are similar to one another. Other types (e.g., work flow) show how things move. These are useful for keeping track of things or having a general understanding. Causal mapping narrows inferential gaps, supporting your ability to enable effective change.

Q: Are there limits to logic?

A: Yes. There are plenty of explanations that *seem* logical but are not really very useful. So you need to support your logic with data (otherwise, you have only a very convincing fiction).

Q: What can you do if stakeholders argue about the validity of the causal connections?

A: Bring in more stakeholders and expand the map. This will show more causal connections—more complex paths that better represent the complexity of real life. You can also do more research to show whether or not the data support the causal connections.

Further Exploration

History of Knowledge Mapping

Wexler, M. N. (2001). The who, what and why of knowledge mapping. *Journal of Knowledge Management, 5*(3), 249–264. Retrieved from http://203.157.7.7/KM/upload_file/data1/to%20what%20why%20of%20 knowledge%20mapping.pdf

Many Approaches to Mapping

Axelrod, R. (1976). *Structure of decision: The cognitive maps of political elites.* Princeton, NJ: Princeton University Press. Retrieved from https://press .princeton.edu/titles/2374.html

For mapping that is more visually dramatic yet useful for communicating complex ideas, please look at the work of Bob Horn, including https://web.stanford.edu/~rhorn/

Bryson, J. M., Ackermann, F., Eden, C., & Finn, C. B. (2004). *Visible thinking: Unlocking causal mapping for practical business results.* Hoboken, NJ: John Wiley & Sons. Retrieved from https://www .wiley.com/en-us/Visible+Thinking%3A+Unlocking+Causal+Mapping+for+Practical+Business+ Results-p-9780470869154

Horn, R. E. (1999). Information design: Emergence of a new profession. *Information design*, 15–33. Retrieved from https://web.stanford.edu/~rhorn/a/topic/vl%26id/artclInfoDesignChapter.html

Concepts and Circles

Fodor, J. A. (1998). *Concepts: Where cognitive science went wrong.* New York, NY: Oxford University Press. Retrieved from http://www.naturalthinker.net/trl/texts/Fodor,%20Jerry/Fodor%20-%20 Concepts%20-%20Where%20cognitive%20science%20went%20wrong.pdf

Causality and Arrows

Pearl, J. (2000). *Causality: Models, reasoning, and inference.* New York, NY: Cambridge University Press.

Sloman, S. A., & Hagmayer, Y. (2006). The causal psycho-logic of choice. *Trends in Cognitive Science, 10*(9), 407–412.

Graphic Recording/Facilitation

Gadsby, T. (n.d.). *What is graphic recording?* Retrieved from https://www.youtube.com/watch?v=Ki1gcoc7Wqg

Shift-It Coach, Inc. (n.d.). Learn graphic facilitation—Online training. Retrieved from https://www.ifvp .org/content/learn-graphic-facilitation-online-training

Integrative Complexity

Suedfeld, P., Tetlock, P. E., & Streufert, S. (1992). Conceptual/integrative complexity. In C. P. Smith (Ed.), *Handbook of thematic Content Analysis* (pp. 393–400). New York, NY: Cambridge University Press. Retrieved from https://www2.psych.ubc.ca/~psuedfeld/Chapter.pdf

(Continued)

(Continued)

Structure of Maps, Models, and More

Rogers, P. J. (2008). Using programme theory to evaluate complicated and complex aspects of interventions. *Evaluation, 14*(1), 29. Retrieved from http://journals.sagepub.com/doi/pdf/10.1177/1356389007084674

Wallis, S. E. (2014). Abstraction and insight: Building better conceptual systems to support more effective social change. *Foundations of Science, 19*(4), 353–362. Retrieved from https://link.springer.com/article/10.1007/s10699-014-9359-x

Wallis, S. E. (2014). Existing and emerging methods for integrating theories within and between disciplines. *Organisational Transformation and Social Change, 11*(1), 3–24. Retrieved from http://neti-net.org/wp-content/uploads/2016/05/Wallis-2014-Existing-and-Emerging-Methods-for-Integrating-Theories-within-and-between-Disciplines.pdf

Wallis, S. E. (2016). Structures of logic in policy and theory: Identifying sub-systemic bricks for investigating, building, and understanding conceptual systems. *Foundations of Science, 20*(3), 213–231.

Wallis, S. E. (2016). The science of conceptual systems: A progress report. *Foundations of Science, 21*(4), 579–602. Retrieved from https://link.springer.com/article/10.1007/s10699-015-9425-z

Wallis, S. E., Wright, B., & Nash, F. D. (2016). *Using integrative propositional analysis to evaluate and integrate economic policies of U.S. presidential candidates* [White paper, 16]. Retrieved from http://meaningfulevidence.com/wp-content/uploads/IPA-of-POTUS-Candidates.pdf

Other Approaches to Structure Using Online Mapping Platforms

Gray, S., & Cox, L. (n.d.). *An introduction to Mental Modeler*. Retrieved July 10, 2018 from http://www.mentalmodeler.org/articles/Mental%20Modeler%20Manual%20for%20Workshop.pdf

KUMU. (n.d.). Metrics [Web page]. Retrieved March 29, 2018 from https://docs.kumu.io/guides/metrics.html

Analyzing Structure for Policy and Programs

Deegan, M. (2011). *Using causal maps to analyze policy complexity and intergovernmental coordination: An empirical study of floodplain management recommendations*. Paper presented at the System Dynamics Society Conference 2011. https://www.systemdynamics.org/assets/conferences/2011/proceed/papers/P1313.pdf

Houston, D., Wright, B., & Wallis, S. E. (2017). Re-structuring evaluation findings into useful knowledge. *Journal of Multi-Disciplinary Evaluation, 30*(29). Retrieved from http://journals.sfu.ca/jmde/index.php/jmde_1/article/view/481

Shackelford, C. (2014). *Propositional analysis, policy creation, and complex environments in the United States' 2009 Afghanistan-Pakistan policy* (Doctoral Dissertation). Walden, Minneapolis, MN. Retrieved from http://scholarworks.waldenu.edu/dissertations/168/

Wallis, S. E. (2010). Towards the development of more robust policy models. *Integral Review, 6*(1), 153–160. Retrieved from http://www.integral-review.org/issues/vol_6_no_1_wallis_toward_the_development_of_more_robust_policy_models.pdf

Entrepreneurship—From the Case Study

Acs, Z. J., Braunerhjelm, P., Audretsch, D. B., & Carlsson, B. (2009). The knowledge spillover theory of entrepreneurship. *Small Business Economics, 32*, 15–30.

Holmes, T. J., & Schmitz Jr., J. A. (1990). A theory of entrepreneurship and its application to the study of business transfers. *Journal of Political Economy, 98*(2), 265–294.

Wright, B., & Wallis, S. E. (2015, July–September). Using integrative propositional analysis (IPA) for evaluating entrepreneurship theories. *SAGE Open*, 1–9. Retrieved from http://journals.sagepub.com/doi/pdf/10.1177/2158244015604190

6

COLLABORATING WITH OTHER RESEARCHERS

istock.com/RawPixel

In this chapter we will cover the following:

- A brief history of fragmentation and its negative (and positive) effects on research and practice

- Addressing wicked problems and the benefits of integration across disciplines

- Where and how to connect with other researchers to find and create new maps

- How to integrate those maps to work against fragmentation and toward better knowledge maps

THE FRAGMENTED WORLD OF SOCIAL SCIENCES

Two thousand years ago, all of science was contained under one title, "philosophy." The scientific revolution, between the 16th and 18th centuries, saw philosophy branch into physics, astronomy, biology, and other areas of the natural sciences. Where once a wise philosopher from ancient Greece could be a respected expert on many subjects, advances in so many directions today means that few individuals can be considered experts in many disciplines.

How difficult would it be for an ancient Greek philosopher to catch up with the knowledge of today? There are untold millions of books and articles piled up in the dusty old storehouse of human knowledge. No person has read any more than a small fraction of them. A quick search on Google Scholar for articles containing the word "science" found over 200,000 publications that came out in the past 12 months. Quite a reading list! Even if we narrow the search, we find too much to read in a lifetime—try it with your favorite topic!

By the 19th century, the social sciences were also branching out with the emergence of political science, sociology, economics, and psychology. Toward the end of the 20th century, each of those fields was rapidly spawning dozens of subfields.

Each subfield has its own jargon, publications, research methods, and theories. Indeed, most subfields also have several sub-subfields (there is even a subfield called "sociology of emotions," which is further divided into sub-subfields). That level of fragmentation means researchers find it increasingly difficult to understand (or collaborate with) researchers from other fields.

Using the techniques in this book (and especially in this chapter), researchers and practitioners will be able to integrate the theories across multiple disciplines to create knowledge maps that will improve our collective ability to make effective decisions and solve the big problems of the world.

Rather than seeing those millions of publications as a confusing liability, they may be seen as assets because knowledge mapping helps us to more easily integrate their theories to make them more understandable and more useful.

istock.com/Henrik5000

Our increasingly fragmented world.

Before we can integrate those theoretical maps effectively, we must recognize the difficulty of working with researchers from different disciplines. It seems that they all speak different languages. For example, while attending an academic conference, I overheard two scholars meeting for the first time. Although they were both sociologists, their research focused on different subfields. They talked for at least 20 minutes just to learn each other's "language" before they could begin talking about a topic! At the Santa Fe Institute (a prestigious interdisciplinary research center), it has been said that the only common language between researchers is "metaphor."

TRAVEL TIP

Some say po-TAY-to, while others say po-TAH-to; what counts is how many are in the bag. When different terms are used for what seems to be the same thing, that confusion may be reduced or eliminated by talking instead about what is being measured.

For a project where researchers are coming from very different fields (such as sociology, psychology, information technology, and biology), the problem of communication becomes much worse. That "Tower of Babel" effect can lead to confusion, conflict, higher research costs, and even project failure as well as missing out on opportunities to collaborate to leverage knowledge from across the academic fields for solving complex problems.

This book bypasses that confusion with a shared language that works across all disciplines. That simple language mainly consists of circles and arrows—"the measurability of concepts" and "the causality of connections between them." In every field, from physics to sociology, researchers can use circles and arrows to create theories, models, mental models, conceptual systems, policy models, and knowledge. By using the language and methods you've learned in previous chapters, interdisciplinary collaboration becomes much easier because we use the "common language" of measuring evidence, causality, structure, and stakeholder collaboration.

This chapter combines insights from Chapter 2 (collaborative mapping) with Chapter 3 (creating maps using existing research). The overarching idea is that by collaborating with other researchers, drawing on their expertise as well as their research, you can rapidly improve your maps.

STOP/REFLECTION/DISCUSSION

Reflect on your own or discuss as a group, what is one big problem that you see in the world?

- What fields and subfields of research know about that problem and solutions to it?

- What solutions might emerge from collaboration among those researchers to integrate their knowledge?

PUTTING THE PIECES TOGETHER

In the world of research, each expert holds a small scrap of the larger map. Researchers have spent their lives learning about the important problems of the world. Far too often, however, that research is not well connected with the numerous other studies across disciplines that are looking at the same topic. This means each isolated study might be relearning what others have already learned rather than adding new knowledge.

More and more, researchers are realizing that the effort to understand the complex problems of the world requires collaboration between researchers. This collaboration may occur between researchers of different disciplines using different methods and drawing on different theoretical backgrounds. Communication between disciplines is difficult, however, when they all speak different "languages."

For an example of linguistic differences, consider the term "zero population growth" from the perspective of two disciplines—psychology and sociology—found on these sites:

https://sociologydictionary.org/zero-population-growth/

https://psychologydictionary.org/zero-population-growth/

The sociology version looks at changes to the population based on immigration and emigration as well as births and deaths. In comparison, the psychology version looks only at population changes from births and deaths. We can go one step further and infer that the idea of zero growth actually allows for a decline in population. Yet, both definitions seem to suggest population *stability* rather than a lack of *growth*.

istock.com/PeopleImages

Working together as researchers, we can find solutions more quickly.

When constructing a map, one might find it entirely reasonable to use one version or the other. The point here is that the versions rely on different underlying assumptions. Those differences can make communication difficult between researchers working in different disciplines.

In this chapter, we will show how to make the process of collaboration among researchers easier by drawing on their expertise, mapping theoretical assumptions, and integrating multiple maps.

INTEGRATION, ACCELERATION, SOLUTION!

In Chapter 2, we talked about bringing stakeholders into a room to make better knowledge maps by drawing on their experiences. Here, similarly, we are talking about bringing researchers together to make better maps drawing on their professional experience including the following:

- Their knowledge as expert researchers (including understanding different research methods)

- The published results of their research

- Their experience within the world of research (including connections with other researchers)

- Their hidden knowledge (unpublished research and related insights)

This is different from collaborative mapping with stakeholders in a few ways (Table 6.1).

When mapping is done by stakeholders, the focus is on a topic that they are very familiar with. That means stakeholders can reasonably rely on their experiences, which are reflected in their opinions and insights. In contrast, when researchers create a map, we like to see their perspectives supported by published research. When stakeholders create a map, they are also the ones who will be using the map to make decisions—for example, in Chapter 2 when

TABLE 6.1 ● Differences Between Mapping With Researchers and Stakeholders	
Stakeholders (other than researchers)	**Researchers**
Map is often made with all stakeholders in the room at the same time.	Map is often made by different researchers working in different places at different times.
Opinions are OK.	Perspectives are best when supported by research.
Those who make the map also use it for making decisions.	The decision makers are managers, community organizations, political leaders, and others who might only see the map after it is finished.
Trust in the map is improved by having good supporting evidence and relevance. Trust between stakeholders is improved during the mapping process when participants see each other's perspectives.	Trust in the map is improved by having good supporting evidence and a high level of structure.

members of an energy consortium created a map to better understand the changes in their industry. In contrast, when researchers make maps, the resulting maps are typically given to stakeholders (who might be elected officials, clients, managers, students, and others) who then use the map to support their decisions.

Trust between people is an important issue. Without trust, we could not work together effectively. It is also important to trust our knowledge map. Without that trust, we would not follow it or use it to help guide our decisions. When stakeholders create a map, the process of mapping helps to build trust in both directions—both in the map and between stakeholders. Trust is built in the map because they see how the map is structured, supported by evidence, and relevant to the situation (Chapter 1). Trust is built between the stakeholders because each person involved in the mapping process can see how the other stakeholders are perceiving the situation as they place concepts and arrows onto the map—placing their cards on the table, so to speak. With researchers, in contrast, the stakeholders are handed a map made by experts. Because the stakeholders are not directly involved in the mapping process, it is possible that they may not trust the map as much. Therefore, it is important that researchers should make their maps with good supporting evidence (Chapter 3) and a high level of structure (Chapter 5).

A Cycle of Collaboration

Since their inception (or, perhaps, their proliferation), the social sciences have advanced only slowly. While they have generated many new theories, we have not seen a similar advance in the effectiveness of those theories. In comparison, the pace of change in the rest of the world seems to be accelerating—new technology, new diseases, new political situations. It seems that the problems of the world are increasing faster than our ability to understand them, let alone to solve them. To win this race, we must accelerate the development of the social sciences.

However, accelerating the social sciences means more than doing "more research." Solving the big problems of the world means integrating theories from many disciplines.

TRAVEL TIP

Additional perspectives support objectivity and accuracy. For example, when the authors of this book are integrating theories for research projects, we sometimes find theories that are not clearly explained in the text. Working independently, we each map our own interpretation of what the author seems to be saying. Then, we compare our maps. If they match, great. If they don't, we talk about our interpretations to reach a mutually satisfactory map. If we can't agree, we might agree that that part of the map is too ambiguous to be included. The mapping process is often easier when you are working within a team of researchers.

As a researcher, your job is to work with people to create better knowledge maps and present those better knowledge maps to the decision makers at all levels—from a local organization, to your city council, all the way to the United Nations.

TRAVEL TIP

Because each field has its own language, it is often easier to integrate theories within each discipline as a first step. Then, integrate those integrated theories between the disciplines. For example, say you are working on a project to support economic development in your state, you might have theories from four disciplines (let's say, sociology, psychology, business, and economics). You should integrate the theories of each of those four disciplines first. Then, integrate those four theories into a final knowledge map.

Collaborating with other researchers means more than using their theories. It also means that (through them) you will have access to their experience in their field of research. You can save a lot of time and effort by drawing on the expertise of other researchers. They will be aware of recent trends in research and may surface interesting research questions that you had not considered.

The process of interdisciplinary collaboration (shown in Figure 6.1) often begins by identifying a problem or topic for study. When you realize that the problem is

FIGURE 6.1 ⬡ Interdisciplinary Research Cycle

- Assigned by your teacher
- Assigned by your supervisor
- Chosen by your client
- Developed from previous maps
- Your own area of interest!

Define the situation/ problem

Identify the relevant disciplines

- What comes to mind—think about it!
- Ask others what they think
- Use the situation/problem as a search term in a database such as Google Scholar to see what relevant disciplines have done work on the topic

- Use knowledge mapping
- Use gap analysis
- Report results and identify potential actions
- Find areas needing additional research

Synthesize theories and identify next steps

Identify experts and gather theories

- Search for researchers in each discipline
- Find those who are already working on the problem
- Find their publications—and theories

larger than your expertise, the next step is to identify additional disciplines that might provide useful insights into understanding the situation. Next, you would search for researchers in those disciplines (including additional researchers in your own discipline) who might be willing to support your research project (much like looking for stakeholder groups in Chapter 2). Finding experts is not difficult. Perhaps the easiest way is to contact the authors of the articles you found on your topic. Another way is to contact professional organizations (for example, the American Evaluation Association, American Psychological Association, American Management Association—you get the idea—just start a web search) and ask. After assembling your team, you create the map, drawing on the formal research (Chapter 3), surfacing their tacit knowledge through interviews (Chapter 4), and creating a highly structured map (Chapter 5).

For many students (and more than a few researchers), the process of integration (also known as synthesis) is a difficult and even mysterious process. Some people fumble about, as if they were trying to assemble a jigsaw puzzle while blindfolded. As a researcher working in collaboration with other researchers, your expertise in knowledge mapping is very important to the success of the team and the project.

COLLABORATION ACROSS INDUSTRIES

Another helpful form of collaboration is when scholars work with teams of practitioners. One approach to that process is consortial benchmarking (CB). CB is a four-step process for sharing key information between managers working for different companies.

1. Formulate the key research question and make connections with other managers who are interested in learning more.

2. Create a questionnaire and choose a set of companies that are recognized as having the best practices.

3. Visit those companies and interview their managers.

4. Discuss the results and integrate them, then share with other managers.

Due to the difficulty of scheduling, the entire process may take as long as two years. Each visit may last one to two days and include presentations by managers of the host firm, informal meetings between managers, formal meetings between managers, and interviews.

From a researcher's perspective, CB is a solid approach to building and refining theory that will be useful in practical application. From a practitioner's perspective, it is a great way to connect with new colleagues and develop better business practices.

While the focus is on sharing knowledge between business managers, there is also a place for academic theory. As part of the first step, academic researchers share their understanding of the research question. Then, as the group moves forward, new insights are compared with the academic model, discussed, and added. By the end, managers' perspectives are integrated with academic perspectives to form a more complete map.

FINDING PEOPLE, FINDING MAPS

There are a lot of researchers out there. And, there are a lot of maps. While you may be able to find the best theories, that process is more difficult when you are searching a database full of unfamiliar jargon. Rather than taking the time (months or years) to learn a new discipline, it is often easier to find researchers who already have that expertise.

In time, you will build a network of colleagues across the country.

As you may remember from previous chapters, you can create maps from stakeholder perspectives (Chapter 2) or find existing maps in the academic literature (Chapter 3) and/or conduct interviews (Chapter 4).

You can also look for meta studies (studies that aggregate the data from multiple previous studies) or existing literature reviews about your topic (Chapter 3). While they may not be complete or sufficiently comprehensive for your research, they are one good place to find your experts (in addition to the places that we mentioned above). That literature might show you authors who you could contact and professional associations whose members you might contact.

When choosing a team of experts for your collaboration, there are a few key questions to ask to find researchers with greater expertise in their field and expertise that is more relevant to your study:

- Who has more citations around their work?

- Whose research is most recent (if you are looking for recent information)?

- What research topic is most similar to your research?

- What methods of research do they use (depending on whether you want a mix of methods or not)?

- Ask for a copy of their CV/resume.

With expertise, those researchers may

- More easily identify theories in their field that are most relevant for your research project

- Have access to unpublished data

- Know other researchers who may be helpful for your project

- Have tacit/hidden understanding of your topic

Steps to Integrating Maps

Integrating separate maps into one is possible as long as the maps have at least one or two points in common, as shown in Figure 6.2.

For combining maps, either within one discipline or between multiple disciplines, it is best to have one or more circles/concepts that are the same on both maps (see section on "bridging and explaining," following, for other technique for integrating maps). For example, in Figure 6.3 you will see three theories. Theory 1 and Theory 2 may be

FIGURE 6.2 ● Connecting Maps Where They Overlap

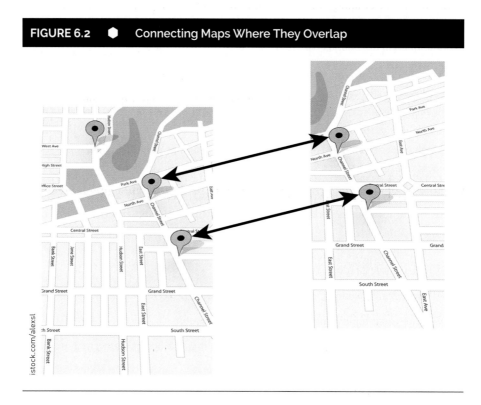

istock.com/alexsl

integrated because both include concept C. Or to put it another way, C is the overlap—the concept where the two maps may be joined.

In much the same way we create maps by integrating propositions from multiple stakeholders and studies, we also create new maps by integrating propositions from multiple maps by finding where they overlap.

Collaborators can help you integrate maps by helping you find maps that are likely to overlap and by engaging in conversations to clarify similarities between concepts.

DEFINITION

An **overlap** is when the same concept is found on two (or more) maps. Ideally, they should have the same word or words to represent the concept and the same way to measure it.

Bridging and Explaining to Support Integration

If you do NOT have a concept that is the same on two maps, you still have at least two options that may be legitimately used to integrate maps: bridging and explaining.

Bridging is used when two theories do not have any overlapping concepts and when a third theory (the bridging theory) contains concepts that overlap with both the other maps. For example, see Figure 6.4.

If you have two maps that don't overlap, you can ask your collaborators to suggest bridging theories.

Explanation is used if you want to argue that *different* concepts on two or more maps actually do overlap—and so may be legitimately used to integrate those maps. Explanation is easiest when those seemingly different concepts have the same measure. For example,

---

FIGURE 6.3 ● Two Theories Integrated Into One

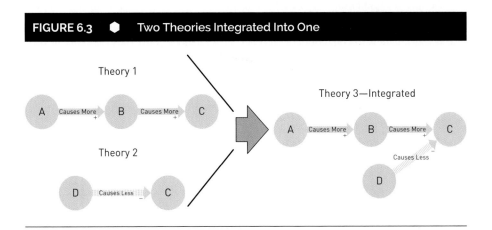

FIGURE 6.4 ● **Two Theory Maps Integrated With a Bridging Theory**

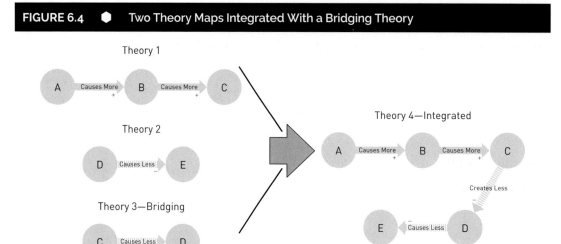

consider a concept from Theory 1 called "Democracy;" it is measured by "Percentage of the eligible population voting in the election." A concept from Theory 2 is called "Voter Turnout" and is measured the same way. Although the concepts have different names, they are measured the same way. So, it is reasonable to say that the concepts are a good overlap. We could merge those two concepts to form a new concept called "Democracy/Voter Turnout."

If you must resort to providing an explanation for integrating maps with differing concepts, you may lose some credibility if others do not accept your argument. Your team of collaborators can help you create and improve your explanations.

An example of explanation may be found in the Test-Drive section later in this chapter. There, the authors argued that similar concepts could be considered to be overlapping. The key idea here is to collaborate with other researchers to boost the credibility of your map (and your own credibility). You can talk with colleagues to see if they agree with your argument.

You can also contact the researchers who wrote the original paper. See if you can get them to talk to you and provide some clarification. They will often be willing because, hey, who doesn't want to talk about their research?

Another way to argue in favor of your overlap is to shift the "scale of abstraction" for one or more concepts (more on this in Appendix A). For example, if Theory 1 has a concept "fruit" and Theory 2 has a concept "apple," you might reasonably argue that those concepts overlap (to integrate maps) if you shift the Theory 2 concept from apple to fruit. Now that they are both the same, and the overlap works. Don't forget to revisit Theory 2 because shifting the abstraction of one of its concepts may raise the need to shift the abstraction of other concepts. Read all causally connected concepts to see if they still make sense.

The result of integrating theories is the creation of a new theory—a new knowledge map with greater structure (breadth, depth, transformative concepts, loops, and leverage points) than the source theories (Chapter 5).

Showing the Results—and the Progress of Integration

Using measures of structure (Chapter 5) lets you show that your work at integration has resulted in a better theory. For example, Figure 6.5 shows the breadth and depth scores for four theories and an integrated theory incorporating the four starting theories.

Integrating those theories results in a clear improvement in the breadth of the theory, and the new depth is higher than the average of the source theories. Although it is only a small improvement, the potential exists for integrating the new theory with additional theories (and/or conducting your own research). That next level of integration will likely result in a theory of still greater depth.

While a map developed by a team of researchers may end up being rather large, the process of creation is made easier by each researcher focusing on only one "zone" of the map, as in Figure 6.6. The manager of the map (or coordinator, or project manager) can then focus on the connections and overlaps between disciplinary zones.

FIGURE 6.5   ●   Progress in Integrating Four Theories Into One

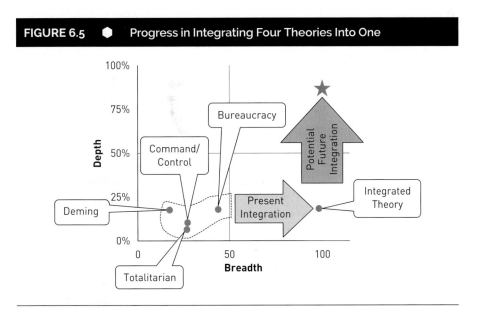

FIGURE 6.6 ● Different Zones of Focus for Researchers in Different Fields

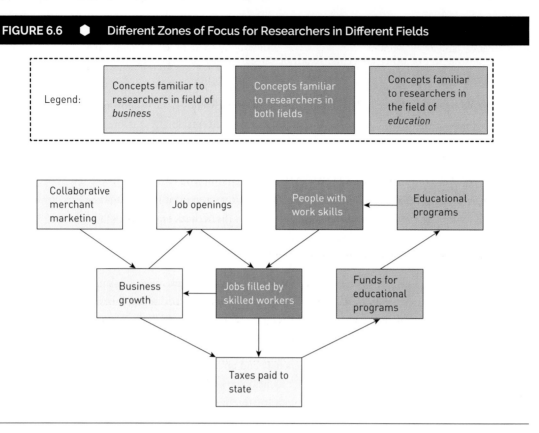

By this point in the journey, you might be starting to think that this is not a "one shot" deal. Indeed, this is an *iterative* process. That is, once you take all the steps, go through the full process, and arrive at the other side with a completed map, you can (and should) do it all again. Importantly, each time you do, you will integrate additional theories and improve your map, along with your expertise and your reputation as a researcher.

CASE STUDY: COLLABORATION AMONG RESEARCHERS

This case study is based on the work of one of the authors (Steve Wallis) in collaboration with researchers in Italy, which culminated in the following publication:

Panetti, E., Parmentola, A., Wallis, S. E., & Ferretti, M. (2018). What drives technology transitions? An integration of different approaches within transition studies. *Technology Analysis & Strategic Management*, (online), 1–22. Retrieved from https://doi.org/10.1080/09537325.2018.1433295

In this case study, we look at a group of researchers collaborating to better understand how nations (and other regions) can accelerate economic growth by encouraging the development and spread of innovative technology. With that improved understanding, stakeholders (including business leaders, policy analysts, and government leaders) will be able to make better decisions about how to improve the economic conditions of their organizations and nations.

Rearview Mirror

From ancient times to the present, practitioners have tried to improve economic growth. Even before the revolutions in technology of the 19th century, innovations in technology (such as the wheel and the plow) had improved productivity and increased standards of living. Since the middle of the 20th century, people had made many efforts at encouraging economic growth through the development and diffusion of technology.

On the scholarly side, researchers have studied efforts at economic improvement through the lenses of multiple disciplines, including business, economics, policy, and more. Despite the research and practice, however, efforts have resulted in "hit and miss" results. Policies often fail, and most business start-ups fail within a few years. Those results show that we do not yet understand how to support long-term change to a more sustainable economy. This presents an opportunity for researchers to research this situation and develop better theories.

On-Ramp

For many in the scholarly world, an ongoing challenge (and daily job) involves conducting research (including reviewing many existing studies) and getting the results published in reputable journals (with the hopes that practitioners will read and use them). Those problems make it difficult for academia to fulfill its role of supporting practitioners because policy makers and organizational leaders rarely read those kinds of journals.

Many research projects begin with a literature review (Chapter 3). The general idea is that by reading a large number of existing papers, the researcher will find relevant insights that will help practitioners make more informed decisions and provide background to understand how their study fits in with other knowledge in the field. Although many literature reviews have provided useful understandings, the social sciences fields have lacked a rigorous way to integrate understandings (theories) across studies to develop measurably better theories (as noted earlier this chapter). So instead of advancing better understanding and ability to resolve wicked problems, each literature review may be adding to the piles of fragmented studies.

Clearly, the time has come for a new direction.

Eva Panetti leads a discussion of graduate students.

Surrounding Scenery

At the Department of Economic and Legal Studies at the University of Naples-Parthenope, experts, professors, and students have explored a wide range of topics, from organizational management to international policy and more.

Among the experts at Parthenope, Eva Panetti is a PhD candidate who is focused on studying how local innovations in technology may be managed. Adele Parmentola is an associate professor with a focus on internationalism and innovation in less-developed areas. Marco Ferretti is a full professor there. His research is focused on strategic management, innovation, and academic spin-offs through venture capital.

Those researchers faced problems common to their colleagues around the world. Their expertise in one field of study made it difficult for them to completely grasp all the nuances of related knowledge from other fields. That, in turn, made it difficult to collaborate, explore the literature, and make effective recommendations to practitioners.

Their shared interest for this project was to draw on four different streams of research (and their different theories from different fields). The team recognized that while each stream contained some useful insights, each also provided incomplete explanations. Further, there appeared to be overlaps, points of similarity, between the theories.

If they could succeed at integrating those four paths, they could develop a new and more useful theory that practitioners could use to guide their nations to greater economic prosperity.

Bumpy Road Ahead

When multiple researchers work together, they often face difficulties because each has a different understanding of the fields and subfields than the others. You might even say that they speak different languages.

Alternate Route

Because knowledge mapping provides a common language of measurability and causality, enabling easier collaboration and more effective integration of theories across disciplines, a colleague suggested that would be a good tool to use.

Steve Wallis, one of the authors of this book, was invited to join the project and had the honor of travelling to Naples as a visiting scholar at the University of Naples-Parthenope.

There, he gave lectures and engaged in conversations with professors and doctoral students.

After discussing the basics of the project in Naples (wine and pizza were involved), Dr. Wallis returned home to California and began corresponding via email. Eva took the lead, with help in writing and rewriting from Dr. Parmentola and Dr. Ferretti as subject matter experts, while Dr. Wallis provided support on the methodological side. All shared a single Word document with "track changes" enabled to keep track of who wrote which parts and what had been changed. Kumu was used as an online platform for mapping (Chapter 7).

The focus of the project and paper was to better understand what drives "transitions in technology." That is, if a society wishes to improve their productivity, they can manage those improve-

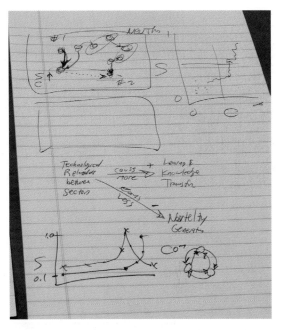

Some notes from discussions on the project.

ments more effectively, sustainably, and efficiently if they know what "drives" or causes those transitions to occur. That broader field of technology transitions has been referred to using different names to represent different strands of research. Those include multi-level perspective (MLP), strategic niche management (SNM), transition management (TM), and technological innovation systems (TIS). Each strand has its own theories.

Eva and her colleagues chose theories from academic publications (in peer-reviewed journals) from each of those four strands of research. Following IPA (Chapter 5), the theories from those four strands were integrated and evaluated according to their breadth and depth. Then, we integrated those four strands to create a final integrated theory. Figure 6.7 shows the scores for each of the four strands of research. The integrated theory is in the lower right quadrant, indicating a greater breadth than any of the individual paths or theories. By providing a greater breadth, the integrated theory provides greater understanding of—and hence greater ability to impact—transitions in technology. The final map is shown in Figure 6.8.

All participants were quite happy with the success of the project. We were particularly excited to discover multiple feedback loops and leverage points that did not exist in the source theories. As you may recall from Chapter 5, loops indicate where practitioners can apply their efforts to promote positive and sustainable change. Leverage points show where smaller efforts can support larger goals. This paper showed that policy makers should focus on entrepreneurial experimentation, knowledge development and diffusion, market formation, and legitimation (some jargon there—for more information, read the paper).

FIGURE 6.7   ⬡   Ranking of Theories According to IPA Scores of Breadth and Depth

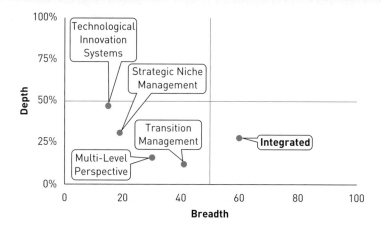

FIGURE 6.8   ⬡   Causal Knowledge Map Integrated Through Collaborative Effort From Four Paths of Research

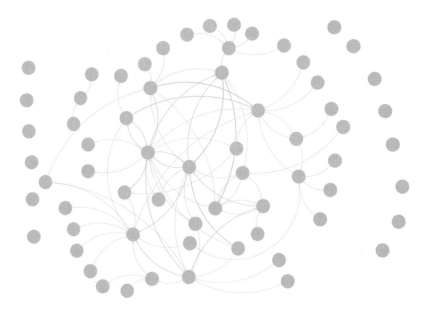

Source: Adapted from original figures in Panetti et al., "What drives technology transitions? An Integration of different approaches within transition studies." *Technology Analysis and Strategic Management*, 2018, https://doi.org/10.1080/09537325.2018.1433295.

Note: Text not included due to space restrictions.

Speed Bumps

No project is without some kind of problem, and this one was no different. When the paper was submitted to a journal, we hit a bump. The reviewers were not familiar with IPA or its special approach to knowledge mapping or as a tool for integration, and the paper was not accepted for publication. When the paper was submitted to a second journal, the reviewers recognized the value of our approach and approved the paper for publication in the prestigious journal, *Technology Analysis & Strategic Management* (Panetti, Parmentola, Wallis, & Ferretti, 2018).

Easy Street

In Table 6.1, we noted some differences between collaborative mapping with stakeholders (covered in depth in Chapter 2) and collaborative mapping with researchers (this chapter). The collaborative process presented in this case study worked very well. The primary researcher (Eva Panetti) chose a topic and assembled a team of researchers based on their interest, availability, subject matter expertise, and methodological expertise. Most of the researchers were already colleagues from the same university, so they worked well together. Future research could involve more researchers, thus adding additional areas of expertise.

It was very useful to have a face-to-face meeting to kick-start the collaborative process. That could have been improved by communicating in advance around possible topics for collaboration.

Integrating the theoretical perspectives becomes easier when researchers have a "common language." In this case, IPA provided the language for integration. That language is easier to apply when at least one member of the team is an expert in the methodology. In this case, that team member was Dr. Wallis. The subject matter experts on team were useful in choosing which streams and theories to use.

The results could be improved by conducting one or more interventions that test the application of the theory in actual practice. The results of that intervention (by policy and/or business professionals) would provide data that add to the researchers' expert perspectives. Also, results may have been improved by drawing on the unpublished research of the experts.

As it is, the map developed in this paper should be used by practitioners to guide their decision-making for the creation of new economic policy. The map should also be used by researchers with an interest in this topic, who could start with the published paper and build on it to improve the map.

In the following Test-Drive, we provide a step-by-step example of collaboration between researchers. This collaboration may not fit your "normal" view of people sitting together in the same room at the same time, working on the same project. Instead, this collaboration was more like a relay race—with runners handing-off the baton.

Test-Drive

"I dare you" is a challenging (and potentially dangerous) way to start a test-drive or road trip. Yet, such a dare came from a colleague of one of the authors of this book, Steve Wallis.

Drawing on his many decades as a distinguished scholar, Dr. Gerhard Fink had written a chapter for an academic book. The purpose of the book was to explore how people might improve their collective ability to manage complex organizations. Dr. Fink's chapter involved presenting and comparing four theories. Each theoretical perspective provided some explanation of the use and abuse of power in organizations. Those four were "totalitarian" (such as the former Soviet Union), "command/control" (top-down management used in some business settings), "bureaucratic" (commonly used in managing governments around the world), and a more enlightened approach to management developed by Deming for more cooperative organizations.

At the end of his chapter, Dr. Fink challenged researchers to use IPA as a way to evaluate, integrate, and improve those theories so they would become more useful. Taking that challenge personally, Dr. Wallis began evaluating those theories and, working in collaboration with Liz Johnson, writing a paper based on the results. Using IPA, it quickly became clear that Dr. Fink's concern was correct—there existed a significant opportunity to improve our collective understanding of power.

The IPA scores in Table 6.2 show that using any one of those theories would be unlikely to provide the deeper understanding needed for supporting sustainable improvement in an organization. Efforts to support positive change in real-world organizations provide some supporting evidence. For example, research shows that attempts to change organizational culture are successful only about 20% of the time.

The next step was to integrate the maps (for part of one of the starting maps, see Figure 6.9). Steve Wallis took the lead on that work, and the results were reviewed and approved by Liz Johnson. It began by identifying the concepts that seemed most similar between the four theories. For example, the concepts "fear" and "trust" were found on more than one map, so those made good overlapping circles.

TABLE 6.2 ⬡ IPA Scores for Four Theories of Power in Organizations			
Theory	**Breadth**	**Number of Transformative Concepts**	**Depth**
Bureaucracy	48	8	17%
Command/control	29	3	10%
Deming	19	3	16%
Totalitarianism	31	2	6%

FIGURE 6.9 ● Part of a Map From Command and Control Management Theory

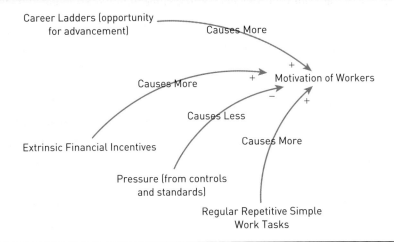

Source: Wallis, Steve, and Johnson, Liz. "Using Integrative Propositional Analysis to Understand and Integrate Four Theories of Social Power Systems," *Journal on Policy and Complex Systems* 4:1, Spring 2018. doi: 10.18278/jpcs.4.1.9.

They were also able to identify concepts that were essentially similar, even though different terms were used. For example, "workers" and "citizens" seemed reasonably similar for this integration. That is because for each of these, the term referred to the people at the "bottom of the ladder"—those who were subject to the abuse of power. It is worth noting that these concepts might not overlap in a different mapping project. For example, if we were creating a map about how workers became citizens, it would make sense for those to be separate concepts on the final map.

Looking more carefully, they also identified concepts that were good overlaps, even though they might appear to be opposites. For example, "collaboration" relates to how people work together. In contrast, "conflict" relates to people not working well together. So anything that causes "more collaboration" might be seen as causing "less conflict." Both were renamed as "Adversarial relationships," as a title which represented less collaboration and more conflict.

TRAVEL TIP

Remember, if you are unsure about how to interpret the similarity of concepts, you can always ask a colleague for their interpretation. If you are working with confidential data, you will need to first get permission before sharing that data with colleagues, and you may need to remove any personally identifying information (see Chapter 1, Right of Way: Research Ethics).

TRAVEL TIP

The integrated map had IPA scores of breadth = 109, transformative = 19, depth = 17%. So, the process of integration showed progress in two directions. First, the increased breadth of the map compared with the individual theories (with breadth scores ranging from 19 to 48). Second, the increased number of transformative concepts from 16 (the sum of transformative concepts among all source theories) to 19, indicating some increase in useful knowledge. The depth of the integrated map (17%) was the same as for the highest depth source theory.

Steven Wallis wondered if the original chapter really captured the full understanding of the author. So Dr. Wallis wrote to Dr. Fink asking if he would review the maps—essentially asking, "Is the diagram an effective representation of the text?" Due to the limits of time, Dr. Fink chose to focus on Deming's map (as described in Fink's book). Following Steve Wallis's instructions to look for causal relationships, Dr. Fink added some causal connections based on his decades of expertise. As a result, the map saw significant improvement. Instead of 16%, the depth was now at a much more useful 47%.

That improvement shows the benefit of collaboration in the world of research because published academic works do not carry all the knowledge in the minds of the experts. We can conduct interviews (Chapter 4) to surface that knowledge to make better maps. We need merely ask.

With Dr. Fink's additions, the Deming map was then integrated with the other maps. The overall map was improved to reach scores of breadth = 109, transformative concepts = 24, depth = 22%. Although the words are too small to read, you can see something of the structure of that map in Figure 6.10.

The final paper was published in the *Journal on Policy and Complex Systems* (Wallis & Johnson, 2018). The paper also noted how such maps could be helpful for those creating computer models. More resources on the process of computer modelling can be found here: https://policyandcomplexsystems.wordpress.com/simulations/.

The Road Does Not End Here

In addition to those improved IPA scores, the final integrated map included a feedback loop. As you recall from Chapter 5, loops improve our understanding and are necessary for supporting sustainable change.

From your reading in this and previous chapters, you will realize that the map can be improved by integrating additional theories (Chapter 3) and conducting additional research (Chapter 4) to identify causal connections and ultimately increase the breadth and depth (Chapter 5) of the map so that it becomes more useful.

FIGURE 6.10 ⬡ Integrated Map, Including Dr. Fink's Insights

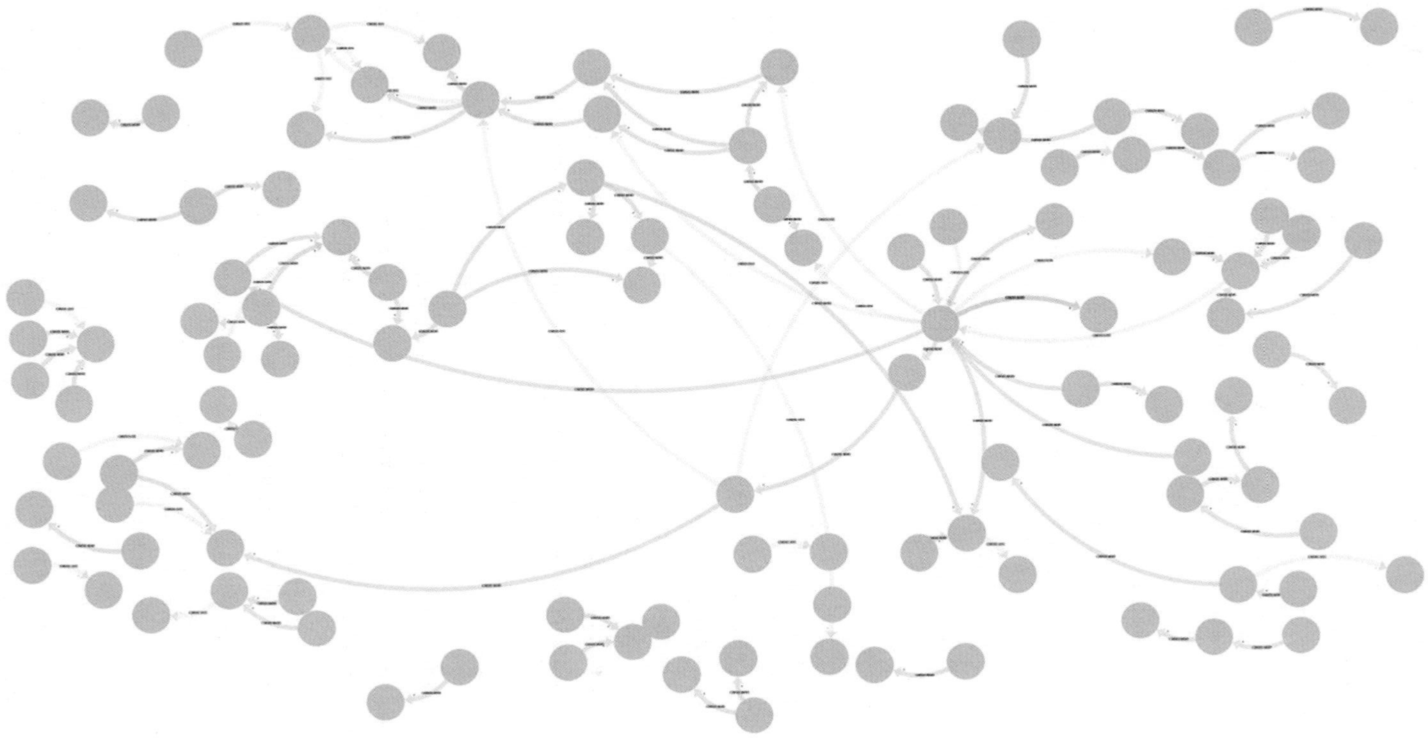

Source: https://kumu.io/Steve/integratedplusfink#integratedplusfink-copy/causes-more

Note: Text not included due to space restrictions

In this test-drive, we showed a step-wise process of collaboration—where maps that were created by research long ago (theories of power in organizations) are analyzed and brought together (by Dr. Gerhard Fink), analyzed and integrated using IPA (by Steve Wallis and Liz Johnson), improved by adding insights from Dr. Fink's expert perspective, and then published.

Collectively, we are accelerating the advance of science. Future researcher collaborations could add ways to continue that collaboration and that progress including the following:

- Integrating more theories into the map

- Interviewing more experts to improve the map

- Building computer models to test the map

- Conducting additional research through individual and group interviews (Chapter 4) and collaborative knowledge mapping (Chapter 2) involving stakeholders in different kinds of organizations

- Implementing the map by practitioners to see if it works as expected

Online platforms can support those collaborations and many others (more on that in Chapter 7).

None of us were around when the social sciences emerged a couple of centuries ago. From that start, there has been a chain of formal and informal collaboration as each generation of researchers have built on the work of previous generations to advance science and practice. That process is accelerated by using the methods of collaboration in this chapter. You are now part of that great process.

Activity Ahead

CLASS ACTIVITY 6.1

Integrating Multiple Maps

In this activity, students collaborate to integrate the maps you created in Class Activities in Chapters 4 and 5 (alternatively, you may use other maps).

First, students work individually (or in small groups) to integrate the two maps. Next, students present the integrated maps to the class. Presenters should pay particular attention to the circles at the overlap between the maps. Explain how you chose those circles. Why do you believe that they are sufficiently similar to be counted as overlaps?

The class then discusses the results, evaluates the work, and suggests improvements. Does the class agree with the choices of circles as overlaps? If not, what changes might be made?

Finally, for each map, draw on the insights and tools found throughout this book (and developed during your class) to discuss evaluating and improving that map for practical application and resolving difficult problems. What additional improvements might be made (generally and specifically) by doing the following:

- Involving more stakeholder groups (Chapter 2)

- Integrating additional theories (Chapter 3)

- Conducting your own research (Chapter 4)

- Improving structure (Chapter 5)

- Integrating expert understanding (Chapter 6)

In this chapter, you've learned about integrating maps by yourself and in collaboration with others. These collaborators may be students today but soon may include a wide variety of academic experts, knowledgeable practitioners, and other researchers.

As you advance in your career, you can connect with other researchers by being active in professional associations of researchers and attending conferences and other professional events. You may also use online platforms to find researchers who might be interested in collaborating with you on your project. Some good online platforms to start include the following:

- Research Gate—https://www.researchgate.net

- Academia.edu—https://www.academia.edu

- LinkedIn—https://www.linkedin.com

- Google Scholar—https://scholar.google.com

- Websites for universities and research centers

- Publishers' websites

You can simply use the concepts found in the maps you made of difficult problems as search terms. Then use the search function for each platform to find and connect with researchers.

Challenges to Interdisciplinary Collaboration

While collaboration across disciplines is a powerful way to create better knowledge maps, it does entail challenges.

- Some researchers may respond slowly to your requests—or not at all.

- Some researchers might produce low quality results.

You can reduce (or eliminate) these problems with a few simple tips.

- Be ready to cut some slack—the non-responsive researcher may be having a temporary problem due to work load or family emergency. Hey, it's easy to ask people to clarify what is going on.

- Be ready to cut the cord—if the collaboration is not working for you, find someone else to work with. If the other researcher is a coworker and you have been assigned to work together, feel free to talk with your supervisor or manager. If you do, remember the following:
  - Be clear and direct. Stick with the facts, such as "Bob set his own deadlines and missed them four out of five times."
  - Avoid "global language," such as "Mary is *always* late."

As you work with other researchers on various projects, you will build relationships simply through day-to-day interactions—you will begin to form a team. Team development is an interesting topic all by itself. We've all worked with teams on school projects. In the real world it is much the same, except that you might be working together on various research projects for many years! There are generally thought to be four stages to good team work:

1. When the team first gets together, they are often very polite. Everyone is on their best behavior. That can be a problem if people don't say what is on their minds. Instead of expressing to the others on the team what they want and need, they stay quiet—and the frustration grows.

2. When the frustration gets too much, there may be horrendous arguments. These can be beneficial because the truth is finally out—everyone's cards are on the table. On the other hand, those arguments can damage relationships—leading to hurt feelings and poor team performance.

3. If properly managed (it's good to get a team coach or facilitator to help), the people on your research team develop a shared understanding of what counts as good communication, quality research, timely delivery—all necessary for a good research project.

4. Finally, when the team comes together, it is a beautiful thing. High quality work gets done according to schedule, and when problems arise (because they always do), everyone on the team talks openly and honestly as the team works to find solutions.

In short, one of the most important tools for working together as a team is establishing clear agreements. Each person on the team should tell the others about their strengths and weaknesses, wants and needs, capacities and limitations. Written agreements should be made about everything relevant to the project—the quality of work, schedule availability, preferred communication channels, response time for communications, and what to do when things go wrong.

Chapter 6 Key Points

- Fragmentation means having more and more disconnected bits of knowledge spread across more and more people, organizations, and academic disciplines.

- While that fragmentation is a problem, we can reap great potential benefits if we can effectively integrate that knowledge.

- We can integrate more effectively if we can collaborate with other researchers, scholars, and practitioners.

- By reaching out through your network (and publications, professional associations, and online communities of researchers), you can connect with other researchers to help you find and create new maps.

- Using IPA, you can more easily integrate your knowledge maps to work against fragmentation and toward better knowledge maps.

Frequently Asked Questions

Q: How much kindness can I expect from strangers?

A: If you send an email to an expert asking, "Please provide me with a list of the best sources for my topic," they will laugh and tell you to do your own homework. If, on the other hand, you show them a map of your research and identify how their expertise might fill a key gap, they are likely to be more receptive!

Q: How can I connect and network with other evaluators?

A: Check out the American Evaluation Association (AEA) at http://www.eval.org/. You can also get lots of great tips such as http://aea365.org/blog/improve-your-evaluations-through-informal-peer-review-by-bronwyn-mauldin/.

Q: Is a map based on the opinions of researchers better or more valid than a map based on the opinions of stakeholders?

A: Researchers and stakeholders provide two different perspectives. Having both of those perspectives is better than having only one or the other. Generally, stakeholder views are more valid for understanding a specific situation. In comparison, researchers' views are more valid for understanding a broader range of situations because researchers' insights come from a wider range of research material. That

(Continued)

(Continued)

difference should be noted in any report or presentation. Remember also that concepts and causal relationships based on the opinions (even the "informed opinion" of researchers and experts) are not as strong a source of evidence as concepts and causal relationships that are supported by both informed opinion *and* data from research.

Q: What if you are trying to integrate two maps where the only concept in common is something that seems very important yet is not measurable—for example, "culture"?

A: If you don't want to invent a new device that measures the (previously) unmeasurable, you might just accept that there will be an unmeasured concept on your map. You might be better off talking with the original authors and asking them how they might measure it. If they provide the same measure— great. Alternatively, you may want to explore that unmeasurable concept in more depth by making it the topic of a new map. If not, perhaps you might want to rename one of the concepts.

Q: What if one expert disagrees with another?

A: Let's say you are looking at a proposition A ➜ B. If one expert says "yes, that is so" while another says "no, that is wrong," the easy answer is to go with the one who says "yes"—mainly because it is pretty difficult to prove a negative. You can also place a question mark on that causal link to indicate that this is an area of disagreement or uncertainty. This shows where more information might improve your map. On the other hand, the expert with a "no" answer might have a more complex map in mind. It might be worth conducting an interview and finding what that map looks like.

Further Exploration

Fragmentation of the Sciences Due to Soft or Ad Hoc Integration of Theories

Wallis, S. E. (2010). The structure of theory and the structure of scientific revolutions: What constitutes an advance in theory? In S. E. Wallis (Ed.), *Cybernetics and systems theory in management: Views, tools, and advancements* (pp. 151–174). Hershey, PA: IGI Global. Retrieved from https://www.researchgate.net/publication/271526139_The_structure_of_theory_and_the_structure_of_scientific_revolutions_What_constitutes_an_advance_in_theory

Wallis, S. E. (2014). Existing and emerging methods for integrating theories within and between disciplines. *Organisational Transformation and Social Change, 11*(1), 3–24. Retrieved from –http://journals.isss.org/index.php/proceedings56th/article/viewFile/1943/657

Wallis, S. E. (2014). A systems approach to understanding theory: Finding the core, identifying opportunities for improvement, and integrating fragmented fields. *Systems Research and Behavioral Science, 31*(1), 23–31. Retrieved from https://onlinelibrary.wiley.com/doi/pdf/10.1002/sres.2159

Collaboration Among Researchers for Interdisciplinary Progress

Bammer, G. (2013). *Disciplining interdisciplinarity: Integration and implementation sciences for researching complex real-world problems*. Acton, Australia: ANU E Press. Retrieved from http://www.oapen.org/download?type=document&docid=459901

Holbrook, J. B. (2013). What is interdisciplinary communication? Reflections on the very idea of disciplinary integration. *Synthese*, 1–15. https://search.proquest.com/docview/1356913781?pq-origsite=gscholar

Newell, W. H. (2007). Decision making in interdisciplinary studies. *Public Administration and Public Policy, 123*, 245. Retrieved from https://www.researchgate.net/profile/William_Newell/publication/260675265_Decision_Making_in_Interdisciplinary_Studies/links/00b49531f3e433a1b4000000/Decision-Making-in-Interdisciplinary-Studies.pdf

Szostak, R. (2002). How to do interdisciplinarity: Integrating the debate. *Issues in Integrative Studies, 20*, 103–122. Retrieved from https://our.oakland.edu/bitstream/handle/10323/4393/07_Vol_20_pp_103_122_How_to_Do_Interdisciplinarity_Integrating_the_Debate_%28Rick_Szostak%29.pdf?sequence=1&isAllowed=y

Szostak, R. (2007). How and why to teach interdisciplinary research practice. *Journal of Research Practice, 3*(2), 17. Retrieved from http://jrp.icaap.org/index.php/jrp/article/viewArticle/92/89

Wallis, S. E. (2018). *The missing piece of the integrative studies puzzle*. Manuscript submitted for publication, available upon request.

Collaborative Research in Business

Bennet, A., Bennet, D., Fafard, K., Fonda, M., Lomond, T., Messier, L., & Vaugeois, N. (2007). *Knowledge mobilization in the social sciences and humanities*. Frost, WV: Mqi Press. Retrieved from https://www.researchgate.net/publication/273062902_Knowledge_mobilization_in_the_social_sciences_and_humanities_moving_from_research_to_action

Schiele, H., & Krummaker, S. (2010). *Consortial benchmarking: A method of academic-practitioner collaborative research and its application in a b2b environment*. Paper presented at the 26th IMP Conference. Retrieved from https://www.impgroup.org/uploads/papers/7542.pdf

Some Sites About Supporting Collaboration in Communities

Banks, S., Herrington, T., & Carter, K. (2017). Pathways to co-impact: Action research and community organizing. *Educational Action Research, 25*, 4. Retrieved from https://www.tandfonline.com/doi/full/10.1080/09650792.2017.1331859

Koné, A., Sullivan, M., Senturia, K. D., Chrisman, N. J., Ciske, S., J., & Krieger, J. W. (2000). Improving collaboration between researchers and communities. *Public Health Reports, 115*. Retrieved from https://www.ncbi.nlm.nih.gov/pmc/articles/PMC1308719/pdf/pubhealthrep00022-0141.pdf

Learning Circle Five Resources. (n.d.). http://www.hunter.cuny.edu/socwork/nrcfcpp/pass/learning-circles/five/LearningCircleFiveResources.pdf

Some Sites About Learning to Collaborate Better in Teams

Abrahamson, D., (2016). *Team coaching: Why, where, when & how*. [WABC white paper—Best Fit Business Coaching Series]. Retrieved from http://www.wabccoaches.com/white_papers/20161130/WABC-White-Paper-Team-Coaching--Why-Where-When-and-How-Nov-2016.pdf

(Continued)

(Continued)

Center for Creative Leadership. (n.d.). *The dynamics of team coaching*. [Podcast]. Retrieved from https://www.ccl.org/multimedia/podcast/the-dynamics-of-team-coaching/

Pentland, A. (2012, April). The new science of building great teams. *Harvard Business Review*. Retrieved from https://hbr.org/2012/04/the-new-science-of-building-great-teams

Stein, J. (n.d.). *Using the stages of team development*. Retrieved from Human Resources website at http://hrweb.mit.edu/learning-development/learning-topics/teams/articles/stages-development

More Sources for Connecting With Researchers

Futurearth. (n.d.). *Early career professionals*. Retrieved from //www.futureearth.org/early-career-professionals

Mendeley. (n.d.). Mendeley website. https://www.mendeley.com/research-network/community

Examples of Integrating Theories

Wallis, S. E. (2006). *A study of complex adaptive systems as defined by organizational scholar-practitioners.* Santa Barbara, CA: Fielding Graduate University.

Wallis, S. E. (2015). Integrative propositional analysis: A new quantitative method for evaluating theories in psychology. *Review of General Psychology, 19*(3), 365–380.

Wallis, S. E., & Johnson, L. (2018). Response to a challenge: Using integrative propositional analysis to understand and integrate four theories of social power systems. *Journal on Policy and Complex Systems, 4*(1). Retrieved from http://www.ipsonet.org/publications/open-access/policy-and-complex-systems/policy-and-complex-systems-volume-4-number-1-spring-2018

Wallis, S. E., Wright, B., & Nash, F. D. (2016). *Using integrative propositional analysis to evaluate and integrate economic policies of U.S. presidential candidates* [White Paper]. Retrieved from http://meaningfulevidence.com/wp-content/uploads/IPA-of-POTUS-Candidates.pdf

Wright, B. & Wallis, S. E. (2015, July–September). Using integrative propositional analysis (IPA) for evaluating entrepreneurship theories. *SAGE Open,* 1–9. doi:10.1177/2158244015604190

Case Study for This Chapter

Panetti, E., Parmentola, A., Wallis, S., & Ferretti, M. (2018). What drives technology transitions? An integration of different approaches within transition studies. *Technology Analysis & Strategic Management, (1–22).* Retrieved from https://doi.org/10.1080/09537325.2018.1433295

Test-Drive Resources

Fink, G. (2017). Power systems: How power works in different systems. In F. Maimone (Ed.), *Evolution of the post-bureaucratic organization* (pp. 41–60). Hershey, PA: IGI Global.

Wallis, S. E., & Johnson, L. (2018). Response to a challenge: Using integrative propositional analysis to understand and integrate four theories of social power systems. *Journal on Policy and Complex Systems, 4*(1). Retrieved from http://www.ipsonet.org/publications/open-access/policy-and-complex-systems/policy-and-complex-systems-volume-4-number-1-spring-2018

7

COMMUNICATION, COLLABORATION, AND ACTION

istock.com/MonkeyBusinessImages

In this chapter you will discover the following:

- Tactile and online tools for making maps

- Techniques for presenting maps to stakeholder groups

- Activities for collaborative decisions and action

- Steps to tracking progress toward desired results

THE ROAD AHEAD

In this, the final chapter, we have nearly reached our destination. You have found your way through fields of data, structures of logic, and gatherings of stakeholders. Now, we will take those maps and put them to work for communication, collaborative decision-making, and action.

Having a better map means that decision makers can move forward with greater confidence. It also means that there can be greater trust, transparency, and accountability between stakeholders—as long as everyone shares their maps!

In this chapter, we will start by reviewing "low-tech" tools for creating maps "by hand." Then, we'll get into "high tech" tools for mapping that you can find on your computer and online. Next, we'll provide some techniques you can use for making effective presentations of your maps to clients (and in the classroom). We'll also talk about how you can guide conversations around those maps to help groups engage in action planning.

TOOLS FOR MAKING MAPS

In this section, we'll talk about low-tech tools, computer-based tools, and online platforms that you can use for creating and presenting maps. Several tactile and electronic tools can help you create a more presentable map from the concepts and causal relationships you identified in your research and/or collaborative mapping activity. Much of this section is from "Low-Tech and High-Tech Tools for Mapping Your Strategic Plan" (Wright, Rostami, & Lewis, 2016).

Low-Tech Tools

By this point in the book, you are familiar with one or more of these low-tech options for turning your research results or stakeholder perspectives into maps:

- Paper, pencil, and pen

- Flipchart and markers

- Whiteboard

- Big wall space or floor space

- Sticky notes

- Index cards

For making more interesting and dynamic presentations, consider using a combination of these tools. For example, at an interactive poster presentation at a conference, we started with a laminated poster board. When people walked by, we encouraged them to add sticky notes, which we'd previously made, showing concepts from the literature. They also wrote and added their own concepts on sticky notes and drew arrows connecting the concepts with markers (Figure 7.1).

FIGURE 7.1 ⬡ Whiteboard and Sticky Notes Used for an Interactive Presentation at an Academic Conference

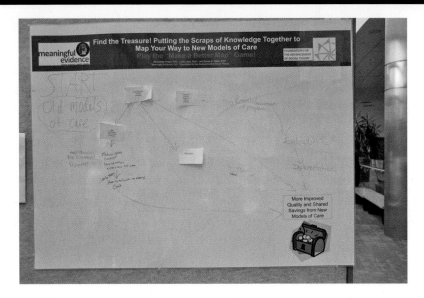

Useful features and possible downsides of low-tech mapping tools

Useful Features	Caution—Possible Downsides
• Can be done at little or no cost • Intuitive—easy to work with • Some people just like the feel of real objects	• Requires everyone working on a map to be in the same room (not designed for collaborating with remote teams) • Requires time and effort to set up your own tools for making your map

The ASK MATT Tabletop Game

This is a gamified approach to making a map to your strategic goals that we developed (Figure 7.2).

FIGURE 7.2 ⬡ An ASK MATT Tabletop Map

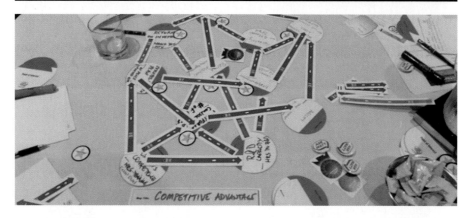

Useful features and possible downsides of ASK MATT Tabletop mapping game	
Useful Features	**Caution—Possible Downsides**
• Includes all materials needed to create a strategic knowledge map (game pieces, markers, timer)	• Requires everyone working on a map to be in the same room (not designed for collaborating with remote teams)
• Provides a structure for evaluating your map (score card, pieces to indicate positive feedback loops, etc.)	• Not easy to move the map from one place to another (although you can take a picture)
• Gamified approach makes the process of creating and refining your map fun	
• Some people just like the feel of real objects	

Desktop Tools

You can use commonly available software such as Word or PowerPoint to make your maps. Basically, to add a new concept to your map, select Insert, Shapes, and a circle (or whatever shape you like). Then enter the name of your concept (e.g., "Customer Service") in the shape. To add a connecting arrow between concepts on your map, select Insert,

Shape, and select an arrow. Then move the arrow as needed so that it's connecting the concepts. To add your own pictures to your map, select Insert, Picture.

Useful features and possible downsides of desktop tools	
Useful Features	**Caution—Possible Downsides**
• Many people already have PowerPoint and Word installed on their computers and are familiar with how to use it • You can make large size slides (e.g., poster size) for diagramming large maps (select Design, Slide Size)	• Not designed as an online tool for collaboration with remote teams (you would need a separate document sharing tool for that) • Not designed to create interactive maps (e.g., a map where clicking on a concept/circle takes you to more information about that concept) • No automated legend feature • Arrows may not automatically move when you move boxes, so moving things around can be cumbersome • Map surface is limited to the size of the page or slide, so adding more concepts to expand your map can be cumbersome • No feature for linking together multiple related maps across pages

Online Mapping Tools

Generally, the main benefit of placing your maps online is that they are easier to share. Many platforms are available (many of them free) for creating online maps. Each comes with its own terminology, learning curve, and features. Some platforms that we have found useful for creating and sharing maps are Insight Maker, Stormboard, and Kumu. Here, we'll provide some tips, benefits, and limitations for those three. Then, we'll go into more depth about how to use Kumu.

Insightmaker.com

At insightmaker.com, you can create a free account and create a new map (called an "insight" in Insight Maker). To add a new concept to your map, right-click to create a "variable" (or other "primitive"), then name it with the name of your concept (e.g., "Customer Service"). To add connecting arrows between concepts, drag your cursor from one concept (variable) to another. You can add your own pictures if they are online: right-click and select Create Picture. Insight Maker also has many built-in pictures that you can add to your map.

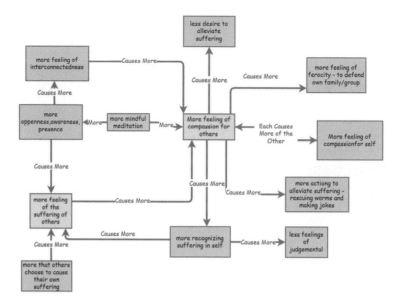

Source: Sample map from Insight Maker. Wright, B., Rostami, A., & Lewis, L. (2016). Low-Tech and High-Tech Tools for Mapping Your Strategic Plan. Meaningful Evidence, LLC. http://meaningfulevidence.com/wp-content/uploads/Tools-for-Mapping-Your-Strategic-Plan.pdf

Useful features and possible downsides of Insight Maker

Useful Features

- Online tool, can add collaborators to edit map
- Option to create a public map that is visible to anyone or a private map that only you and your collaborators can see
- "Storytelling" feature to walk through your map step-by-step and publish your story as an "article"
- Can zoom in to get a larger size map, which you can then copy using Print Screen on your keyboard and save as a picture by pasting it into a picture editing program
- Includes a simulation modeling feature
- Free

Caution—Possible Downsides

- No automated legend
- Arrows may not automatically move when you move concepts (circles), so moving things around can be cumbersome
- Map surface is limited in size, so adding concepts to expand your map can be cumbersome
- Can't import/export to/from Excel for further analysis
- Limited space to add information about each connection or concept on your map
- No feature to group/cluster together related concepts or connections from multiple maps

Stormboard.com

In Stormboard (at Stormboard.com), you can create an account and create a new map (called a "Storm" or "board" in Stormboard). To add a concept to your map, double-click on the board (map) to add a "sticky" (concept). To add a connecting arrow between concepts on your map, click on one of the arrow points on the starting concept (sticky) and drag your cursor to the concept (sticky) that you want to connect it to.

Useful features and possible downsides of Stormboard

Useful Features	Caution—Possible Downsides
• Online tool; can invite people to access your map (storm) (they will need a Stormboard account)	• Limited choice of legend templates; can't add connectors to legend
• Can add data or other information about a concept on your map in comments for the concept	• Free version has very limited features; monthly/annual fee for full version
• Can import/export to Excel for further analysis	• No ability to make a public map (only you and people who you invite to access your map can see it; all users must have a Stormboard account)
• Can move map surface to easily create very large maps	
• Includes legend feature to show what your color coding means for stickies (concepts)	
• Voting feature provides a way for people to vote on concepts and to show the number of votes for each concept	
• Option to show concept creators and their avatars	
• Can create "substorms" within storms to show more detail for concepts	
• Chat feature provides a place for team members to discuss issues related to your map	
• Free version available for up to five users working as a group	

A Strategic Knowledge Map for a Health Club to Increase Revenue

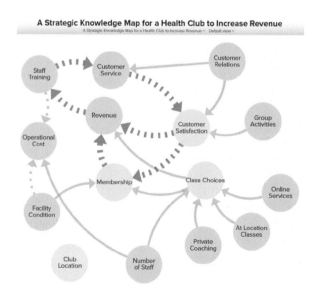

Source: Example online interactive strategic knowledge map (storm) created in Stormboard. Wright, B., Rostami, A., & Lewis, L. (2016). Low-Tech and High-Tech Tools for Mapping Your Strategic Plan. Meaningful Evidence, LLC. http://meaningfulevidence.com/wp-content/uploads/Tools-for-Mapping-Your-Strategic-Plan.pdf

Kumu.io

In Kumu (at Kumu.io), you first create an account, log in, and create a new map. Then, to add a concept to your map, click the green "+" button, then choose "add element." To add a connecting arrow between concepts, select the concept (element) that you want to connect from, click the green "+" button, and choose "add connection." You can add your own pictures to concepts if the pictures are online (create a new field called "Image" and add a link to the image).

Source: Example online interactive strategic knowledge map created in Kumu. Wright, B., Rostami, A., & Lewis, L. (2016). Low-Tech and High-Tech Tools for Mapping Your Strategic Plan. Meaningful Evidence, LLC. http://meaningfulevidence.com/wp-content/uploads/Tools-for-Mapping-Your-Strategic-Plan.pdf

Useful features and possible downsides of Kumu

Useful Features	Caution—Possible Downsides
• Online tool, so you can add collaborators who may also edit the map	• Functions take time to learn
• Can import/export map data to/from Excel for further analysis (select the three dots in the lower right corner of the screen for "More," then select "Export .xlsx")	
• Can add fields to show customized information for a concept/connection on your map and "decorate" concepts and connections (change shape size, color, etc.) by field (e.g., make all concepts representing outcomes the same color)	
• Can automatically create a legend to show what your decorations mean based on the fields that you created	
• Connecting arrows between concepts (circles/elements) automatically move when you move concepts on your map	
• Maps are not limited to one page, can create a very large map	
• Includes "presentations" feature to walk through your map step-by-step	
• "Capture screenshot" feature lets you easily save pictures of your map	
• Can create customized map views to show different parts of your map	
• "Issues" feature provides a place for team members to discuss issues related to your map	
• Includes social network analysis tool	
• Free for public maps in individual accounts	

For resources on mapping tools and a list of online mapping tools, see the Further Exploration section at the end of this chapter.

Test-Drive—Mapping in Kumu

In this section, we provide a step-by-step example of how to create a map in Kumu. We decided to use Kumu (https://kumu.io/) because many of our students and clients like how it may be used to create attractive presentations.

We created a Microsoft Excel file to meet Kumu's requirements for uploading data in a way that would automatically create a map. That file contained two worksheets. The first worksheet, "Elements," contained information on each concept/circle, called an element in Kumu. Figure 7.3 shows the Elements worksheet, where we entered the label for each element. The label is the name of the concept that will appear on each circle.

The second worksheet, "Connections," contained information on each arrow between the elements in the first worksheet. Figure 7.4 shows the Connections worksheet, where we entered information for each causal proposition, one row for each causal connection.

- In the first column ("From"), we entered the name of the concept that the connection was starting from (the concept with an arrow pointing away from it). We were careful to include only concepts that we had already entered in the

FIGURE 7.3 ● Spreadsheet With Information About Concepts (Elements in Kumu)

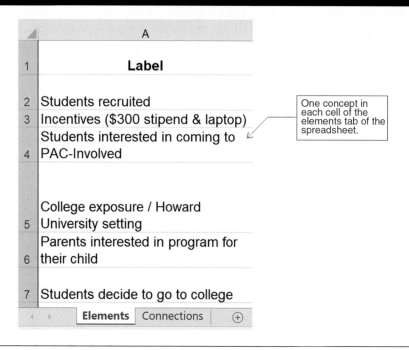

Elements worksheet (good to copy-and-paste here or use Excel's Data Validation feature so that all elements are entered into the Connections worksheet in exactly the same way as they are in the Elements worksheet).

- In the second column ("To"), we entered the concept that the arrow was pointing to. We were again careful to include only concepts that we had already entered in the Elements worksheet.

- In the third column ("Type"), we entered "+" for relationships in which more of the concept in the "From" column caused more of the concept in the "To" column. We entered "-" for relationships when more of the concept in the "From" column caused less of the concept in the "To" column. We could have entered any type that we wished, such as "Causes more" and "Causes less." We could have also added labels for these, such as entering the data sources for each connection (see Chapter 4). These labels would appear as text on the arrows.

- In the fourth column ("Description"), we pasted details of our research findings supporting that proposition.

- We created a fifth column ("# data sources") to track how many data sources supported the proposition, calculated by adding the numbers in the columns to the right. We also created the next five columns, one for each evaluation method. In those columns, we entered "1" if the proposition had data from that method. As Figure 7.4 shows, this lets us quickly see that one of the four propositions has data from three sources (student focus group, project team interviews, and student survey) and the other three propositions each have data from one method.

We can use this same system to create additional columns to record any information about concepts and connections that we wish to include in our map.

Creating a Map in Kumu

Next, log into your Kumu account. From the Dashboard, create a "new project." When asked, select "directed" as the default for connections.

Within the new project, open the advanced editor, enter the text shown in Figure 7.5 into the editor, and click "save." This sets up the map to use dotted lines for "-" (causes less) relationships and solid lines for "+" (causes more) relationships. It also formats the circles and arrows similar to how they look in the examples in this book.

Next, we clicked the three dots in the lower right of the screen to bring up the "More" menu, then selected "Import Data" (Figure 7.6). We then imported our Excel file containing data about the concepts and causal connections in our knowledge map.

FIGURE 7.4 ● Spreadsheet With Information About Causal Relationships ("Connections" in Kumu)

From	To	Type	Description	#data sources	Data: Structured Observation	Data: student focus group	Data: Project team interviews	Data: Student journal	Data: Student survey
College exposure/ Howard University setting	Parents interested in program for their child	+	A teacher who we spoke with mentioned that the Howard University setting got parents excited about their children participating.	1			1		
Incentives ($300 stipend & laptop)	Students interested in coming to PAC-Involved	+	On the pre-survey, when asked what most interested them about PAC-Involved, participating students frequently mentioned receiving the prizes/ incentives/rewards (6 of 20 students). Two of 11 students mentioned the incentives on the post-survey. All students who answered these survey questions and mentioned prizes/incentives/rewards also mentioned other aspects of the program that most interested them. In the focus group, when first asked what interested them the most, one student mentioned the incentives. When asked why else they were in PAC-Involved, students then most frequently mentioned the laptop/tablet (8 students) and/or money (9 students) provided at the end of the program (12 students total). One of the project team members mentioned that the incentives—the computer and $300 stipend—were selling points in recruiting students.	3		1	1		1

From	To	Type	Description	#data sources	Data: Structured Observation	Data: student focus group	Data: Project team interviews	Data: Student journal	Data: Student survey
College exposure / Howard University setting	Students interested in coming to PAC Involved	+	PAC-Involved students who completed the pre-survey most frequently mentioned the college campus experience/Howard University as what interested them the most about the program (7 students).	1					1
College exposure / Howard University setting	Students decide to go to college	+	In the student focus group, when asked if they would recommend the program for other students, one student said they would recommend it because "for friends who are not going to school/college, this trip to Howard University may change their minds."	1		1			

FIGURE 7.5 ● Formatting Your Map in the Advanced Editor in Kumu

CURRENT VIEW

Core map

If you're comfortable with code, we strongly recommend using the
advanced editor. Check out our ADVANCED VIEWS guide to get started.

☑ Automatically apply changes

```
 1   @import "base";
 2
 3 ▾ @settings {
 4       element-size: 120;
 5       element-font-size: 180;
 6       element-text-align: center;
 7       arrow-height: 6;
 8       arrow-width: 8;
 9       font-size: 20;
10       connection-size: 30;
11
12   }
13
14
15
16   |
```

SWITCH TO BASIC EDITOR

Source: Howard University PAC-Involved Project.

FIGURE 7.6 ● Importing Data Into Kumu to Create a Knowledge Map

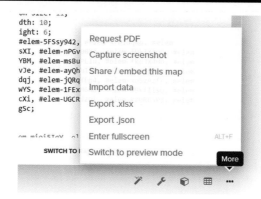

```
           ... size: ..,
dth: 10;
ight: 6;
#elem-5FSsy942,
sXI, #elem-nPGv
YBM, #elem-msBu
vJe, #elem-ayQh
dqj, #elem-jQRq
WYS, #elem-1FEx
cXi, #elem-UGCR
gSc;

om miniSTcY  o1
```

SWITCH TO |

Request PDF

Capture screenshot

Share / embed this map

Import data

Export .xlsx

Export .json

Enter fullscreen   ALT+F

Switch to preview mode

More

TRAVEL TIP

You can also import data to Kumu by dragging and dropping your Excel file onto the map space.

Once we uploaded our data, Kumu instantly turned the data into a knowledge map (Figure 7.7).

For Figure 7.7, the map is so complex that we had to shrink it down to fit on this page. Due to the space constraints of this book, Figure 7.7 does not show the text on the circles, but you get the idea (we'll talk about creating submaps to make maps more readable below).

FIGURE 7.7 ⬢ The Resulting Knowledge Map in Kumu

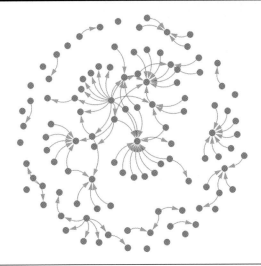

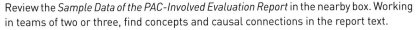

Source: Howard University PAC-Involved Project.

CLASS ACTIVITY 7.1

Creating an Online Map

Review the *Sample Data of the PAC-Involved Evaluation Report* in the nearby box. Working in teams of two or three, find concepts and causal connections in the report text.

Next, following our example in the above "Test-Drive," complete the Elements worksheet and the Connections worksheet on the "Handout for Class Activity 7.1" with information about each concept and causal relationship you find.

(Continued)

(Continued)

In the Elements worksheet, enter the name of each concept in the Label column.

In the Connections worksheet, enter each causal relationship, one row per causal arrow:

- In the "From" column, enter the concept (from your Elements worksheet) that the arrow is pointing away from.
- In the "To" column, enter the concept (from your Elements worksheet) that the arrow is pointing to.
- In the "Type" column, enter "+" (or "Causes more") if more of the first concept causes more of the second concept. Enter "-" (or "Causes less") if more of the first concept causes less of the second concept. Enter "?" for any causal relationships that are uncertain or mixed.
- In the "Description" column, enter the supporting data for the causal relationship.
- In each of the five rightmost columns, enter "1" in the column for each data source that supports the causal connection. Then, enter the total number of data sources for the causal connection in the "# data sources" column.

Compare and discuss your understandings.

If you wish, create an account in Kumu and upload your completed handout to instantly create a map. Then format your map to fit your artistic inclinations.

SAMPLE DATA OF THE PAC-INVOLVED EVALUATION REPORT FOR CLASS ACTIVITY 7.1

During the observation, students appeared to be engaged at several times, such as during the demo with the toy cars, while watching the videos about scientific topics—for example, the "twins paradox"—and during some of the lectures, during which they asked questions (e.g., when the professors was explaining the "twins paradox"). The students also seemed engaged in choosing names for their groups for the video project and while they were working in groups on their video project. At some points, some students seemed not engaged or student engagement was mixed, in particular before lunch, which arrived late, and during some of the lectures.

In the final round of project team interviews when asked about the biggest impact of the program, one team member said that getting students involved was the biggest impact. This team member reported some students came for the incentives and then got involved because they enjoyed it. Once they got engaged, their primary purpose seemed to be to learn. One team member mentioned that some of the students who were not initially interested were actively engaged in the sessions, while other students who they thought would be interested were not as interested as the program went forward.

HANDOUT FOR CLASS ACTIVITY 7.1

Label	

| ‹ | › | | **Elements** | Connections | |

Elements Worksheet

From	To	Type	Description	# data sources	Data: Structured observation	Data: Student focus group	Data: Project team interviews	Data: Student journals	Data: Student surveys

| ‹ | › | | Elements | **Connections** | ⊕ | ⋮ ◂ | |

Connections Worksheet

Download an electronic version of this handout at https://practicalmapping.com

MAKING PRESENTATIONS

There are many situations in which you may find yourself making presentations. You might be sharing information between stakeholder groups, explaining your research to clients, or giving a talk at an academic conference. Whatever the situation, the purpose of a presentation is to inform the audience. That information prepares them for conversations, decisions, and action.

Keep in mind that most stakeholder groups will only want a very brief overview of your methods, data, and implications for future research—the exception being other researchers and academicians. Most stakeholders will be more interested in the implications for action.

Here are a few basic guidelines for making effective presentations:

- Rehearse your presentation ahead of time.

- When you speak, make sure you are heard.

- Modulate your voice—to highlight key points and to show your interest in the topic.

- Avoid long lists of details (instead, provide a handout for those who might be interested).

- Make sure the audience can see and read the text on the screen by using large size font and by not including too much detail on a slide.

- Use the map to guide listeners from point to point. Start with the goals and work backward to action items.

- Use stories, examples, and quotes to reinforce the data.

- At each major step, ask if there are clarifying questions.

- Bring other voices into the room by asking stakeholders to present their parts of a shared map.

Presenting Data With Maps

Having the supporting data easily accessible during your presentation gives you the ability to switch seamlessly between map and supporting evidence—which makes for a more impressive presentation.

For example, you can use larger circles and wider arrows to show concepts and relationships that are supported by more interviews, more studies, or more methods. Keep in mind that (for Kumu) you will need to manually create fields (columns in your Excel file) for the number of data sources and record that information, then manually customize your map settings to resize circles and arrows based on that field. Kumu may also be set up so that clients and stakeholders can click on a concept or arrow for details about the supporting data in a pop-up box (called a "popover" in Kumu, see https://blog.kumu.io/introducing-popovers-cf091fedde78) or in a sidebar.

Here are a few more ideas for using the arrows on your map to visualize the level of data supporting them:

- Percentage or number of survey respondents who made the causal claim

- Percentage or number of interview participants/focus group participants who made the causal claim

- Number of study sites (e.g., number of cities) in which the causal claim was found

- Number of data types (e.g., surveys, observation, interviews, literature review) in which the causal claim was found

Depending on your research, you may end up with a map that looks like a giant hairball. Not only will viewers find it difficult to unravel, they may find it impossible to read. Here are a few ways to deal with that messiness and make your maps more accessible to your clients.

Submaps

One way to deal with a large map is to look at only a small portion of the map or create separate views—"submaps"—then walk people through the map one piece at a time. This is similar to how you would organize a large research report into different sections. Figure 7.8 shows a hairball map —the whole map of U.S. presidential candidates' economic policies that we developed for a study (Wallis, Wright, & Nash, 2016).

Figure 7.9 shows that map again – where we are focused on a few select concepts (the darker ones), with the rest of the concepts shaded into the background. That helps somewhat, but the concepts that we're interested in are still too small to see, they are not together in one place, and they might not be arranged in the order that we want them. So, we'll use another solution.

While Figure 7.10 shows a submap of only those few concepts, here, we've created a new "view" of the map that includes only our selected concepts, all together in one place. Now we have a presentable piece of a map that our audience will be able to read and understand.

FIGURE 7.8   ⬡   Hairball

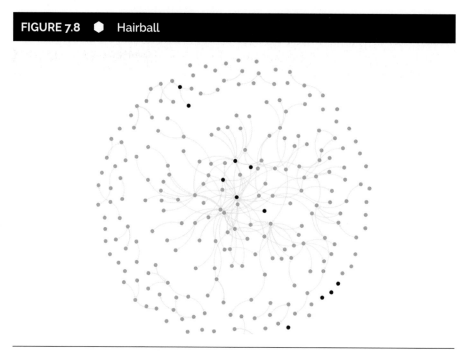

Source: Wallis, S. E., Wright, B., & Nash, F. D. (2016). Using Integrative Propositional Analysis to Evaluate and Integrate Economic Policies of U.S. Presidential Candidates. Center for Scientific Analysis of Policy. http://meaningfulevidence.com/wp-content/uploads/IPA-of-POTUS-candidates.pdf.

FIGURE 7.9   ⬡   Key Concepts Highlighted

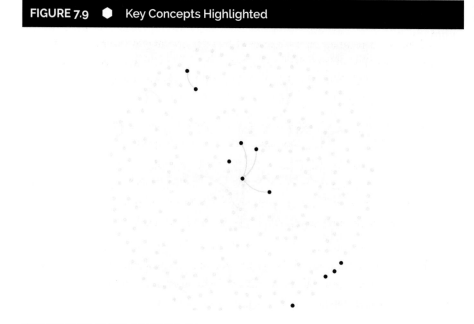

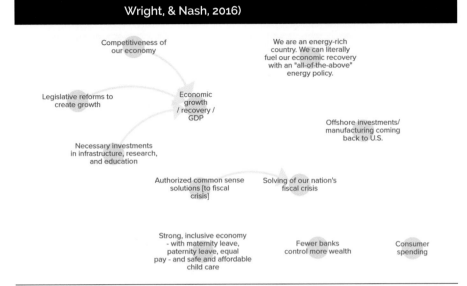

FIGURE 7.10   ⬡   Submap (From Our Analysis of Economic Policies of 2016 Candidates for President of the United States; Wallis, Wright, & Nash, 2016)

Source: Wallis, S. E., Wright, B., & Nash, F. D. (2016). Using Integrative Propositional Analysis to Evaluate and Integrate Economic Policies of U.S. Presidential Candidates. Center for Scientific Analysis of Policy. http://meaningfulevidence.com/wp-content/uploads/IPA-of-POTUS-candidates.pdf.

We sometimes find it useful to present different parts of the large map to different stakeholder groups (always retaining key information so all groups get the same general message). If you are working with experts, their maps will likely be more complex than those submaps—depending on their level of comfort creating and working with larger maps (such as the one in Figure 7.11). You, as the researcher, will walk people through the map by discussing the data behind each concept and the connections between them, as they relate to achieving desired goals.

In contrast, you might add pictures for the concepts on your stakeholder-facing map (Figure 7.12). Well-selected pictures make your map more engaging.

Because the professional-facing map in Figure 7.11 was developed to represent community development, the pictures in Figure 7.12 were chosen to reflect that theme and provide viewers with a general feel of a neighborhood. Here, the roads show connections whose causal relationships would be explained by the presenter.

In the interest of transparency, it is a good idea to make more information (such as the hairball map and related data) easily available to all stakeholders in an easy-to-navigate format. This may be done with handouts and/or by having the information available online, one submap at a time.

Here are a few more techniques for making complex maps easier to navigate.

FIGURE 7.11   ●   Professional-Facing Map

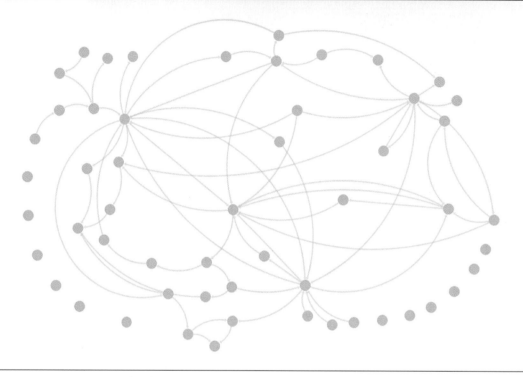

Source: Neighborworks America (NWA).

Nested Maps

In addition to creating submaps to view details of the larger map, you may also create a relatively simple map that has more detailed maps "nested" in the circles of that simple map.

Like individual people are nested within teams, teams within departments, and departments within organizations, we can also think of knowledge maps as nested within other knowledge maps. For example, a board of directors might create a "board-level" map in which each concept might represent high-level functions (e.g., accounting, fundraising, human resources). That high-level map could show how more fundraising leads to more staffing to provide services. While such a map might be very useful for the board in understanding the operation of a large organization, it might not be so useful for the individual departments in understanding and improving their own operations. So, each department, might create their own "department-level" map, focused on their own function, which could be seen as "nested" within the board-level map.

Similarly, an organization might be researching a very large and complex problem such as city government strategies for reducing homelessness. That information could help

FIGURE 7.12 ● Stakeholder-Facing Map With Pictures to Supplement the Concepts

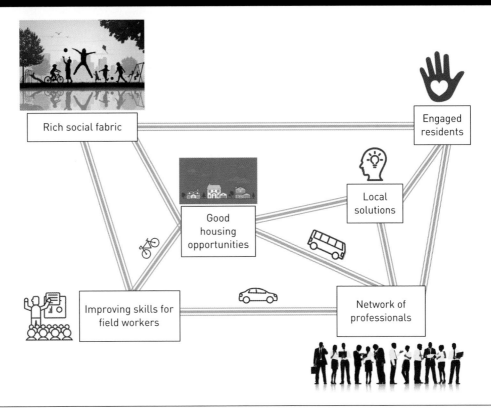

Source: Neighborworks America. Icons: istock.com/paci77; istock.com/bananajazz; iStock.com/RawPixel; iStock.com/-VICTOR-; iStock.com/-VICTOR-; iStock.com/matsabe; istock.com/filo.

advocacy groups to plan effective strategies for influencing policy in their cities. That city-level map might include concepts such as "housing support for veterans" or "collaboration among care providers." Each of those concepts may become the topic or focus of a group-level map that could be nested within the city-level map.

Figure 7.13 shows an abstract map that might be made by a city-wide coalition, with another abstract map nested within in—as might be made by a group focused on unemployment.

With nested maps, various people and groups can each create and use the maps that are most meaningful for them. And by seeing how their nested map fits into the larger map, they can see how those maps might be related to maps of other groups to support collaboration.

When making presentations, you can show a simple "overview" (or "key findings") map. Then, show a nested map that provides more details for each of the overview concepts. A key findings map is a way to present a key findings report in visual form. See Chapter 4

FIGURE 7.13 ⬗ Map Nested Within One Concept of High-Level Map

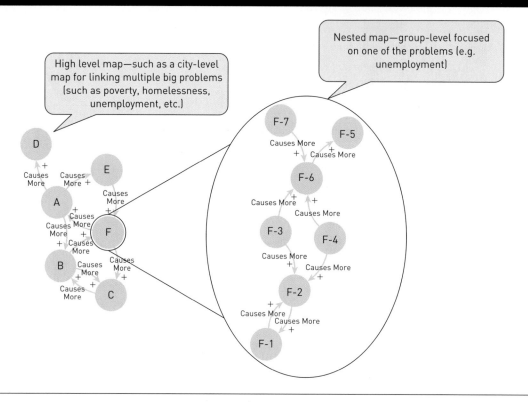

for a brief introduction to creating a key findings report. See Appendix B for an example key findings map and detailed maps.

Presentations are about providing people with useful information. The next step is for those people to engage in conversations around that information and what it means for their activities.

GUIDING CONVERSATIONS AROUND A MAP

In some projects, clients may want you to help the group in moving to the next step—supporting stakeholders in conversations around a map that leads to plans and action.

In conversations, people share their feelings and information. That process generates excitement for the topic, along with creative ideas for collaboration and action. Your role here is as a facilitator—a person who works to make the conversation successful for the participants.

You might find yourself facilitating a management team, a board of directors, a mixed group of stakeholders—the possibilities are almost endless.

Facilitation is as much art as science. And to be a good facilitator often requires significant education, experience, and effort. Often that equates to months of training and years of practice. Here, we will touch on a few of the basics. We encourage you to develop your skills by following the reading suggestions in the Further Exploration section at the end of this chapter.

In those conversations, the map serves as a "touchstone" to provide information and to focus the conversation. For these conversations, you start by using the presentation techniques already discussed in this chapter to help people understand complex maps more easily. For example, rather than showing the whole maps, you might show a series of slides such as the nested maps in Figure 7.13 or the submap in Figure 7.10. Next, you can stimulate conversation by asking the participants questions such as the following:

- Who are the stakeholders related to this part of the map?

- Are they all represented in the room now?

- What is new, interesting, or surprising for you about this map?

- What circles represent your short-term and long-term goals?

- What loops are there to support sustainable success?

- Where are the leverage points—circles where loops intersect?

- What circles are actionable for you?

Also, it is worthwhile to keep the group focused on the "core" of the map (Appendix A). The core is where concepts are more connected so more likely to provide useful knowledge and guidance for action. In contrast, you want to avoid having conversation drift to concepts around the "belt," unless the conversation is about how that concept might be brought into the core (see exception to this below)—for example, if the group is talking about conducting additional research to find connections between concepts because additional research there will help make the belt concepts become more useful (and move them toward the center).

TRAVEL TIP

For problematic situations, use the tips in "Dealing With Difficult Dynamics" in Chapter 2.

Conversations around the map flow directly into decision-making. Indeed, the two are often intertwined. You may go back and forth between the two as the group talks about various parts of the map and reaches conclusions about various action items.

TRAVEL TIP

It is entirely possible that one or more participants may suggest new circles and arrows that could or "should" be added to the map. In that case, you can "reflect" the question back to the group. Do they want to return to mapping at this time or move forward with planning?

Collaborative Decisions

A collaborative decision is made when two or more stakeholder groups agree on a course of action.

In Chapter 6, we talked about how fragmentation in the academic world has been making it increasingly difficult to communicate and collaborate across disciplinary boundaries. The same fragmentation is common in the world of practice—between each person and each stakeholder group. We live in a world of specialization—doctors, lawyers, technicians, each with their narrow area of expertise on the world and its problems. When those views are integrated on a knowledge map and those stakeholders gathered together, they can look at the map and identify their action items—what they will do—and identify potential collaborators.

For example, take a look at Figure 7.14 showing actionable concepts that teachers, parents, and other stakeholders might change to improve school attendance. You can

FIGURE 7.14 ●   Many Paths to Shared Results: Many Possibilities for Collaboration (Howard University PAC-Involved Program)

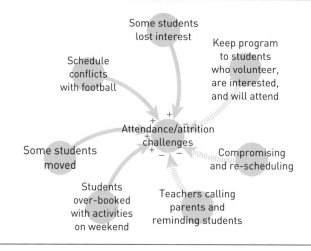

Source: Howard University PAC-Involved Project.

ask participants to look at the gaps—the spaces between the circles where there are no arrows.

Each gap represents an opportunity for collaboration between stakeholders as you ask the key question: *"How might you collaborate with each other to more effectively reach that shared goal?"*

If you have a large number of stakeholders, they might divide into teams, with each team exploring the opportunities. For example, teams of participating students, teachers, the football coach, and program managers might meet to talk about how best to fit the program into students' schedules.

ACTION PLANNING

As participants talk about the map, their changing understanding of the situation, and possible stakeholder collaborations, ask them to identify specific circles where they will take action. Ask and find out the following:

- What the specific actions will be
- When those actions will be done
- Who they will work with
- What resources they will need
- What the expected short-term and long-term results are
- When those results will emerge
- Who will report the results back to the group

DEFINITION

Planning is the process of considering alternative actions and choosing the best option.

As people answer those questions, make a record of their answers (who said it, expected actions, timeline, etc.) on a large sheet of paper (or on a large projection screen) so everyone can see. Here, the group is creating a shared commitment to action. In future meetings, those key points can be used to keep track of progress.

TRAVEL TIP

The map is also a great focal point of reference for scenario planning. Ask participants to develop "what if" scenarios. Starting at one point on the map, suggest how changes in one concept will lead to changes in the other.

TRAVEL
TIP

Using Figure 7.14 as an example, you ask participants questions such as

- Identify which circles in Figure 7.14 are best to measure (e.g., you might measure the level of attendance at PAC-Involved)

- For each circle, confirm how it will be measured (e.g., number of students missing each PAC-Involved session)

- Decide who will obtain and share the data (let's say the professor teaching the PAC-Involved session or the evaluator observing the sessions)

- Gain consensus on the current level of each (for example, in the observed session, about a third of the 32 students who registered for PAC-Involved were absent)

- Choose objectives for the year (increasing attendance to, let's say, five students absent per session)

- Create a first quarter (90 day) goal (hey, let's make it doable here, something like reducing the average number of students missing each sessions by two students each month for those first three months)

Short-Term and Long-Term Goals

If your participants have backtracked through many concepts, it is usually a good idea to identify short-term goals that will contribute to longer-term goals. For example, if the ultimate goal is Z and their actions are A, it might take a very long time for those actions to cause the desired results. So it is worthwhile to measure progress along the way!

Reporting Relationships

There is an interesting "side effect" of using a knowledge map for planning and action. Because of the interconnected nature of all those parts (and the people working on those parts), it not so important to have one person "in charge" of the whole operation. Instead of that kind of hierarchical "chain of command," the interconnected structure suggests that it is more important that each person (working on a concept in a circle) should report to the people who are working on concepts in other circles that are connected by arrows. That kind of relationship, in turn, supports "flat" organizations, which are known for better communication, coordination, decision-making, and removal of layers of management.

You can also suggest to the team that you

- Meet with the team on a monthly basis

- Help them (as and if appropriate) to avoid potholes, get out of ruts, track data (a monthly meeting is good)

- Revisit the map at the end of the year to improve it by bringing in new perspectives and data

You also have the opportunity to discuss more traditional work of organizational development or industrial/organizational psychology to improve the organization. For example, the following might be part of action planning:

- Revising job descriptions based on changed responsibilities

- Training

- Succession planning

- Facilitating change management

- Team building

- Quality control

- Changes in management responsibilities

- Communication

- Performance evaluation

- Conflict management

For additional information on those and other approaches to facilitation and improving organizations consider visiting the following websites:

https://www.odnetwork.org/

https://www.apa.org/ed/graduate/specialize/industrial.aspx

In follow-up conversations, you might encourage the group to reflect on each of the action items—what worked, what did not, what can be done better next time.

The End Is a New Beginning

Every end is the start of a new journey, exploration, discovery, and mapping—all finding new paths for solving the wicked complex problems of the world.

TRACKING RESULTS

istock.com/NicoElNino

Key Performance Indicators (KPI)

KPI are those things you want to keep track of during the year (usually on a monthly basis) to show how your project or program is doing. Some organizations have "typical" KPI from their industries that they regularly track, relating to productivity, costs, and such. You might also have other measures you consider important such as employee turnover, unit cost, or even smiles per day!

Each KPI **must** be measurable. Be careful to measure things that are important to your success rather than measuring those things that are convenient (recall the story of the

Sharing KPIs online to support progress and connect stakeholders.

drunk looking for his keys under the streetlight). Also, while we want most or all things on the map to be measurable, please don't try to keep track of everything—that requires a lot of time and resources.

TRAVEL TIP

Remember, if a concept does not seem actionable—if some stakeholders cannot "make it happen"—you should remind them to do some back-mapping until they identify what actions they can take to be successful. That is, to continue mapping "backward" until they identify what actions can be taken relatively easily . . . so the results will flow down the chain of causality and concepts so that you get the desired results.

Recall, way back in Chapter 1, that we are working to improve our collective understanding of each big problem to such a degree that we can gain a consensus among scholars and practitioners across many fields. This will lead to greater collaboration and shared success. In this endeavor, researchers are the knowledge mapmakers; a new generation of explorers and leaders.

Chapter 7 Key Points

- You can use a variety of tactile tools (cards, markers, sticky notes, etc.) and online tools (Kumu, Stormboard, etc.) for making maps.

- Using clear graphics (as found in many online platforms) to focus on key parts of the map and effective communication techniques (voice modulation, pacing, etc.) for presenting maps to stakeholder groups, your presentations can be more useful to your audience.

- You can facilitate conversations among stakeholders (for example, by asking them to consider what circles on the map represent short-term and long-term goals) to help them find opportunities for collaboration and action.

- By encouraging your clients to keep track of their progress toward desired results, you can help them reach those results and create a bank of data that can be useful for the next evaluation.

Frequently Asked Questions

Q: Hey, the book is almost over and I'm hungry to explore some more. Where should I go?

A: Recommended reading related to this book can be found in the Further Exploration sections of each chapter. You can find lots of our publications and webinars here: http://meaningfulevidence.com/news-resources

Q: What if the client doesn't follow my recommendations for action and research?

A: That's their choice. Remember that, while your research is very important, it only represents part of the client's understanding of the world. They have many other things to consider. So just relax. Also, often the process of conducting research and creating a map, in itself, can be valuable. Evaluators call this "process use." Developing research questions, examining data, and developing a shared understanding of the issue often inspires adjustments that increase program success (while you are not looking).

Q: What if I'm supposed to make a short presentation but I have a super-large map?

A: Take the same approach that you would use to make a short presentation about research that resulted in a lengthy written report. Use your knowledge of the research results and your knowledge of the client's priorities to focus your presentation on the most important parts—that is, a short summary of the findings as they relate to the client's research questions. Talking with the client to find out what information they most want you to cover is also a good idea.

Further Exploration

Tools for Creating Maps

ASK MATT tabletop game. Available at: https://askmatt.solutions/

Brown, A. (2017). Different software for developing and visualising theories of change. Retrieved from *LinkedIn*, https://www.linkedin.com/pulse/software-developing-theories-change-ann-murray-brown/

Wright, B., Rostami, A., & Lewis, L. (2016). Low-tech and high-tech tools for mapping your strategic plan. *Meaningful Evidence*. Retrieved from http://meaningfulevidence.com/wp-content/uploads/Tools-for-Mapping-Your-Strategic-Plan.pdf

Here are some additional software programs/online tools that we found. While this is not an exhaustive list, it should be enough to start your exploration of additional options for mapping your strategy/concepts and causal connections. Remember, some of these have steep learning curves.

- Changeroo, https://changeroo.com/ (see also BetterEvaluation.com, "Changeroo" https://www.betterevaluation.org/en/resources/tools/Changeroo)

- Cmap, http://cmap.ihmc.us/

- Concept Spotlight, https://www.wazoku.com/features/

- Concept Systems, http://conceptsystems.com/software/

- Crowdicity, http://crowdicity.com/en/

- DoView, www.doview.com

- FreeMind, http://freemind.en.softonic.com/

- Gephi, https://gephi.org

(Continued)

(Continued)

- iMindMap, https://imindmap.com/software/

- iMindQ, https://www.imindq.com/

- InVision, https://www.invisionapp.com/

- Justinmind, http://www.justinmind.com/

- Loopy, https://ncase.me/loopy/

- LucidChart, www.lucidchart.com

- Marvel app, https://marvelapp.com/

- Mental Modeler, http://www.mentalmodeler.org/

- Metamap, https://www.crlab.us/

- Mindjet, https://www.mindjet.com/

- Nodebox3, https://www.nodebox.net/

- OmniGraffle, https://www.omnigroup.com/omnigraffle

- Plectica, https://www.plectica.com/

- Realtimeboard, https://realtimeboard.com/

- SmartDraw, https://www.smartdraw.com/

- TheoryMaker, http://theorymaker.info/

- TOCO (Theory of Change Online), http://www.theoryofchange.org/toco-software/

- Vensim, http://vensim.com

- VISEO, http://www.viseo.com/en

- Visio, https://products.office.com/en-us/visio/flowchart-software

- Wisemapping, http://www.wisemapping.com/

- Xmind, http://www.xmind.net/

- yEd, http://www.yworks.com/products/yed

Presentations

American Evaluation Association. (n.d.). Potent presentations resources (p2i). https://www.eval.org/p2i

Salmons, J. (n.d.). Academic ≠ boring: Presenting your research [Blog post, SAGE Publishing, *Methodspace*]. https://www.methodspace.com/academic-%E2%89%A0-boring-presenting-your-research/

Nested Maps

Alexander, J. C., Giesen, B., Munch, R., Anderson, W. T., & Smelser, N. J. (Eds.). (1987). *The micro-macro link*. Chicago, IL: University of Chicago Press.

Hutchins, E. (1995). *Cognition in the wild.* Cambridge, MA: MIT Press.

Wallis, S. E., Wright, B., & Nash, F. D. (2016). Using Integrative Propositional Analysis to Evaluate and Integrate Economic Policies of U.S. Presidential Candidates Center for Scientific Analysis of Policy. Retrieved from http://meaningfulevidence.com/wp-content/uploads/IPA-of-POTUS -Candidates.pdf.

Facilitating Decisions in Groups

Doyle, M., & Straus, D. (1982). *How to make meetings work*. New York, NY: Jove.

Kaner, S. (2014). *Facilitator's guide to participatory decision-making*. Hoboken, NJ: John Wiley & Sons.

Senge, P., Kleiner, K., Roberts, S., Ross, R. B., & Smith, B. J. (1994). *The fifth discipline fieldbook: Strategies and tools for building a learning organization*. New York, NY: Currency Doubleday.

Tracking Results With Dashboards

With data from your KPI you can create an online "dashboard" to show the continued benefits of your efforts. Here are a few free online sources for dashboards:

- Arcadia Data, https://www.arcadiadata.com/product/

- Chartblocks, https://www.chartblocks.com/en/features

- Dash, https://www.thedash.com/

APPENDIX A

Advanced Strategies for Making Maps More Useful

This appendix briefly presents a range of advanced techniques for clarifying, improving, and working with knowledge maps. Each section will explain how to use each technique and why the technique is important.

These may be read in any order. For practice, we suggest that you apply each technique to excerpts of maps provided in the book and/or maps you've developed along the way.

As you are conducting knowledge mapping for research projects, you can use this appendix as a guide to techniques that might be useful. Some techniques may not be relevant to every study. In some situations, you may need to make trade-offs between these techniques. The important thing is that you choose and apply the techniques that are suitable for your specific situation and are able to explain why you used each technique.

BRIDGES

For tabletop mapping, you may want to connect two concepts that are on different sides of the table, but adding so many arrows might make things a little crowded. In this case, consider using a "bridge." Bridges are like causal arrows, but rather than showing a direct connection, they point at concepts far away. For people working on a tabletop map who wish to connect concepts that are far apart on the map, they may use a bridge instead of a long line of arrows.

In Figure A.1, participants have placed bridge pieces to show causal links between different sides of the map. They placed one bridge piece at the concept where the bridge starts. They placed another bridge piece at the concept where the bridge ends. After building their map by placing the pieces on large sheets of paper, they then used markers to draw "A" on the paper at the bridges to highlight how the connection should work.

FIGURE A.1 ⬡ **Creating a "Bridge" on a Tabletop Map to Avoid Congestion in the Middle**

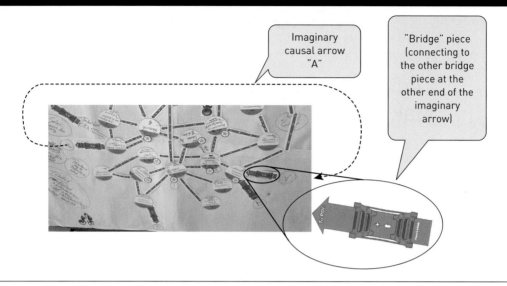

Imaginary causal arrow "A"

"Bridge" piece (connecting to the other bridge piece at the other end of the imaginary arrow)

TIME

In some situations, your map might include activities occurring at different speeds or time scales. In forestry management, for example, some activities might occur relatively quickly (such as a manager attending community meetings on a monthly basis and sharing information). Other activities might occur more slowly (such as the years needed to grow the trees). In these situations, a map may be improved by taking into account the passage of time. You can show time on a tabletop map by placing a sticky note on a causal arrow to indicate the time delay between the cause and the effect (Figure A.2).

Here, the more trees you plant, the more timber you will harvest—but not anytime soon!

Many mapping platforms have a similar ability to place a note or graphic on or near an arrow.

FIGURE A.2 ⬡ **Sticky Note on a Tabletop Map Indicating the Passage of Time**

Sticky Note

Planting Trees → 20 years → Harvestable Timber

CORE AND BELT

An important part of any research study is interpreting the data and discussing what the findings mean as they relate to your research questions. In practical research, this also includes discussing the implications of your findings for making practical decisions and perhaps providing recommendations. Focusing on the core and belt of your map helps you to discuss your findings in a meaningful way.

The *core* of a knowledge map is that cluster of concepts that have more causal connections between them (Figure A.3). The *belt* includes those concepts with fewer connections (or none). You can identify the approximate core and belt visually. You can also identify the core and belt systematically by creating a spreadsheet of the concepts on your map and the number of arrows pointing to each concept. Then, sort the concepts by the number of arrows to find which concepts have the most arrows pointing to them. Those concepts represent the core.

If your research leads you to create a large "hairball" of a map, some people will find it difficult to read and understand. One technique to reduce the confusion is to focus your presentation on the concepts at the core of the map. You can explain to the client that your presentation will focus on those things that are better understood. That is to say, you

FIGURE A.3 ● **Core and Belt of an Economic Policy Map**

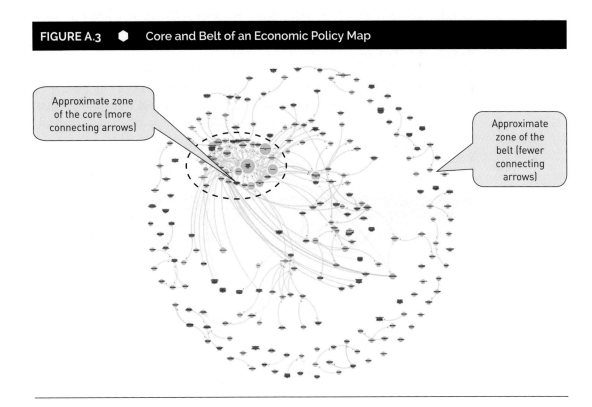

Approximate zone of the core (more connecting arrows)

Approximate zone of the belt (fewer connecting arrows)

will focus on the transformative concepts that are more actionable and so have greater chance of being achieved.

In that case, you can create and show to the client an overview map that shows the core concepts only. Then, for each of those core concepts, create and walk your audience through one or more submaps showing the concepts that lead to and result from that concept, based on your mapped research results. See Appendix B for an example.

Because concepts in the belt are not well connected, they have little depth, so they will not be useful for informing effective action. Instead, those disconnected concepts show where research can identify causal relationships and develop more useful knowledge.

LOOKING FOR SUB-STRUCTURES

While breadth and depth (see especially Chapter 5) are useful measures of structure for evaluating the map as a whole, you can also look at sub-structures *within* the map to gain new insights.

Studies have identified five structures of logic: atomistic, linear, circular, branching, and transformative. Each structure is defined by the causal relationships between the concepts within the model. Please note that it is not important for these structures whether those causal connections are "causes more" or "causes less."

Atomistic Structure

The first structure is *atomistic* or structurally disconnected (Figure A.4) (see Chapter 5). Each atomistic concept may be thought of as a truth claim that may or may not be supported by data and is not supported by logic. Concrete examples include "We should all oppose the plan to allow more parking in our neighborhood," and "Our staffers are highly qualified." By itself, an atomistic concept is not very convincing. Also, without causal relationships between the concepts, the map will have no depth. We sometimes think of these as "causal orphans," and we try to find connections for them through research.

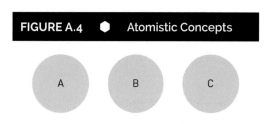

FIGURE A.4 ● **Atomistic Concepts**

A   B   C

Linear Structure

Second, you might see a *linear* structure within your map (Figure A.5). A linear structure shows a single causal pathway, with all arrows pointing in the same direction. These are more causally connected than the atomistic concepts (which have no causal connections at all).

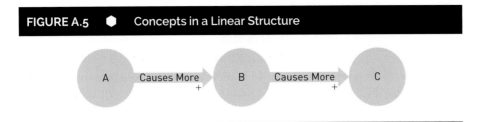

FIGURE A.5 ⬡ Concepts in a Linear Structure

However, linear structures (by themselves) are not highly useful because they suggest a simple, direct cause-and-effect world. The real world is much more complex and interconnected. So when you see a linear structure in a map, you should be thinking in two directions: first, to add more concepts and connections (by conducting more research or stakeholder conversations) so that the concepts have more than one arrow pointing to them; second, to check for and remove any redundant intermediate concepts (see the section on "Reducing Redundancy" in this appendix).

Circular Structure

Third, for a *circular* logic (Figure A.6), a change in any concept will lead back to itself. In practical application, we like these kinds of loops because they suggest sustainable change—where efforts will build on themselves. But we may be fooled into thinking that, simply because we have a loop, we are guaranteed to have success. That limitation is highlighted when we hear loops being used in arguments. There, a loop may be considered a kind of tautology—a relationship that is generally held to be of little worth. For example, in Figure A.6, more A will cause more B, which will cause more C, and that will lead to more A. Or in short, one could say that more A leads to more A.

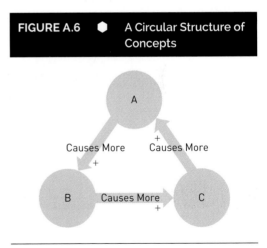

FIGURE A.6 ⬡ A Circular Structure of Concepts

When you see a loop on your map, look for ways to connect it with other loops—especially loops that work "against" your loop. That anti-loop shows forces that "undo" what your loop is showing how to "do." Remember also that this applies to "simple" loops made of concepts with few other connections. If some or all of the concepts in your loop are transformative, you are in much better shape!

FIGURE A.7 ● Branching Structure

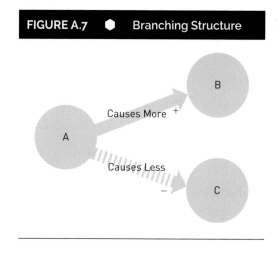

Branching Structure

Fourth (Figure A.7) is the *branching* structure of logic (e.g., more A causes more B *and* causes more C). Changes in one thing (concept) may truly cause many effects. However, in the real world, we find that each effect must have more than one cause. That is why a branching structure, when not part of a larger structure, is associated with wishful or "magical" thinking—if we do this "one thing" (A), we will reach many results. Try to avoid having too many of these by identifying (through research and stakeholder contribution) how those concepts may be combined with other structures to build transformative structures and interconnected loops.

Transformative Logic Structure

Fifth, a *transformative* logic (Figure A.8) is a kind of "dual description." Understanding a single object from two or more perspectives is preferable to understanding it from any single view. You may gain more understanding of a concept when it is causally resulting from multiple other concepts. For example, if you are seeking to understand "C," that understanding is relatively limited if one only looks at changes in C as a result of changes in B. In contrast, if one looks at the changes in C as a result of changes in A *and* changes in B, one will have a better understanding of C. Within the transformative *structure*, "C" is the transformative *concept*.

FIGURE A.8 ● Transformative Structure

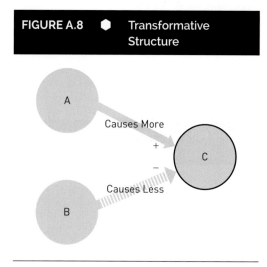

As before, it does matter which direction the arrows are pointing, but it does not matter if those arrows are indicating "causes more" or "causes less."

TRAVELLING FROM OPTIMISM TO REALITY

In our experience, stakeholders making maps tend to be a little optimistic. We need that optimism if we are going to take on the seemingly impossible problems of the world. For a map to be useful, however, it cannot be *overly* optimistic.

One sign of excessive optimism is when your map has many feedback loops—so many, that you cannot do anything "wrong." Every action will lead to multiple positive benefits.

For example, the loop in Figure A.9, viewed by itself, makes it seem like everything will be perfect! But does the real world work that way?

In addition to the "optimist loop," add a few "pessimistic connections." What concepts work to reduce or limit each of those? That process can be thought of as "balancing your loops." This is an opportunity for more research and more stakeholder conversations.

For those striving for more sophisticated maps, what kinds of "limits" might you encounter? What kinds of "unanticipated consequences?" Look for answers to those questions to add to your map.

For example, a concept in Figure A.9 is "fundraisers." If you hold too many fundraisers, you may find that you will also start to see donor fatigue and volunteer fatigue. By identifying those kinds of connections, you will create a map that is more useful because you will have a deeper understanding. With those new insights you can, for example, look for additional ways to raise income besides fundraisers, to prevent donor fatigue.

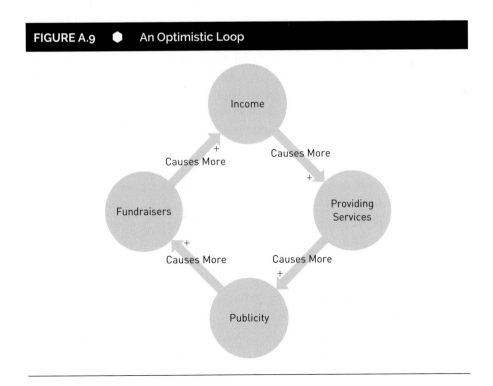

FIGURE A.9   ●   An Optimistic Loop

SCALE OF ABSTRACTION

In Chapter 6, we briefly discussed a *scale of abstraction*. Here, we go a bit deeper into that idea. The general idea is that we can think of any concept as being part of a scale or ladder of abstraction, consisting of more concrete and more abstract concepts (Figure A.10). Maps tend to work better for improving understanding and guiding decisions when most of the concepts are closer together in terms of their level of abstraction.

Most of the time, when maps are created by stakeholders in a collaborative tabletop mapping process, in our experience the scale of abstraction is appropriate for their level of work. To put it another way, each level of an organization will tend to create knowledge maps that are appropriate and useful to their understanding and ability to take action. Maps made at the level of the board of directors will generally be more abstract than maps made by supervisors or line workers. Creating maps at that kind of "natural" level of abstraction is what generally works best. However, when integrating maps of different perspectives, you may find concepts that are at very different levels of abstraction. That can cause confusion.

You might know the old adage, "We should compare apples to apples and oranges to oranges." The reason for this is because it is easier to identify more nuance and gain greater insights when comparing things of similar type. In contrast, it is not very useful to compare "apples" with the concept of "fruit" because the "category of fruit includes apples. So we can improve our maps by understanding and adjusting where each concept stands on the scale of abstraction.

When integrating multiple maps, one map might include apples (low level of abstraction) while another might include fruit (medium level of abstraction). You can shift the concepts on your map so that they are all at the same level of abstraction (or at least closer) in a few different ways:

- *Shifting one or both concepts to match the other.* This makes it easier to find overlaps and connections between models. The more concrete model (containing the concept of apple) might be made to better match the abstract model (containing the concept fruit) if the concept apple were changed to fruit. Of course, both might be changed to "plant," which would be more abstract still! While that process may reduce the breadth of the map, it may also increase the depth—as more concepts are connected.

- *Creating an overview map and submaps.* The more abstract concepts, such as fruit, could be part of an overview map showing the overarching concepts on your map. Then, the submap could show the concrete concepts within that abstract concept, such as a submap for fruit showing apples and oranges. For knowledge mapping from related research, this approach retains all of the authors' meaning while keeping concepts on each map or submap at the same level of abstraction (see Inter-Mapper Consistency).

- *Moving one or both concepts to explanatory text.* For example, you could keep the concept fruit on the map and remove the concepts of apples and oranges from the map, and you mention in your explanatory text accompanying your map that the studies mentioned apples and oranges as kinds of fruit. For knowledge mapping from related research, this approach retains all of the authors' meaning while keeping concepts on the map at the same level of abstraction (see Inter-Mapper Consistency).

The general goal for this section is to create maps in which most of the concepts are closer to each other on the scale of abstraction.

Try this for one (or more) of your maps.

- Start by grouping the concepts into related themes (e.g., animals). This will let you more easily see where you might have different levels of abstraction for the same concept.

FIGURE A.10   ●   Scale (or Ladder) of Abstraction

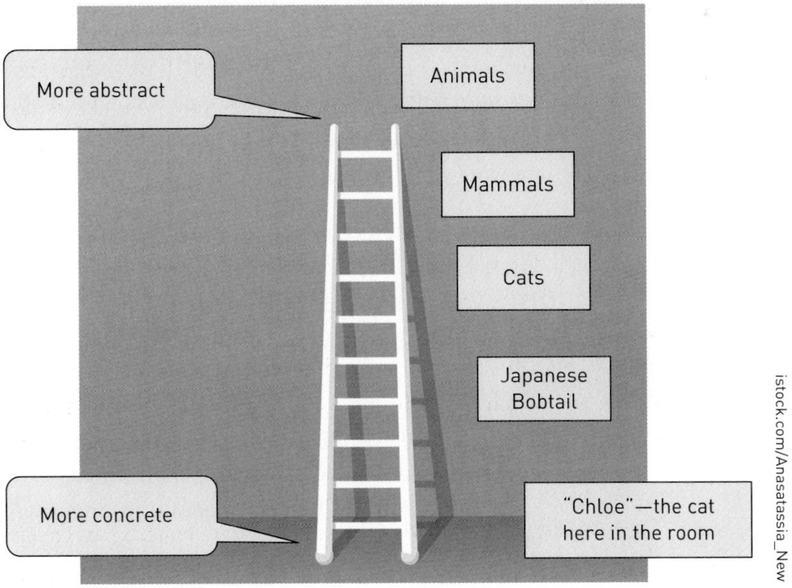

istock.com/Anasatassia_New

- Look at the concepts within each theme. For each concept, consider (compared with other concepts), does *this* concept seem to be higher, lower, or about the same level of abstraction? If you are doing this as a group exercise, this is a great opportunity for some interesting and enlightening conversation.

- With the agreement of the mapping group, change each concept so that it is closer to the others in terms of abstraction.

- Once you have changed a concept, consider the causal arrows connecting it with other concepts. Do they still make sense? Or should they be changed?

Remember to keep the map at a level of abstraction that is most *useful* for the stakeholders—something they can operationalize.

Another thing to keep in mind is that *everything* is an abstraction. So whether you are working on your own or facilitating a group, it is useful to ask if we are looking at the *right* abstractions? For example, apples and oranges are both fruit. But is fruit the important thing? Why not "sweetness" or "popularity" or color of the fruit? Sorting out that issue is a topic for conversation with the group.

REDUCING REDUNDANCY

Another way to reduce the crowding of a map (while only slightly affecting its explanatory power) is to remove redundancies. There are (at least) two forms of redundancy: *atomistic* and *linear*.

While removing redundancies may reduce the number of concepts on a map (and so reduce the breadth), that may be an acceptable trade-off for improving the readability of the map. Be careful about removing concepts that might be important to stakeholders.

An *atomistic redundancy* is when two (or more) concepts are essentially the same thing (as in Figure A.11). Then, they should be combined on the map. This is similar to the process of coding qualitative data (Chapter 3). You review your initial codes and combine redundant codes that are saying the same thing.

FIGURE A.11   Three Concepts With Atomistic Redundancies

For an example of *linear redundancy*, Figure A.12 shows that more A causes more B, causes more C, causes more D. In collaborative mapping with stakeholders, the group might just as easily say that more A causes more D. This makes the diagrammed model much clearer and more concise—without losing

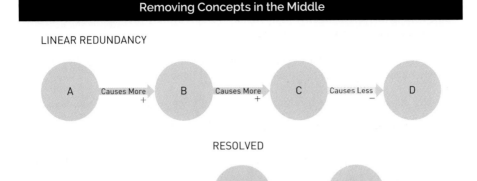

FIGURE A.12 ⬡ Linear Redundancy (Above—From A to D)—Resolved by Removing Concepts in the Middle

significant meaning. On the other hand, if the intermediate concepts (B and C) are very important to the stakeholders or if they are connected to other concepts on the map (besides A and D), then we may want to keep those concepts on the map (considerations of relevance).

In mapping from related research and materials, you can reduce linear redundancy on your map and still retain the authors' meaning (see Inter-Mapper Consistency) in a couple of different ways:

- Conduct additional research to find more arrows that can point to the intermediary concepts

- Remove the intermediary concepts from the map but keep them in your explanatory text describing the map (see Appendix B for an example report presenting a map with explanatory text)

UNANTICIPATED CONSEQUENCES

In Chapter 1, we mentioned the idea of unanticipated consequences. These include those unforeseen situations in which policies or programs end up causing more problems than they cure. At least one program to reduce pollution actually led to an increase in the level of smog; efforts to support economic improvement have resulted in massive unemployment; pushing for economic empowerment has increased violence against women in some situations . . . the list goes on. Unanticipated consequences may also refer to situations when a solution for one thing ends up having other positive benefits that you hadn't anticipated. The list of positive unanticipated consequences is much shorter—possibly because many people tend to notice the negative more rapidly—but they have been spotted on occasion (such as the invention of sticky notes or the microwave oven). For a common example, it has been recognized that when you get people together for training in a particular skill, this sometimes has the effect of building their shared sense of community.

Generally, having more structure (more breadth and depth) will reduce the chances of unanticipated consequences. With greater breadth, there are more concepts "on the map." So if stakeholders can monitor all of them, they will have a better idea of what is happening. So they will be less likely to get caught by surprise when something does not go right. On the other hand, each thing that is not on the map that the stakeholders are not watching is a place where something unexpected may emerge. This suggests that a good map will go beyond the "bare bones" or minimal basics and include a wider variety of concepts—think big!

Similarly, when a map shows greater depth, policies based on that map will be more likely to reach their goals and less likely to generate unanticipated problems.

To improve your map and reduce the chances for unanticipated consequences, the first thing is to follow the recommendations in this book for creating a map with more data, more structure, and more stakeholders representing diverse views on the policy.

You can also ask your mapping group questions such as, "What negative effects might this have?" and, "What other positive effects might it have?" Additionally, you can have a diverse group of people brainstorm "what if" scenarios. Ask the group, "What might go wrong?" When they come up with causal relationships, add them to the map. Then, reassess the map for structure, participation of potential stakeholders, and evidence.

INTER-MAPPER CONSISTENCY

When researchers are reading text (such as research papers, articles, and program documents) to create knowledge maps, it is important to be sure that those maps effectively reflect the original authors' meaning. This rigor enhances the quality of the map and so improves the usefulness of your analysis.

For novice analysts, a good way to develop your mapping skills is to work with other analysts in groups of two or three. Have each person read the original text, then talk with each other as you work through interpreting and mapping propositions in the texts.

For more advanced analysts, two or three people can analyze the same text and (working independently) create their maps. Next, compare the maps to identify those concepts and causal arrows that you hold in common. Then, discuss the differences and attempt to reach agreement.

If two analysts cannot reach agreement, a third might be brought in as a tie-breaker. Alternatively, the final map may be marked to reflect the uncertain understanding. Another approach is to contact the original author to gain clarification.

OFF THE SHELF

This book has focused on creating your own map—through collaborative mapping, from existing literature, and/or from your own research. What happens, instead, if you are leading an organization and you are advised to use an "off the shelf" approach to your programs?

A likely scenario is that a program has been in operation at some distant place and they have found some level of success there. The director (working at the national level) gives you a "program model" or "logic model" outlining the resources, activities, and short-term and long-term results. There is an expectation "attached" that your branch of the organization (working at your local level) will be able to follow their model and achieve the same results.

There is some cause for concern here. What if that other organization was located in a major metropolitan area with a reliable funding stream and your organization is located in a rural area with uncertain funding? You certainly want to make the most of their model; however, their model might not work well with your organization and your stakeholders.

Here is a path you might follow:

1. If the "off-the-shelf" model is not in the form of a causal knowledge map, use the tools in Chapter 4 to create a causal knowledge map from that model. If the existing model is already in the form of a causal knowledge map, proceed to Step 2.

2. Gather a group of stakeholders and review the map. Consider each causal arrow—does it seem reasonable for your situation? Get a consensus from the stakeholders for each individual arrow. If an arrow does not receive stakeholder consensus, either remove that arrow from your map or add a question mark to it to mark it as an area of uncertainty.

3. Expand on the map by adding additional concepts and connections that are relevant to your situation.

4. Consider whether or not your organization has the resources to take effective action and track the results for all the concepts on the map. If so, great! If not, you may

consider bringing in collaborators with the needed resources and/or focusing your efforts on only parts of the map.

5. If the map is highly complex, it may have a "core" of highly interconnected circles and a "belt" of concepts that are not well connected (see Appendix A "Core and Belt"). Focus your efforts on the core of the map.

6. You can make a map more relevant by looking at it through different views of abstraction.

7. Report back to decision makers on what seems like it will work and what is less likely to be effective in your specific situation.

For example, let's say there is a nation-wide organization whose mission is to support entrepreneurship. You are serving as the director of a branch office for that organization. Your national leadership has sent you a new "model for successful entrepreneurship" that has worked well for some other branches. Your job is now to implement that map in your area.

You are not sure, however, that the map will work to support entrepreneurship in your area. One part of the map tells you to partner with a national organization that supports education (because that organization can help you teach people about entrepreneurship), but they don't have any offices in your area! Thinking on a more abstract level, you realize that you could benefit by partnering with any organization that supports education. Then, going back down the ladder of abstraction, you quickly think of organizations and individuals that you might partner with—such as the community college, high school, and employment development department of the federal government.

Now, you can redraw the national-level-map to make it more useful on your local level. This process of customizing an existing map for your situation is important for ensuring cultural relevance for your local community.

Further Exploration

Time

A deep and interesting read on time—focused on theories of psychology—may be found here:

Tateo, L., & Valsiner, J. (2015). Time breath of psychological theories: A meta-theoretical focus. *Review of General Psychology, 19*(3), 357. Retrieved from https://www.researchgate.net/profile/Luca_Tateo/publication/283173448_Time_breath_of_psychological_theories_A_meta-theoretical_focus/links/56518d4608ae4988a7acf870.pdf

Core and Belt

Wallis, S. E. (2009). Seeking the robust core of organisational learning theory. *International Journal of Collaborative Enterprise, 1*(2), 180–193.

Wallis, S. E., Wright, B., & Nash, F. D. (2016). *Using integrative propositional analysis to evaluate and integrate economic policies of U.S. presidential candidates* [White paper, 16]. Retrieved from http://meaningfulevidence.com/wp-content/uploads/IPA-of-POTUS-Candidates.pdf

Looking for Sub-Structures

Wallis, S. E. (2016). Structures of logic in policy and theory: Identifying sub-systemic bricks for investigating, building, and understanding conceptual systems. *Foundations of Science, 20*(3), 213–231.

Scale of Abstraction

Wallis, S. E. (2014). Abstraction and insight: Building better conceptual systems to support more effective social change. *Foundations of Science, 19*(4), 353–362. doi: 10.1007/s10699-014-9359-x

Unanticipated Consequences

Wallis, S. E. (2011). *Avoiding policy failure: A workable approach*. Litchfield Park, AZ: Emergent Publications.

Wallis, S. E., & Valentinov, V. (2016). A limit to our thinking and some unanticipated moral consequences: A science of conceptual systems perspective with some potential solutions. *Systemic Practice and Action Research, 30*(2), 103–116.

Wallis, S. E., & Wright, B. (2016). Integrative propositional analysis: The missing link for creating more effective laws. *Science of Laws Journal, 2*(1), 10–15.

Wallis, S. E., Wright, B., & Nash, F. D. (2016). *Using integrative propositional analysis to evaluate and integrate economic policies of U.S. presidential candidates* [White paper, Center for Scientific Analysis of Policy]. Retrieved from http://meaningfulevidence.com/wp-content/uploads/IPA-of-POTUS-Candidates.pdf

Inter-Mapper Consistency

Wright, B., & Wallis, S. E. (2015, September 3). Using integrative propositional analysis (IPA) for evaluating entrepreneurship theories. *SAGE Open*, July-September, 1–9. Retrieved from https://journals.sagepub.com/doi/abs/10.1177/2158244015604190

Off-the-Shelf

Castro, F. G., Barrera, M., & Martinez, C. R. (2004). The cultural adaptation of prevention interventions: Resolving tensions between fidelity and fit. *Prevention Science, 5*(1), 41–45.

Janevic, M. R., Stoll, S. C., Lara, M., Ramos-Valencia, G., Stephens, T. B., Persky, V., . . . Malveaux, F. J. (2016). Peer reviewed: The "retrofitting" approach to adapting evidence-based interventions: A case study of pediatric asthma care coordination, United States, 2010–2014. *Preventing Chronic Disease, 13*(E114).

APPENDIX B

Sample Report

This appendix provides a short example excerpt of a report that students and professionals can use to inspire their presentations. It is based on an actual report that we prepared for the NMAC Strong Communities project. The purpose of that research was to help NMAC to better understand actions that healthcare and social service organizations could take to address and improve racial equity. NMAC requested that the report be in the form of a map because their staff and the organizations they work with found the map format to be a good way to communicate information.

Please note that, instead of a written report, you can also use this same kind of format for a presentation (Chapter 7). Keep in mind that the visual part of the presentation will be focused on the maps, while you use the text of the report to inspire the oral part of your presentation.

Here, the report starts with an overview of the study purpose, scope, and methods. It then presents the "big picture," an overview map of the main concepts we found during the research. Then, a series of "detail pictures" of the causal connections directly related to each one of those main concepts.

The big picture helps clients understand the key research findings. The detail pictures help clients see how they can more easily operationalize each of those main concepts so they can reach their desired goals.

This sample report contains the following:

- Cover page
- Report overview
- Legend/orientation for reading maps
- Overview map showing the key concepts

- Text explaining the overview map
- For each of the key concepts
  - Detail map showing causal pathways *leading to* the concept
  - Text explaining the detail map of causal pathways *leading to* the concept
  - Detail map showing causal pathways *resulting from* the concept
  - Text explaining the detail map of causal pathways *resulting from* the concept
- Summary and conclusion
- References

Throughout the sample report you will find callout boxes pointing out key ideas.

FIGURE B.1 ● **Cover Page**

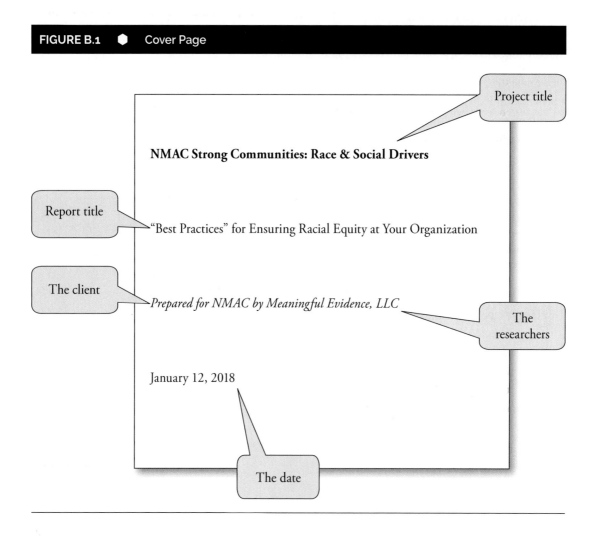

Project title

NMAC Strong Communities: Race & Social Drivers

Report title

"Best Practices" for Ensuring Racial Equity at Your Organization

The client

Prepared for NMAC by Meaningful Evidence, LLC

The researchers

January 12, 2018

The date

FIGURE B.2 ⬤ Report Overview

About This "Best Practices" Report

The purpose of this paper is to support community-based organizations and clinics to assess and ensure racial equity at their organizations.

> Research purpose

We identified the effective practices from our analysis of data from eight sources:

- Literature review (11 studies and materials)

- Open-ended-question survey (35 respondents)

- Conversations with providers and clients at organizations providing HIV-related services in communities of color, in six cities

> Research methods and participants

  o Atlanta, GA (3 interviews/focus groups)

  o Birmingham, AL (4 interviews/focus groups)

  o Fort Lauderdale, FL (6 interviews/focus groups)

  o Houston, TX (5 interviews/focus groups)

  o Jackson, MS (3 interviews/focus groups)

  o New Orleans, LA (5 interviews/focus groups)

This report focuses on the nine best practices for organizations to ensure race equity at their organizations that three or more of the sources mentioned. These show areas where we have the most evidence to support them and thus greatest confidence in chances for successful action in many organizations and communities.

> Report focus and how readers can use it

For each of these practices, we show the techniques for making them happen, and the effects they can have, based on the literature, survey, and interviews, with example quotes. These ideas can support organizations as they assess and collaboratively develop solutions for their specific situations.

FIGURE B.3 ⬡ Legend for Reading Maps

Notes for Reading the Maps

Solid arrows = causes more.

Dashed arrows = causes less.

Darker circles and arrows = mentioned by 3 or more sources.

Lighter circles and arrows = mentioned by 1 or 2 sources.

> Be sure to have a Legend/Orientation explaining how to read your maps

FIGURE B.4 ⬡ Overview Map

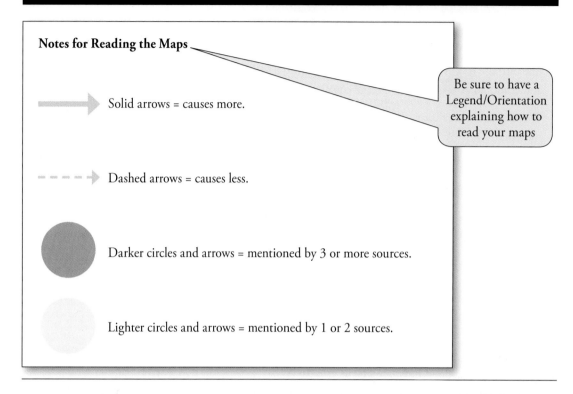

1. Assessing equity at organization

2. Community participation in designing services

3. Designing solutions to address equity

4. Policies on cultural competence

5. Providing health literacy interpreter services, translated materials

6. Training on equity, cultural competence

7. Staff diversity, reflecting, community demographics

8. System for and acting on complaints about racial inequities

9. Conversations on race

Figure 1. Overview of Frequently Mentioned Practices for Ensuring Equity in Your Organization

> Overview map—This is like the executive summary of your report. It shows the key concepts emerging from your research.

> Always be sure to have a caption explaining what the figure is about.

FIGURE B.5 ⬢ Text Explaining the Overview Map

The nine recommended practices for ensuring equity within your organization that three or more sources mentioned were

1. Assess equity at organization

2. Engage community participation in designing services

3. Design solutions to address equity

4. Have policies on cultural competence

5. Provide health literacy, interpreter services, translated materials

6. Provide staff training on cultural competence

7. Ensure staff diversity, reflecting community demographics

8. Have a system for and act on complaints about racial inequities

9. Hold conversations on race

The following sections detail ways of making each of these nine effective practices happen and how each of these practices leads to race equity at your organization. We'll also show the connections between these nine practices.

It is important to have text explaining each map.

FIGURE B.6 ⬡ Detail Map Showing Causal Pathways Most Closely Leading to Concept 1, Based on the Research

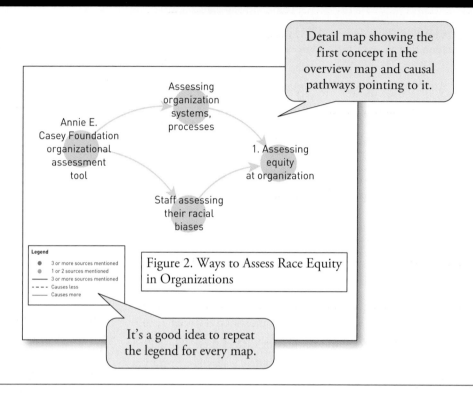

Detail map showing the first concept in the overview map and causal pathways pointing to it.

Annie E. Casey Foundation organizational assessment tool

Assessing organization systems, processes

1. Assessing equity at organization

Staff assessing their racial biases

Legend
- 3 or more sources mentioned
- 1 or 2 sources mentioned
— 3 or more sources mentioned
---- Causes less
— Causes more

Figure 2. Ways to Assess Race Equity in Organizations

It's a good idea to repeat the legend for every map.

FIGURE B.7 ● Text Explaining the Detail Map of Causal Pathways Pointing to Key Concept 1

1. Assessing Equity at Your Organization

This section explains the map in the previous figure (we like to have figures followed by text).

The idea here is to walk readers through the details of your research findings.

Our research found three ways to assess equity at your organization (Figure 2):

1. The Annie E. Casey Foundation (2011)
    Race Matters: Organizational Self-Assessment Tool

This is a tool for organizations to assess their racial equity score. It includes 9 questions about staff competencies and 10 questions about organizational operations.

2. Assessing organization systems, processes

A Houston interview participant suggested organizations checking their systems and processes:

> "Checking bias at organization. Check systems to see who you are serving, whether you are serving the people who really need it, and, if not, how you can change your processes so that they will come or you will go to them."

3. Staff assessing their racial biases

A person who we interviewed in New Orleans suggested individual providers, such as doctors, could assess their subconscious racial bias:

> "Providers have to check their subconscious biases toward clients. . . . how you treat a patient when they come in could be based on those unconscious biases."

That interview participant mentioned a study in which doctors stood farther away and showed less empathetic expressions when reporting bad news to patients of color than to white patients.

> "There was . . . some sort of study . . . they compared patients of color to white patients, and they monitored when a doctor had to go in and either report bad news to the client or good news or relate information. . . . And the result of the study was that for clients or patients of color, the doctors stood farther away, usually held their clipboard, and didn't have those empathetic expressions towards those clients."

Note how we start with the key idea from the detail map, explain each related concept, then support it with quotes from the participants and the literature.

The full report would include a similar section for each of the concepts listed in the overview map.

FIGURE B.8 ⬡ Detail Map Showing Causal Pathways Resulting From Key Concept 1

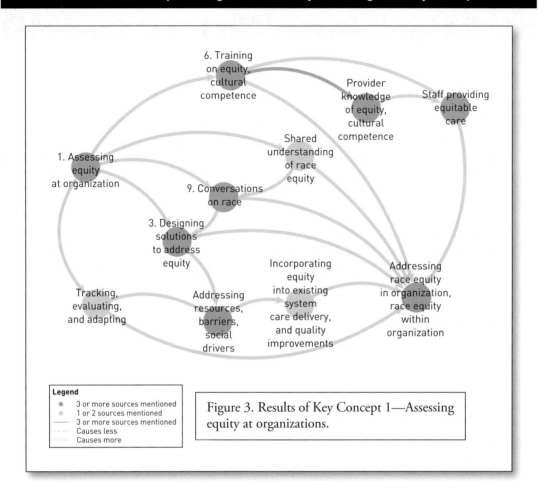

6. Training on equity, cultural competence

Provider knowledge of equity, cultural competence

Staff providing equitable care

1. Assessing equity at organization

Shared understanding of race equity

9. Conversations on race

3. Designing solutions to address equity

Incorporating equity into existing system care delivery, and quality improvements

Addressing race equity in organization, race equity within organization

Tracking, evaluating, and adapting

Addressing resources, barriers, social drivers

Legend
- ● 3 or more sources mentioned
- ● 1 or 2 sources mentioned
- —— 3 or more sources mentioned
- ----- Causes less
- —— Causes more

Figure 3. Results of Key Concept 1—Assessing equity at organizations.

FIGURE B.9 ● Explanatory Text for Detail Map of Causal Pathways Resulting *From* Key Concept 1. Note: the Full Report Would Include Explanatory Text for Each of the Arrows in the Detail Map.

As shown in Figure 3, assessing racial equity at your organization leads to increasing race equity at the organization in several ways:

A Houston interview participant suggested that organizations use assessment of racial bias at their organization to develop health equity training. The IHI tool (Wyatt et al., 2016) included training on equity ("Staff . . . receive adequate training on implicit bias") as a component of race equity ("decrease institutional racism within the organization").

The Annie E. Casey Foundation (2011) stated that organizational self-assessment, among other things, tracks organizational change. The Annie E. Casey Foundation's Action Guide (2014) lists continuously evaluating effectiveness and adapting strategies as one of the seven steps for advancing racial equity within your organization. The guide notes, to effectively advance racial equity, organizations need to set goals for the equity outcomes you are seeking, track results, measure progress, and implement needed course adjustments.

The Annie E. Casey Foundation (2011) states that organizational self-assessment also starts focused conversations. A Fort Lauderdale interview participant noted that conversations on race can lead to more race equity in an organization.

"And it was nice to get to be heard, we get different opinions . . . with our clients. . . . Like they say, 'When I came in, it was an icy feeling to come into the organization.' Then you think, 'Oh wow, we have to change that.' Then the providers make the changes happen." (Fort Lauderdale interview D)

A survey respondent and an interview participant mentioned that conversations on race as a path to designing solutions to address equity. The Annie E. Casey Foundation's Action Guide (2014) for advancing race equity within your organization includes as part of step 5, identifying strategies to address root causes of inequities. The guide notes, organizations should develop racially equitable solutions that "have an explicit goal of eliminating racial disparities and increasing racial equity."

> For each detail map, provide explanatory text and details along with quotations and sources for each of the arrows between concepts.

FIGURE B.10   ●   Summary and Conclusion

Summary and Conclusion

This best practices report detailed nine practices for promoting racial equity in HIV services, from the literature and conversations with service providers and people of color with HIV.

We recommend that you discuss the practices presented here with your colleagues and people you serve, to collaboratively choose actions that are relevant to your organization and community.

For more information on how to make those activities happen, see the sources referenced in this paper. For example, if you are interested in assessing racial equity at your organization, you may wish to use the Annie E. Casey Foundation (2011) Race Matters: Organizational Self-Assessment Tool.

Like any research, this study had limitations. The 11 publications that we reviewed do not include all potentially useful publications. The findings from those publications may not apply to every situation. The perspectives shared by the service providers and people receiving services who we interviewed may be different from the perspectives of others who we did not interview. In addition, interview participants may have other ideas and experiences that they did not share during the interviews.

As you gain new information from additional conversations with stakeholders, additional research, and learning from experience, you will be able to use the new knowledge you gain to improve your map. The better your map, the greater your chances for success in putting your map into action to reach desired goals.

> Summary and Conclusion; pretty much self-explanatory.

> Include recommendations for action and research—along with any "caution" notes that may seem appropriate.

> You should also include limitations of your research based on the methods used and results obtained.

FIGURE B.11 ⬡ References

References

The Annie E. Casey Foundation. (2011). *The race matters: Organizational self-assessment.* Baltimore, MD: The Annie E. Casey Foundation. Retrieved Jan 12, 2006 http://www.aecf.org/resources/race-matters-organizational-self-assessment/

The Annie E. Casey Foundation. (2014). *Race equity and inclusion action guide. Embracing equity: & steps to advance and embed race equity and inclusion within your organization.* Retrieved from http://www.aecf.org/resources/race-equity-and-inclusion-action-guide/

Wyatt, R., Laderman, M., Botwinick, L., Mate, K., & Whittington, J. (2016). *Achieving health equity: A guide for health care organizations.* [IHI white paper]. Retrieved from Institute for Healthcare Improvement: http://www.ihi.org/resources/Pages/IHIWhitePapers/Achieving-Health-Equity.aspx

For references, use whatever format is standard for the client. If they don't have a standard, Harvard or APA 6th are commonly used.

APPENDIX C

Some Research Methods for Building Better Maps

You have a variety of research methods available for your use—including interviews (Chapter 4) and the analysis of existing research and program documents (Chapter 3). Different methods are suited for addressing different questions. This appendix provides some additional methods. These methods might also be called designs, strategies, techniques, or approaches. Researchers sometimes distinguish between these terms. However, in practice, they frequently overlap. For example, interviews could be an entire research design in one study and a method that is part of a larger design in another study. Therefore, here we will use those terms interchangeably to refer to what you do to get answers to your research questions.

We can have more confidence in our research results if we have evidence from multiple methods (for example, interviews, and analysis of existing research, and a survey), compared to findings that have evidence from only one method. Many evaluation projects require multiple methods to answer all evaluation questions. In general, however, the more methods you use to answer a question, the stronger body of evidence you build to answer that question. For information on how to map findings from across multiple research methods, see Chapter 4.

> **DEFINITION**
>
> **Research methods** (also research approach, research design, evaluation approach, evaluation design, research strategy) is what a researcher does to conduct a study to find useful information.

Conducting rigorous research requires documenting your specific plans for research as well as documenting the process—how you actually did the research—so that others can interpret and assess your research.

Let's explore some example research strategies that you can use for building better maps. These include (a) strategies for collecting data and (b) strategies for creating and expanding maps. Our purpose here is not to catalogue every evaluation approach. Rather, the purpose of this section is to give you a sense of the broad range of designs that can help answer different questions for understanding and solving complex issues. The Further

Exploration section, at the end of this appendix, lists resources for more information on research strategies.

TRAVEL TIP

When you're conducting practical research and program evaluation, your evaluation methods should fit your specific evaluation questions, available data, and project timeline and budget.

To minimize the weaknesses of any one method, use more than one method.

RESEARCH STRATEGIES FOR FINDING DATA

Following are some research strategies that are good for measuring or testing existing circles and arrows on your map. These strategies can provide a broad range of information, including information for describing the situation (data for circles in your map) and evidence to demonstrate causal effects (data for arrows on your map). The strategies detailed in this section are generally more useful for testing all or some of the circles and arrows that are already on a map. They are not so useful for creating new or expanded maps.

Reviewing Existing Quantitative Data

In some situations, existing data may provide the data you need to show whether your map is working as expected. For example, for a study of student performance in a school, you might use existing standardized test data to compare test scores for students at the school by the students' race, gender, and economic status. The study might also compare results for the school with results for other schools in the local area and the state.

Closed-Ended Survey Questions

Collecting data through closed-ended surveys is a good strategy for documenting an issue using information from a large number of people. Closed-ended survey questions are survey questions that give a limited set of options for how to respond. Below are a few examples.

Examples of closed-ended questions:

- How old are you?
  - Under 18
  - 18–19
  - 20–29

- o 30–39
- o 40–49
- o 50–59
- o 60–69
- o 70–79
- o 80 or older

- How satisfied are you with the services you received?
  - o Very satisfied
  - o Satisfied
  - o Neither satisfied nor dissatisfied
  - o Dissatisfied
  - o Very dissatisfied

- What is your favorite flavor of jelly bean?
  - o Orange
  - o Licorice
  - o Cherry
  - o Banana

Like any method, surveys have limitations. A limitation specific to closed-ended survey questions is that they provide only a narrow range of information because the answers allow for a limited number of options.

Closed-ended survey questions are also subject to general limitations of all surveys such as the following:

- Survey respondents may have different views than those who did not complete the survey
- People may not always remember things
- People may not always give their candid/factual/honest opinions on surveys

Delphi Method

The Delphi method is a systematic approach to using the opinions of informed persons (Helmer, 1967; Hsu & Sandford, 2007; Yousuf, 2007). The basic process consists of three to five rounds of anonymous surveys of experts to reach consensus. Below are details of a Delphi study with a series of four surveys. Electronic technologies, such as teleconferencing and email, can help to speed up the process. Using these technologies in the Delphi process, researchers can collect data and distribute surveys faster, while maintaining respondent anonymity.

Round 1. The Delphi process begins with a survey that asks experts to select or rank priorities from among a list of possible opinions, such as predictions, goals, concerns, or recommended activities. For example, an early use of the method asked experts what year in the future they thought an intelligent computer will be built (responses ranged from 1975 to 2100). If no existing list of possible response options is available, an initial step can be added to generate a list using open-ended survey questions.

Round 2. In the second round, respondents receive a follow-up survey. That survey presents a summary of the responses and asks respondents to respond.

- One way to do this is to show respondents the middle 50 percent of opinions. Respondents are asked to revise their answers if they wish. If their answer is still outside the middle 50 percent of answers, they are asked to say their reason for thinking that the answer should be different from the majority of answers.

- Another approach is to ask Delphi participants to review a summary of the information provided in the first round and to rate to establish priorities. They may also be asked to state their reasons for rating items as high or low priority.

Round 3. In the third round, respondents receive a survey that shows a summary of the responses from round 2. They are then asked to revise their round 2 responses, if they wish, considering the stated reasons. If their answer is still outside the majority opinion, they are asked their reasons for being unpersuaded by the opposing argument and staying outside the majority opinion.

DEFINITION

Delphi method is a technique for collecting and analyzing the opinions of informed people to identify a consensus opinion, through three to five rounds of anonymous surveys.

Round 4. In the fourth and often final round, the experts receive a summary of responses from round 3, such as a list of remaining responses, their ratings, items achieving consensus, minority opinions, and reasons for the opinions. The experts are given a last chance to change their estimates. The final responses are then used to represent a group consensus.

The major limitation of the Delphi method is the same limitation as in any research that relies on people's informed opinions: The experts are not always right. However, sometimes the views of informed experts may be the best source for providing the data you need. In addition, sometimes just knowing what people think, in itself, can be valuable.

Quantitative Observation

Quantitative observation is an approach to quantifying an item of interest using the researcher's own observations. Examples include the following:

DEFINITION

Quantitative observation is a research technique that involves collecting *quantitative data* (data about the amount or quantity of something) using the researcher's own observations (what the researcher sees and detects).

- Counting cigarette butts within prohibited smoking areas on a university campus, to assess compliance with a university's smoking policies (Seitz et al., 2012)

- Shadowing nurses as they go about their day in a hospital to collect data on how much time the nurses spend providing patient care and performing other tasks (Westbrook, Duffield, Li, & Creswick, 2011)

- Recording conversations between groups of men and women to examine whether women get interrupted while speaking more often than men (Tannen, 2016)

- In environmental biology research, visiting an area to look for birds and recording the number and species of birds seen

Quantitative Meta-Analysis

Quantitative meta-analysis is a technique that involves pooling and reanalyzing similar data from multiple studies (Liberati et al., 2009; Wright, 2013a). When many studies have measured the same thing, the results of those studies can be used as data for a quantitative meta-analysis study. A frequent use of this technique has been to combine statistical results from multiple tests of the effectiveness of an intervention, such as clinical trials of a medication.

DEFINITION

Quantitative meta-analysis is a type of meta study that combines and statistically analyzes numerical data from multiple studies.

A limitation of this quantitative meta-analysis is that mathematically synthesizing data from study results is not always possible or desirable (Liberati et al., 2009). The approach may produce misleading results when the treatments vary across studies (Berk, 2011, p. 199). Berk cautioned, "A conventional literature review will often do better."

Randomized Experiments

Randomized experiments, also called randomized controlled trials, are studies in which researchers use a random selection process to assign research participants to a particular group. For an example from medical research, participants in one group would receive a drug that is being tested while the other group would receive a placebo. A randomized experiment generally involves the following steps:

1. Recruit research participants and collect data for the outcome measures and other variables needed for your analysis for all research participants.

2. Randomly assign research participants to two or more groups. Here, "randomly assigning" means using a systematic process, such as applying a random number generator, so that assignment of study participants to groups is strictly by random chance.

3. Carry out the experiment with one group receiving an intervention and the other not or the two groups receiving different things. For example, in many medical studies, one group receives an experimental medicine or therapy, and the other group receives a placebo (no treatment) or "treatment as usual" (such as the medication usually prescribed).

DEFINITION

Randomized experiment (also randomized controlled trial) is a study in which research participants are randomly assigned to one or more groups. If the only difference between the two groups is the thing being tested, then any difference in results for the two groups is likely to be caused by the thing being tested.

4. Collect data for both groups of research participants again and examine the results. If the only thing that was different between the two groups was the intervention that you're testing, then we can conclude that any difference in change between the two groups was likely due to that intervention.

Randomized studies have several potential limitations, particularly for studies involving complex situations (McMillan, 2007) including the following:

- People receiving the intervention and not receiving it may interact (and so influence each other's responses).

- "Blinding" (setting up your study so that people do not know whether a person is receiving treatment or not) is not possible for all experiments. For example, you might be able to use a sugar pill in place of the real medicine for testing a medical treatment, but for a social situation, a person knows if they are attending a class or receiving counseling.

- Randomizing, so that some people receive services while others do not, may be unethical in some situations.

- Randomized experiments can provide limited information because they only collect data for the things that the study is measuring. For example, an experiment to test racial discrimination may be designed to show whether or not employment discriminate happens. That study might also collect data to explore whether other factors such as the job applicant's education and gender influence results. However, that study can't uncover reasons for or solutions to discrimination that the study was not designed to measure.

> **DEFINITION**
>
> A *field experiment* is a randomized experiment with people who are in their everyday environment, such as at work or at school, rather than people who come to a research laboratory to participate in the study.

- Results from a controlled experiment may be different from what happens in the real world.

Quasi-Experiments

Quasi-experiments are like randomized experiments except that the researchers use methods other than random assignment to form the two groups of research participants. Studies have found that several quasi-experimental designs that meet certain conditions are able to recreate results from randomized experiments (Shadish, Galindo, Wong, Steiner, & Cook, 2011; Shadish & Cook, 2009; Cook, Scriven, Coryn, & Evergreen, 2010; St. Clair, Cook, & Hallberg, 2014). Types of quasi-experimental designs include the following:

- *Regression discontinuity design* (Jacob, Zhu, Somer, & Bloom, 2012). This design can work in situations when people are assigned to receive services (or not) based on criteria that are known. Researchers estimate the effects of an intervention by comparing outcomes for people just above and just below the cutoff point. For example, studies have used this method to evaluate educational programs for students who score above or below a certain score on an academic test that is used to determine program eligibility. Another example is evaluations of welfare programs for people with income below the income level needed to qualify for the program.

- *Matched comparison group studies* that meet certain criteria for making sure that the two groups are similar, such as selecting both groups of research participants from the same local area.

- Matched comparison group studies that use *statistical matching techniques*. These are techniques for making statistical adjustments to account for any differences between the groups of study participants.

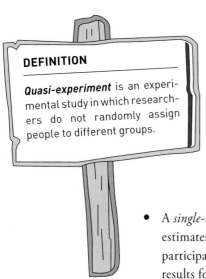

DEFINITION

Quasi-experiment is an experimental study in which researchers do not randomly assign people to different groups.

- *Interrupted time series* studies, in which the researcher collects data for the same result at many points in time, both before and after an intervention. If the trend in results changes at that point of the intervention and nothing else changed, this indicates that the intervention caused the change. This method can work in situations in which (a) data are available at many points in time before and after the intervention, and (b) no other changes happened at the same time that may have influenced results.

- A *single-case design* (also called a single subject design) study is one that estimates the effects of an intervention using results for a single person participating in the intervention. An example is a study that compares results for the intervention participant with results for a similar person who does not receive the intervention. Another example is a study that removes and reintroduces the treatment.

Before-and-After (Pre-Post) Design

Researchers use a before-and-after design, also called a pre-post design, to measure results both before and after an intervention. Researchers then compare the results. If the only thing that changed was the intervention and everything else was the same, then any changes were likely due to the intervention.

This design works best in situations in which researchers can be highly certain that nothing else can explain the change other than the intervention.

The major challenge in using this design is that, in most situations, we cannot rule out alternative explanations for what caused the change. For example, say a federal agency conducts an educational campaign to raise public awareness of safe driving habits. Evaluators compare the number of car accidents before and after the educational campaign and find that the number of accidents declined. Without more information, we can't know whether the decline in car crashes was due to that educational campaign or to something else. Other possible explanations could include cars getting safer, improved road maintenance, better weather conditions, or educational messaging from auto insurance companies, to name a few.

Another potential limitation is the influence of the study itself. The very act of administering a survey before the intervention (the "pretest") may influence people's responses to the survey administered at the end of the intervention (the "posttest.").

Retrospective Pre-Post Design

A retrospective pre-post design (Klatt & Taylor-Powell, 2005; Lang & Savageau, 2017; Geldhof et al., 2018) measures change by asking people to rate how their lives have changed as a result of participating in a program. Two questions are asked and the responses are then compared to show changes. An example would be, at the end of a first aid class, asking the class participants two questions:

1. How do you rate your knowledge of first aid BEFORE the class? (scale of 1 to 5)

2. How do you rate your knowledge of first aid AFTER the class? (scale of 1 to 5)

DEFINITION

Retrospective pre-post design is a study that measures the effects of an intervention or program at the end of the intervention by asking participants two questions: (1) to rate themselves according to some measure before they participated and (2) to rate themselves according to the same measure after participating.

An advantage of this method is that, unlike a pre-post design or a quasi-experimental design, which requires collecting data before the program and again after the program, with a retrospective pre-post design, you only have to collected data once (at the end of the program). This strategy has the same limitations as the general limitations of closed-ended surveys mentioned above.

Cost Analysis Studies

Cost analysis studies (economic evaluations) evaluate a program's economic value. These designs can also be used to compare the value for money of different options:

- A *cost-benefit analysis* compares program costs with monetized benefits. A cost-benefit analysis can compare more than one kind of costs and benefits for more than one stakeholder group, such as costs and benefits for the government, for employers, and for participants. A cost-benefit analysis can also include noneconomic costs and benefits that are expressed in economic terms, such as the estimated monetary value of lives saved.

DEFINITION

Cost analysis study (also called "economic evaluation") is an evaluation of the economic value of one or more programs.

- A *cost-effectiveness analysis* compares program costs with noneconomic effects, such as costs compared with improvements in quality of life gained.

- A *cost utility analysis* compares program costs with stakeholders' ratings of perceived value ("utility").

Social Network Analysis

Social network analysis is "the study of relationships within the context of social situations" (Durland & Fredericks, 2005, p. 9). It focuses on the social context and behavior of relationships among the people under investigation. Unlike causal knowledge mapping that examines *causal* relationships between concepts, social network analysis examines *social* relationships between people. Social network analysis is useful for collecting data to assess progress in program activities such as "developing new friendships within the group," "working together," "collaborating," and "forming work teams."

Social network analysis data are often collected through surveys. For example, a mentoring program might be designed to encourage children to develop new friendships within the group. A network measure could be a survey question asking the children to name their best friends and those they hang out with at the start of the program and at intervals during the program. Changes in the children's networks to include more friendships within the group would indicate that the program was having the desired effect in that area.

DEFINITION

Social network analysis is "the study of relationships within the context of social situations" (Durland & Fredericks, 2005, p. 9). It focuses on the social context and behavior of relationships among the people under investigation.

For another example, a survey might ask people who they primary work with to achieve the goals of their team. Social network analysis might reveal that Team B is split into two cliques that do not communicate with each other. Managers could act on that information.

Statistical Modeling

Statistical models are useful for estimating causal relationships when many things influence desired results. Statistical models can account for many factors that influence results, including aspects of the program and things that happen outside the program.

To conduct statistical modeling that yields meaningful results, you need strong knowledge of mathematical modeling techniques. You also need two things:

- Quantified data for the elements in your map. If you have a clearly articulated map but the items in the map have not been measured with data, you might start with one of the methods above to collect data to quantify the unmeasured elements in your map. These data could come from any number of methods, such as through closed-ended surveys, Delphi method, review of existing data, and others.

- A good understanding or map of what elements (variables) are important to achieving results. If a clear map has not yet been articulated, starting with a research strategy for improving your map can help you identify what the relevant variables and causal links are between them and build a strong statistical model. For building a map, you might use collaborative mapping (Chapter 2), program documents (Chapter 3), interviews (Chapter 4), and the methods for improving your map detailed throughout the book.

> **DEFINITION**
>
> ***Statistical model*** is a mathematical model that researchers use to explore relationships between multiple concepts (variables) of interest.

Many mathematical models fail to make accurate predictions because the data are unreliable, the models do not reflect reality, or both (Knowledge@Wharton, 2009; Krugman, 2014; Kirsch, 2016). Below are some examples of types of statistical models.

- *Hierarchical linear model* (HLM) is a statistical approach that incorporates data that are measured at multiple nested levels, such as data on individual students, classrooms, and schools, referred to as "hierarchical data" (Newton & Llosa, 2010). This approach is good for linking program implementation processes and outcomes that take place at different levels, for example, to model how the school environment and program implementation interact with program participation to affect results for students. For example, Newton & Llosa (2010) describe a study to evaluate a computer-based reading program in low-performing elementary schools. First, several strategies were used to collect data, including a matched comparison group design, testing of students' reading ability before and after the program, classroom observations, review of program usage data, and teacher interviews. The many types of data were used to apply HLM to estimate the effect of various variables on results for students as well as the extent to which results might vary between students within a classroom or between classrooms within a school.

- *Microsimulation modeling* is a type of mathematical model used to predict future activity at the level of individuals. For example, a 2005 study by Kemper, Komisar, and Alecxih used a microsimulation model to predict remaining lifetime need for long-term care services and who would finance those services for people turning age 65. The model included many variables related to family status, work history, retirement income and assets, disability and mortality, use of long-term care services, and financing of long-term care. Microsimulation has the advantage of allowing researchers to simulate all the variables that they wish to analyze. It enables researchers to use the best available data for each variable, drawing on many data sources.

- *Structured equation modeling* is a statistical approach that is useful for estimating multiple causal relationships specified in a logic model or causal knowledge map (Moore, 2010). A map can be adapted into a structural equation model diagram (called a "path diagram") that can be estimated with data. For example, Moore (2010) demonstrated how structural equation modeling could be used to estimate the causal relationships between input, activity, output, initial outcomes, intermediate outcomes, and longer-term outcomes shown in a logic model of an approach to helping parents choose high quality child care, expected to promote child development.

- *Survival analysis* is a statistical approach that examines the effects of various factors on the time that passes before some event occurs (called "survival time"). For example, studies have used survival models to assess the impacts of programs on time spent refraining from offending among juvenile offenders (Bouffard, Cooper, & Bergseth, 2017) and to show what factors predicted the amount of time remaining in the community after discharge from a nursing home (Howell, Silberberg, Quinn, & Lucas, 2007). This method can use new or existing data that are collected over time.

- *Computer modelling* is a form of mathematical modeling used to represent real-world situations, explore alternatives, and predict future events. In fact, if you have played a video game of any kind, you have used a kind of simulation of the real word—one that is based on a kind of knowledge map. You can use your knowledge of mapping to help you build better computer models (and/or collaborate with someone who is knowledgeable about mathematical modeling methods). Specifically, you can use your map to identify concepts and causal connections that are important to include in your mathematical model, to make the model more likely to make accurate predictions.

RESEARCH STRATEGIES FOR CREATING AND EXPANDING MAPS

In this section, we detail some research designs that are good for discovering new circles and arrows, for creating and expanding maps as well as testing maps (or a set of hypotheses). All this research will provide valuable information for your stakeholders and for managers and evaluators of other programs (that are designed to achieve similar goals), by showing which activities, results, contextual factors, and causal relationships may be important to consider in their decision-making.

These strategies are less about finding precise data for one causal relationship and more about identifying what the relevant causal relationships are. A benefit of these strategies is that they provide quotes and stories. This is good because, while many policymakers and other audiences want to see numbers, adding stories and examples often makes your research findings more engaging, informative, and persuasive. A limitation of these methods is that they are not designed to provide precise numbers showing the amount of an effect or the magnitude of a relationship.

Interviews

For in-depth information and resources on interviews, see Chapter 4. Interviews are a great way to get rich understandings of the knowledge, experiences, opinions, and beliefs of interested and knowledgeable people. Unlike casual conversations, effective interview research takes a systematic and documented approach to selecting potential interview participants, recruiting interview participants and arranging interview logistics, protecting research participants, asking questions of the interview participants, and organizing the resulting data.

A limitation of interviews is that people do not always know or remember the information that you are seeking (such as how participating in a program affected them). Also, people may not always share their candid thoughts with interviewers. These limitations can be minimized by carefully planning your interview research and incorporating effective practices for interviewing, such as wording your questions to help jog participants' memories and to encourage candid response.

Focus Groups

A focus group is a type of interview (see Interviews) in the form of a facilitated conversation with a small group. Focus groups are a way to elicit the perspectives of a group of people who can be brought together in the same place and time. A benefit of focus groups is that participants get to hear each other's ideas. Hearing what others have to say may spark new ideas that they did not initially think to share (Williams, 2018). A potential limitation of focus groups is that, in some situations, participants may feel less comfortable sharing their opinion in a group than in a one-on-one conversation. For more information and resources on focus groups and interviews, see Chapter 4.

Review of Narrative Documents

Narrative documents may include participants' written reflections, staff reports, program websites, and meeting minutes. Reviewing existing documents is often faster and less expensive than collecting new data through interviews, observation, surveys, or any of a seemingly endless array of optional methods or a combination of many methods. And it doesn't take any participant time. Narrative documents may provide information on whether activities and outcomes are happening as planned as well as reveal new strategies, challenges, ideas, and effects that you hadn't anticipated.

A limitation of document review is that the documents may not always be up-to-date, accurate, and complete. People writing the narratives may not always remember and report all relevant details.

Qualitative Observation

Observation is when a researcher watches events as they occur at the research site. You can see the activity rather than relying on what people have said about their situations in retrospect. Observation also does not require any participant time. Whereas quantitative observation focuses on counting things (see the previous section), qualitative observation focuses on discovering what is happening. Observation is good for documenting the whole picture of everything happening at the research site. You can see many activities and processes that might affect outcomes, including expected and unexpected contextual factors and processes.

Researchers may conduct observations as participants (participant observation) or as outside observers (nonparticipant observation, like a "fly on the wall").

For example, one of the authors of this book, as part of obtaining background information for her dissertation to evaluate a series of interracial "dialogue/action circles," participated in one of the circles to gain first-hand understanding of the program through participant observation. Later, she observed two other circles (as a nonparticipant), sitting quietly in the back of the room, watching everything going on, and taking notes.

> **DEFINITION**
>
> ***Observation*** is a research method in which the researcher gathers information by watching what is happening at the research site.

A limitation of observation is that people may change their behavior if they know that they are being watched (known as the Hawthorne effect). Taking time to develop a rapport with people can help people feel more at ease with your presence and mitigate the Hawthorne effect. Another limitation is that observers may not notice relevant events or interpret them correctly. In addition, the research project may allow for only conducting a few observations so the observer may not be present to see important events. These limitations can be mitigated by following an observation guide that you develop in advance of the observation; your observation guide specifies what you will look for and take notes on as you observe. Other ways to strengthen observation research includes using more than one observer, observing more sites, and observing more times or for longer amounts of time.

Open-Ended Survey Questions

Open-ended survey questions, unlike closed-ended questions, provide opportunity for revealing responses that you hadn't anticipated. Open-ended questions allow respondents to give any answer. Examples include the following:

- Based on your knowledge and experience, what would you say is the most important thing that needs to happen to achieve racial equality in this country?

- What changes would you recommend to improve the training that you attended?

- Please add any additional comments or suggestions that you would like to make.

Open-ended questions are good for finding out about challenges, effective strategies, outcomes, and ideas for improvement that were not in your original logic model or map.

Surveys are good for gathering information from a large number of people. A limitation is that surveys cannot capture the level of depth and detail you can get with interviews.

Open-ended survey questions are also subject to general limitations of all surveys such as the following:

- Survey respondents may have different views than those who did not complete the survey

- People may not always remember things

- People may not always give their candid/factual/honest opinions on surveys

DEFINITION

Open-ended survey questions are survey questions that respondents answer by providing comments in their own words.

Case Study

Case studies are used to explore complex interconnected activities in one or more contexts (Yin, 1984). They can provide a broad range of information, such as understanding the causes of a problem, identifying effective practices, documenting implementation progress, and demonstrating impact. Examples of a "case" include a program site, a classroom, a university, or a hospital. Case study research may investigate one case or many cases. Case studies may use several sources to collect data about each case, such as observation, interviews, and document review—for example, a study of a nationwide tutoring program might study successful program sites and identify the contextual factors and strategies that made their success possible.

DEFINITION

Case study research is applied to a specific group of stakeholders within a specific context or situation to understand complex interrelated activities and results.

Causal Link Monitoring

Causal link monitoring (Britt, Hummelbrunner, & Greene, 2017) is a cyclical process of developing, collecting data for, and improving a map.

- *Building a map and identifying assumptions.* The first step in causal link monitoring is to build an initial map. You might make this initial map using collaborative mapping (Chapter 2), existing program materials

DEFINITION

Causal link monitoring (CLM) is a research approach that integrates design (mapping) and monitoring (data) to support project enhancement. CLM helps project planners and managers to identify the processes required to achieve desired results and to observe whether those processes take place and how (Britt et al., 2017).

(Chapter 3), and any data that you have already collected. Next, people doing the program and project planning (such as managers and directors) identify assumptions behind the causal links in the map. That is, they specify who will do what and when to make the causal link happen and how the results will be measured.

- *Enhancing map.* In the next phase of causal link monitoring, you enhance the map with diverse perspectives, such as through interviews (Chapter 4).

- *Monitoring map with data.* Next, you choose which circles and arrows in the map to monitor for collecting data. Then you collect the data for those chosen items. These data can come from any number of research strategies, such as surveys, interviews, review of program data collected during the monitoring period, and other methods (See Chapter 7—Key Performance Indicators or "KPI"). Examining the monitoring data shows which concepts and relationships are confirmed and should be kept on the map, what could be removed, and where more information is needed.

- *Enhance the program and improve the map.* Use the data to adjust your activities to increase success in reaching desired goals and revise the map to incorporate changes made and knowledge gained.

Causal link monitoring is well suited for situations when multiple aspects of the program (and factors outside the control of the program) might affect the desired outcomes. The resulting enhanced map can provide a strong basis for additional evaluation using any of a variety of methods for enhancing maps and collecting data.

Contribution Analysis

Contribution analysis is used to demonstrate whether a program was an important influencing factor in driving results, perhaps along with other factors (Scottish Government, 2011). Thus, it is well suited for situations in which many factors (both within and outside the direct control of the program) influence desired results.

Contribution analysis is designed for evaluating programs that are based on a consistent "theory of change" (what we have been calling a knowledge map) and have little or no scope for varying how they are implemented (Mayne, 2008). Thus, they are less applicable to programs that are implemented with wide flexibility and variation.

Contribution analysis (Mayne, 2001, 2008) assesses the effects of one or more influences that contribute to intended effects. Contribution analysis involves six steps to develop a map and collect evidence from various sources to test the map and build and improve a credible "performance story," thereby improving the map. The first three steps are similar to the building a map and identifying assumptions step of causal link monitoring, described above.

1. *Determine the attribution problem to be addressed.* Here, you determine the specific cause–effect question(s) being addressed, the level of confidence required, the type of contribution expected, the other key influencing factors, and the plausibility of the expected contribution in relation to the size of the program (Mayne, 2001).

2. *Develop a map and risks to it that might affect implementation.* This involves

   a. Building a map and a results chain

   b. Determining the level of detail needed in the map

   c. Determining the expected contribution of the program

   d. Listing the assumptions underlying the map, including consideration of other factors that may influence outcomes

   e. Determining how much the map is contested (note what stakeholder groups disagree with the map and what their disagreements are)

3. *Gather the existing evidence on the theory of change (map).* This includes evidence on observed results, assumptions about the map, and other influencing factors. These data may come from any number of types of studies and data sources, such as surveys, case studies, Delphi method, quasi-experiments, analysis of existing data and documents, and other research strategies.

   DEFINITION

   Contribution analysis is a research approach that explores attribution by assessing the contribution a program is making to observed results (Mayne, 2008). It sets out to verify the theory of change (map) behind a program while also taking into consideration other influencing factors.

4. *Assemble and assess the contribution story.* In this step, the contribution story, as developed so far, is assembled and assessed. This shows the robustness of the contribution story (as shown in the map) and will guide further efforts.

5. *Seek out additional evidence.* Identify what new data are needed based on Step 4, adjust/update the map, and gather more evidence. Any number of research strategies and data sources may be used to provide this additional evidence.

6. *Revise and strengthen the contribution story* (going back to Step 4). New evidence is used to build a more credible contribution story, strengthening the weaker parts of the earlier version and suggesting modifications to the map as needed, thereby improving the map.

Further Exploration

Research Strategies and Example Studies

BetterEvaluation.com. (n.d.). Approaches [webpage]. Accessed May 29, 2018. https://www.betterevaluation.org/approaches

BetterEvaluation.com. (n.d.). Randomised controlled trial. Retrieved from https://www.betterevaluation.org/plan/approach/rct

Berk, R. (2011). Evidence-based versus junk-based evaluation research S lessons from 35 years of the Evaluation Review. *Evaluation Review 35*(191).

Britt, H., Hummelbrunner, R., & Greene, J. (2017). *Causal link monitoring*. Retrieved from https://www.betterevaluation.org/en/resources/overview/Causal_Link_Monitoring

Cook, T. D., Scriven, M., Coryn, C. L. S., & Evergreen, S. D. H. (2010). Contemporary thinking about causation in evaluation: A dialogue with Tom Cook and Michael Scriven. *American Journal of Evaluation, 31*(1), 105–117.

Durland, M. M., & Fredericks, K. A. (2005). An introduction to social network analysis. *New Directions for Evaluation, 107.* doi: 10.1002/ev.157. https://onlinelibrary.wiley.com/doi/pdf/10.1002/ev.157

European Evaluation Society. (2007). *The importance of a methodologically diverse approach to impact evaluation—specifically with respect to development aid and development interventions* (Report by the European Evaluation Society) Retrieved from https://www.europeanevaluation.org/about-ees/policy-statements

Fazey, J., Schäpke, N., Caniglia, G., Patterson, J., Hultman, J., van Mierlo, B., & Wyborn, C. (2018). *Energy Research & Social Science, 40*(54–70). Retrieved from https://www.sciencedirect.com/science/article/pii/S2214629617304413

Flyvbjerg, B. (2006). Five misunderstandings about case-study research. *Qualitative Inquiry, 12*(2), 219–245.

Geldhof, G. J., Warner, D. A., Finders, J. K., Thogmartin, A. A., Clark, A., & Longway, K. A. (2018). Revisiting the utility of retrospective pre-post designs: The need for mixed-method pilot data. *Evaluation and Program Planning, 70*, 83–89. Retrieved from https://doi.org/10.1016/j.evalprogplan.2018.05.002

Helmer, O. (1967). *Analysis of the future: The Delphi method.* Santa Monica, CA: The RAND Corporation. Retrieved from https://www.rand.org/pubs/papers/P3558.html

Hsu, C., & Sandford, B. A. (2007). The Delphi technique: Making sense of consensus. *Practical Assessment, Research & Evaluation, 12*(10). Retrieved from https://pareonline.net/pdf/v12n10.pdf

Jacob, R., Zhu, P., Somer, M., & Bloom, H. (2012). A practical guide to regression discontinuity. *MDRC.* Retrieved from https://www.mdrc.org/publication/practical-guide-regression-discontinuity

Klatt, J., & Taylor–Powell, E. (2005, October 29). *Synthesis of literature relative to the retrospective pretest design.* Panel presentation for 2005 Joint CES/AEA Conference, Toronto, Session Title: More on Retrospective Pre-Test: Developing a Taxonomy of Best Practice Uses. Retrieved from http://comm.eval.org/HigherLogic/System/DownloadDocumentFile.ashx?DocumentFileKey=31536e2f-4d71-4904-ae5d-056e3280c767

Lang, D., & Savageau, J. (2017, July 31). Starting at the end: Measuring learning using retrospective pre-post evaluations [American Evaluation Association AEA365 blog]. Retrieved from http://aea365

.org/blog/starting-at-the-end-measuring-learning-using-retrospective-pre-post-evaluations-by-debi-lang-and-judy-savageau/

Liberati, A., Altman, D. G., Tetzlaff, J., Mulrow, C., Gøtzsche, P. C., Ioannidis, J. P. A., & Moher, D. (2009). The PRISMA statement for reporting systematic reviews and meta-analyses of studies that evaluate health care interventions: Explanation and elaboration. *PLoS Med, 6*(7), e1000100. doi:10.1371/journal.pmed.1000100

Mayne, J. (2001). Addressing attribution through contribution analysis: Using performance measures sensibly. *The Canadian Journal of Program Evaluation, 16*(1), 1–24. Retrieved from https://www.betterevaluation.org/en/resources/guide/addressing_attribution_through_contribution_analysis

Mayne, J. (2008). *Contribution analysis: An approach to exploring cause and effect* (Brief from the Institutional Learning and Change (ILAC) Initiative) Retrieved from BetterEvaluation website https://www.betterevaluation.org/resources/guides/contribution_analysis/ilac_brief

McMillan, J. (2007). Randomized field trials and internal validity: Not so fast my friend. *Practical Assessment, Research & Evaluation 12*(15). Retrieved from https://pareonline.net/pdf/v12n15.pdf

Scottish Government. (2011). *Contribution analysis* (Guide 6 in the Social Science Methods Briefings series). Retrieved from http://www.scotland.gov.uk/Topics/Research/About/Social-Research/Methods-Guides/Guide-6

Seitz, C. M., Strack, R. W., Orsini, M. M., Rosario, C., Haugh, C., Rice, R., & Wagner, L. (2012). Quantifying littered cigarette butts to measure effectiveness of smoking bans to building perimeters. *Journal of American College Health, 60*(4), 331–334. Retrieved from https://libres.uncg.edu/ir/uncg/f/M_Orsini_Quantifying_2012.pdf

Shadish, W. R., & Cook, T. D. (2009). The renaissance of field experimentation in evaluating interventions. *Annu. Rev. Psychol., 60*, 607–629.

Shadish, W. R., Galindo, R., Wong, V. C., Steiner, P. M., & Cook, T. D. (2011). A randomized experiment comparing random and cutoff-based assignment. *Psychological Methods*, (2),179–191.

St. Clair, T., Cook, T. D., & Hallberg, K. (2014). Examining the internal validity and statistical precision of the comparative interrupted time series design with a randomized experiment. *American Journal of Evaluation, 35*(3), 311–327. doi: 10.1177/1098214014527337

Stern, E., Stame, N., Mayne, J., Forss, K., Davies, R., & Befani, B. (2012). *Broadening the range of designs and methods for impact evaluations.* Report of a study commissioned by the Department for International Development, London, UK. Retrieved from https://assets.publishing.service.gov.uk/media/57a08a6740f0b6497400059e/DFIDWorkingPaper38.pdf

Tannen, D. (2016, October 7). The sexism inherent in all that interrupting. *The Washington Post.* Retrieved from *Washington Post* website at https://www.washingtonpost.com/opinions/the-sexism-inherent-in-all-that-interrupting/2016/10/07/9ccdd2a0-8c9e-11e6-875e-2c1bfe943b66_story.html?utm_term=.b6efe1eca3a6

Treasury Board of Canada, Secretariat. (1998). *Program evaluation methods: Measurement and attribution of program results* (3rd ed.). Retrieved from http://www.tbs-sct.gc.ca/cee/tools-outils-eng.asp

United States Government Accountability Office (GAO). (1990). *Case study evaluations.* Retrieved from https://www.gao.gov/special.pubs/10_1_9.pdf

(Continued)

(Continued)

United States Government Accountability Office (GAO). (2012). *Designing Evaluations* (2012 rev.). Retrieved from https://www.gao.gov/products/GAO-12-208G

Westbrook, J. I., Duffield, C., Li, L., & Creswick, N. J. (2011). How much time do nurses have for patients? A longitudinal study quantifying hospital nurses' patterns of task time distribution and interactions with health professionals. *BMC Health Services Research, 11*(319). Retrieved from ghttp://www.biomedcentral.com/1472-6963/11/319

Williams, R. (2018). *Creating great focus groups*. American Evaluation Association Coffee Break Demonstration [Webinar #314]. Retrieved from http://comm.eval.org/coffee_break_webinars/coffeebreak/coffeebreak

Wright, B. (2013a). *Reuse, recycle: Rethink research*. Meaningful Evidence. Retrieved from http://meaningfulevidence.com/wp-content/uploads/2014/11/Meaningful_Evidence_LLC_Reuse_Recycle_Rethink_Research-4.pdf

Wright, B. (2013b). *When to use a randomized controlled trial and when not to*. Meaningful Evidence. Retrieved from http://nebula.wsimg.com/d2f44ff8d56007cc94871c36924c2b52?AccessKeyId=16AA239B5DAFF9374305&disposition=0&alloworigin=1

Wright, B. (2016, September 13). *Evaluation approaches: You don't need to choose just one*. Route One Evaluation [Blog post]. https://route1evaluation.com/2016/09/13/evaluation-approaches-you-dont-need-to-choose-just-one/

Wright, B. (2016, December 12). Six steps to effective program evaluation (part 5): Plan your methods. Charity Channel. Retrieved from https://charitychannel.com/six-steps-to-effective-program-evaluation-step-5-plan-your-methods/

Wright, B, & Lewis, L. (2014). *Case studies in action*. Meaningful Evidence (Tip sheet). Retrieved from http://meaningfulevidence.com/wp-content/uploads/2014/12/Case-Studies-in-Action-October-27-1.pdf

Wright, B, & Lewis, L. (2016, May). *Evaluation methods cheat sheets*. Meaningful Evidence. Retrieved from http://meaningfulevidence.com/download-cheat-sheets

Yin, R. K. (1984). *Case study research: Design and methods*. Beverly Hills, CA: Sage.

Yousuf, M. I. (2007). Using experts' opinions through Delphi technique. *Practical Assessment, Research & Evaluation, 12*(4). Retrieved from https://pareonline.net/pdf/v12n4.pdf

Statistical Modeling and Computer Simulation Resources

Bouffard, J., Cooper, M., & Bergseth, K. (2017). The effectiveness of various restorative justice interventions on recidivism outcomes among juvenile offenders. *Youth Violence and Juvenile Justice, 15*(4), 465–480. Retrieved from https://doi.org/10.1177/1541204016647428

Howell, S., Silberberg, M., Quinn, W. V., & Lucas, J. A. (2007). Determinants of remaining in the community after discharge: Results from New Jersey's Nursing Home Transition Program. *The Gerontologist, 47*(4), 535–547. Retrieved from https://doi.org/10.1093/geront/47.4.535

Howick, S., Eden, C., Ackermann, F., & Williams, T. (2008). Building confidence in models for multiple audiences: The modelling cascade. *European Journal of Operational Research, 186*(3), 1068–1083.

Kemper, P., Komisar, H. L., & Alecxih, L. (2005). Long-term care over an uncertain future: What can current retirees expect? *Inquiry, 42*, 335–350. Retrieved from ehttp://journals.sagepub.com/doi/pdf/10.5034/inquiryjrnl_42.4.335

Kirsch. F. (2016). Economic evaluations of multicomponent disease management programs with Markov models: A systematic review. *Value in Health, 19*, 1039–1 0 5 4. Retrieved from https://doi .org/10.1016/j.jval.2016.07.004

Knowledge@Wharton. (2009, May 13). Why economists failed to predict the financial crisis. Retrieved from http://knowledge.wharton.upenn.edu/article/why-economists-failed-to-predict -the-financial-crisis/

Krugman, P. (2014, May 1). Why economics failed. *The New York Times*. Retrieved from https://www .nytimes.com/2014/05/02/opinion/krugman-why-economics-failed.html

Moore, C. (2010). *Christopher Moore on structural equation modeling for theory-driven evaluation.* American Evaluation Association AEA 365 [Blog post]. Retrieved from https://aea365.org/blog/ christopher-moore-on-structural-equation-modeling-for-theory-driven-evaluation/

Newton, X. A., & Llosa, L. (2010). Toward a more nuanced approach to program effectiveness assess- ment: Hierarchical linear models in K-12 program evaluation. *American Journal of Evaluation, 31*(2), 162–179.

Perros, H. (2009). *Computer simulation techniques: The definitive introduction!* Retrieved from http:// www4.ncsu.edu/~hp/files/simulation.pdf

Wallis, S. E., & Johnson, L. (2018). Response to a challenge: Using integrative propositional analysis to understand and integrate four theories of social power systems. *Journal on Policy and Complex Systems, 4*(1).

Presentation with many embedded examples: https://www.acm-sigsim-mskr.org/Courseware/Balci/ Slides/BalciSlides-01-Introduction.pdf

Teaching guide for an introduction to modelling: https://code.org/curriculum/science/files/CS_in_ Science_Module_1.pdf

This has a free online mapping platform for the basics of mathematical modeling. They use "stocks and flows," which are very similar to our "circles and arrows." https://www.iseesystems.com/store/products/ stella-online.aspx

List of simulation software for social scientists: http://cress.soc.surrey.ac.uk/s4ss/links.html

A list of online platforms for simulation: https://www.capterra.com/simulation-software/?utf8=%E2%9 C%93&users=&sort_options=Highest+Rated

GLOSSARY

Note: Some of the terms in this glossary are not defined in the chapters, but we include them here anyway because they are relevant.

actionable concept: A concept relating to something in the real world where "you" (as an individual or organization) may take action to cause change. For example, "research" is something that a person can do while "interstellar travel" is not.

applied research: Research conducted to inform decisions and action.

ASK MATT: Table-top gamified process for the collaborative creation of knowledge maps. The acronym stands for *Accessing Strategic Knowledge Meta-Analytical Think Tank.*

aspect: See *concept.*

atomistic logic: The least structured of logics, such as "A is true" or "profits are important." From a knowledge mapping perspective, such concepts are not causally connected with other concepts.

back-mapping: Starting from a relatively non-actionable concept (something that would be very difficult to do), this is the process of adding concepts and causal connections to a map until you reach actionable concepts. For example, if you have a map of personal development with the concept of "having a great reputation as a researcher," that is something that does not happen by magic. You would need to add concepts to your map (back-mapping), such as "providing high quality research," and to get there, you would need to back-map other concepts, such as "gain a solid education" (which is more actionable than the other two).

back-tracking: The process of following the causal arrows on your map "upstream" (against the direction of the arrows), away from less actionable concepts and toward more actionable ones to find points where you can take concrete action to cause changes "downstream."

branching causal logic: A logic structure in which a change in one concept causes change in two or more other concepts. For example, a branching proposition might say that changes in A will cause changes in B and C. For a more concrete example, "More teamwork will lead to more cohesion *and* more results *and* more frustration."

breadth: An IPA measure of the number of concepts on a knowledge map or the range of conceptual territory covered by the map. Sometimes called "complexity." With more breadth, a map is more likely to be relevant or applicable in more situations. See especially Chapter 5.

case study: Research applied to a specific group of stakeholders within a specific context or situation to understand complex interrelated activities and results. See especially Appendix C.

causal coding: In qualitative research, a type of coding (see *coding*) in which, in addition to assigning codes to concepts (which can include overarching concepts and subconcepts), you take the added step of coding causal relationships between concepts.

causal link monitoring (CLM): A research approach that integrates design (mapping) and monitoring (data) to support project enhancement. CLM helps project planners and managers to identify the processes required to achieve desired results and to observe whether those processes take place and how (Britt, Hummelbrunner, & Greene, 2017).

causal logic: An understanding of the causal relationship between two or more concepts or things—often graphically represented by arrows between circles showing the direction of causality. See especially Chapter 5.

causality: Seen any time two or more things change, and one of those is the cause of the other. For example, rain and sunlight cause plants to grow.

circular causal logic: A logic structure where one cause leads back to itself, such as changes in A cause changes in B cause changes in C cause changes in A. Circular logics may be seen as feedback loops that are held to be very useful in understanding systems. However, they can also be misleading if researchers rely on too few loops to adequately represent the real-world system. Then they may appear as tautologies (e.g., more A causes more A).

closed-ended questions: Questions that elicit answers from a specified set of answer options, such as "yes/no," a ranking scale, or any question in which respondents choose their response from a specified set of possible answers. Contrasts with "open-ended questions."

coding: In qualitative research, the process of assigning words or short phrases (codes) to chunks of text (words, sentences, parts of sentences, paragraphs, etc.) from some source of data (academic paper, interview transcript, industry publication, etc.) to organize and simplify large quantities of data (which helps you and others to make sense of it all).

cognitive science: Interdisciplinary investigation of the human, social, and artificial processes around perception, information, reasoning, and decision-making.

coherentist perspective: Basically, the way we understand each concept better because it is related to other concepts. For example, we can better understand "wealth" when we understand where our money comes from and where it goes. For the other view, see *correspondence perspective*.

collaboration: Working purposefully with others toward goals that are shared (all have the same goal) and/or goals that are interrelated (different but mutually supporting). See especially Chapter 2.

community IRB: An official group that evaluates proposals for community-scale research to reduce the risk to human participants and increase the benefits to the community.

complexity: See *breadth*.

concept: Also called "aspect" or "variable," the part of a causal knowledge map that represents an idea or notion. The concept may be as concrete as in "apple" or as abstract as in "truth." Concepts may be simple as in numbers or complex as "left-handed monkeys with undiagnosed trauma." A concept is typically detectable—that

is to say, empirically measurable—but that is not an absolute standard. Concepts are part of propositions.

conceptual system: A set of interrelated concepts such as knowledge maps. Each may be useful for understanding and enabling effective decisions and actions to reach goals.

consensus: General agreement among members of a group on an understanding or course of action. Consensus does not require that everyone specifically agrees or is in favor of the course of action, only that no member of the group actively opposes it.

contribution analysis: A research approach that explores attribution by assessing the contribution a program is making to observed results (Mayne, 2008). It sets out to verify the theory of change (map) behind a program while also taking into consideration other influencing factors.

correspondence perspective: Essentially developing an understanding based on the relationship between a concept and some measurable thing in the real world. For example, you can understand "wealth" based on the number of dollars you have in the bank. For the other side, see *coherentist perspective*.

cost analysis study: An evaluation (also called "economic evaluation") of the economic value of one or more programs.

cybernetics: The study of communication and control within and between human, organizational, and natural systems. Typically involving one or more feedback loops.

data: The facts or information gained from research and measurement or experience. Examples include survey results, interview results, and everything you see and hear. See especially Chapter 1.

Delphi method: A technique for collecting and analyzing the opinions of informed people to identify a consensus opinion, through three to five rounds of anonymous surveys. See Appendix C.

depth: An IPA measure of a map's potential for useful application based on its systemic structure. More depth (also called "systemicity") means decisions made with the map are more likely to lead to successful results. See especially Chapter 5.

discipline: An area of academic study (also called "field") such as physics, economics, or psychology (including the research methods, projects, results, and people).

evaluation: See *program evaluation*.

evaluation question (EQ): See *research question*.

facilitator: Person who guides conversations, interactions, and activities within and between groups to help them more easily reach new and useful insights and directions for action.

field: See *discipline*.

field experiment: A randomized experiment with people who are in their everyday environment, such as at work or at school, rather than people who come to a research laboratory to participate in the study.

focus: See *topic*.

focus group: A type of interview (see *interview*) that consists of a facilitated conversation to surface the knowledge, experiences, opinions, and/or beliefs of a small group.

gamification: The process of taking something serious (such as knowledge mapping or strategic planning) and making it into a game or game-like process so it's a lot more fun (also leading to seriously useful insights). See especially Chapter 2.

institutional review board (IRB): A formal group (generally part of a university or research organization) that sets standards and procedures for ethical research. IRBs evaluate research proposals to maintain high ethical standards for the safety of the participants.

integration: The process of synthesizing theoretical propositions (such as merging their corresponding circles and arrows where they overlap on a knowledge map). See especially Chapter 6.

integrative complexity (IC): A measure of the intellectual style used by individuals or groups in processing information, problem-solving, and decision-making. IC looks at the structure of one's thoughts, based on books, articles, fiction, letters, speeches and speech transcripts, video and audio tapes, and interviews. See http://www2.psych.ubc.ca/~psuedfeld/index2.html

integrative propositional analysis (IPA): A six-step process for the rigorous and reasonably objective deconstruction into propositions of formal texts and the re-integration of propositions from those texts; also a process of analysis for evaluating knowledge maps to

determine their breadth and depth and so their potential usefulness (based on structure).

interdisciplinary: Including research and insights from across multiple disciplines (social science, natural science, humanities, etc.). Often includes taking purposeful collaborative action across multiple professions.

interview: A systematic process of asking questions of an individual or a group to surface their knowledge, experiences, opinions, and/or beliefs as they relate to the research questions. See especially Chapter 4.

interview questions: Specific questions presented to interview participants to generate data in the form of answers. Typically, these are more specific and detailed than "research questions."

knowledge: The understanding of a topic that potentially enables effective action. While that understanding may be in our minds, communicated verbally, or in writing, this book focuses on *diagrams* (maps) of knowledge. Knowledge maps make it easier to clarify *logic*, identify *data*, and confirm *meanings* for making better decisions for reaching important goals. See especially Chapter 1.

knowledge map: A diagram representing knowledge (such as a theory or model). Also called "maps," knowledge maps make it easier to clarify logic, identify data, and confirm relevancies for making better decisions for reaching important goals.

linear causal logic: A causal logical structure describing one-directional causal relationships between two or more concepts—for example, "More A causes more B causes more C."

logic: Represents an understanding of the relationships between things.

logic model: A diagram/visualization that shows an understanding of how a policy, program, or other action functions (or will function) to achieve results. May be represented in many forms, including as a causal knowledge map or a table.

logic structure (structure): The interconnectedness between multiple concepts. A set of concepts with more connections between them would have more structure.

map: See *knowledge map*.

meaning: A dimension of knowledge referring to the relevance and importance of the concepts on a knowledge map to the people involved and the situation at hand. See especially Chapter 1.

mental model: A mental representation about how the world works that may be useful for understanding and decision-making. Mental models may be surfaced and clarified through interviews, knowledge mapping, and other methods.

meta study: A study that combines data from multiple studies.

model: A model is a simplified representation of a system at some particular point in time or space intended to promote understanding of the real system. As an abstraction of a system, it offers insight about one or more of the system's aspects, such as its function, structure, properties, performance, behavior, or cost. For more information, see http://sebokwiki.org/wiki/Representing_Systems_with_Models

observation: A research method in which the researcher gathers information by watching what is happening at the research site.

open-ended survey questions: Survey questions that respondents answer by providing comments in their own words.

overlap: When the same concept (or causal relationship) is found on two (or more) maps. Ideally, they should have the same word or words to represent the concept and the same way to measure it. See especially Chapter 6.

participants: See *research participants*.

planning: The process of considering alternative actions and choosing the best option. See especially Chapter 7.

policy: A plan of action to reach general and/or specific goals.

policy model (policy theory): A type of knowledge map or model representing "how the world works" or the understanding of a community or organization as it relates to a policy. With a policy model, the organization can create a plan (a policy) to use their resources and engage in activities to achieve their goals. Policy models may be developed at any level of scale (global, national, state, regional, local) for any purpose (health, transportation, education, etc.).

policy research: Research performed to inform new or existing policy.

practitioner: A person such as a worker, manager, supervisor, or leader who makes decisions and takes action to accomplish goals. See especially Chapter 1.

principal investigator (PI): The person who leads and manages a whole research project.

program: A set of activities, such as a project, initiative, or intervention, run by one or more organizations, groups, and/or individuals to purposefully improve lives and communities.

program evaluation: Research conducted to provide information for shaping effective programs, policies, and other actions to purposefully bring about social or environmental change. Program evaluations explore a broad range of questions, such as whether a program is reaching its goals, what unanticipated impacts it is having, and how to design and implement action for the greatest chance of success. In practice, these studies are conducted by researchers from a variety of disciplines (e.g., sociology, education, public policy), and they are not always labelled as a "program evaluation." While program evaluations are conducted for the primary purpose of informing specific decisions, many also contribute to broader knowledge of the issue that can benefit others in the field.

proposition: A sentence expressing a relationship about concepts. For example, "More travel leads to more discovery." Or, "Apples are good."

qualitative data: Qualitative data describe the things, people, or events in your study. These data are non-numerical; the focus is on describing things rather than counting them. Qualitative data tell you "what is happening," rather than "how often" or "how much" it is happening.

qualitative research: Research that relies primarily on non-numerical data, such as text from literature, program documents, interviews, and observation.

quantitative data: Data that are expressed in the form of quantities or numbers.

quantitative meta-analysis: A type of meta study that combines and statistically analyzes numerical data from multiple studies. See Appendix C.

quantitative observation: A research technique that involves collecting quantitative data (data about the amount or quantity of something) using the researcher's own observations (what the researcher sees and detects). See Appendix C.

quantitative research: Research that focuses on investigating the qualities or nature of something.

quasi-experiment: An experimental study in which researchers do not randomly assign people to different groups.

randomized controlled trial: See *randomized experiment*.

randomized experiment: A study (also called a randomized controlled trial) in which research participants are randomly assigned to one or more groups. If the only difference between the two groups is the thing being tested, then any difference in results for the two groups is likely to be caused by the thing being tested.

related research: Publications and other materials (e.g., webinar recordings, conference presentations, program brochures) developed prior to your current study that provide information for better understanding your topic. See especially Chapter 3.

research: A scientific process of investigation and discovery that may include program evaluation and policy analysis. See especially Chapter 1.

research methods: Also called research approach, research design, evaluation approach, evaluation design, or research strategy. The research methods are what a researcher does to conduct a study to find useful information.

research participants: People who complete surveys, answer interview questions, engage in participatory research, or otherwise provide data for studies. See especially Chapter 1 and Chapter 4.

research question (RQ): A general or specific question that a researcher is attempting to answer by conducting research. In evaluation research, may be called an "evaluation question."

research topic: What a researcher will seek to understand, within a broader context or situation. May include multiple research questions.

researcher: A person who conducts research.

retrospective pre-post design: A study that measures the effects of an intervention or program at the end of the intervention by asking participants two questions: (1) to rate themselves according to some measure before they participated and (2) to rate themselves according to the same measure after participating.

social network analysis: "[T]he study of relationships within the context of social situations" (Durland & Fredericks, 2005, p. 9). This research strategy focuses on the social context and behavior of relationships among the people under investigation. See Appendix C.

social/behavioral sciences: The study of human interaction across fields such as sociology, economics, policy, psychology, business, ethics, management, organizational development, social anthropology, and human development.

stakeholder: In research, a person with a personal and/or professional interest in a situation, topic, or subject that is being studied or whose life may be impacted by that situation in the future. May include, for example, participants, advocates, family members, program managers, social service workers, researchers, funders, elected officials, and representatives of partnering organizations. See especially Chapters 1 and 2.

statistical model: A mathematical model that researchers use to explore relationships between multiple concepts (variables) of interest.

structure: See *logic structure*.

survey: In research, a set of questions used to elicit the knowledge, experiences, opinions, and/or beliefs of multiple people.

systemicity: See *depth*.

systems thinking: A way of thinking based on an understanding that the world is made of systems (conceptual, physical, biological, etc.). Systems thinkers seek to understand commonalities among various kinds of systems and so develop deeper interdisciplinary knowledge.

theory: A set of interrelated concepts such as a knowledge map or policy model.

topic: What a knowledge map or research study will focus on. Also called "focus." See also *research topic*.

Toulmin logic model of argument: The idea that a good argument includes data, claim, warrant, qualifiers, rebuttals, and backing. See https://web.cn.edu/kwheeler/documents/Toulmin.pdf

transcript: Text made from recording—often of an individual or group interview.

transformative causal logic: A logic structure found within a proposition in which two or more concepts are described as causing change in a third concept—for example, changes in A *and* B will cause changes in C.

transformative concept: A concept (or circle) that has multiple causal arrows pointing directly at it. See especially Chapter 5.

usefulness: The potential ability of a knowledge map (theory, model, etc.) to help stakeholders make effective decisions and take effective action to reach their goals.

variables: Concepts that are measurable and may change (vary) over time.

REFERENCES

Britt, H., Hummelbrunner, R., & Greene, J. (2017, April). *Causal link monitoring*. Retrieved from https://www.betterevaluation.org/en/resources/overview/Causal_Link_Monitoring

Durland, M. M., & Fredericks, K. A. (2005). An introduction to social network analysis. *New Directions for Evaluation, 107*. doi: 10.1002/ev.157. https://onlinelibrary.wiley.com/doi/pdf/10.1002/ev.157

Mayne, J. (2008). *Contribution analysis: An approach to exploring cause and effect*. The Institutional Learning and Change (ILAC) Initiative. Retrieved from the Better Evaluation website at https://www.betterevaluation.org/resources/guides/contribution_analysis/ilac_brief

INDEX

Note: Page numbers in **boldface** indicate definitions.

Abstraction, 160
Abstract map, 221, 222
Abstracts, 77, 80
Academia.edu, 75, 193
Accessibility of collaborative mapping sessions,
    42–43
Accuracy, in research, additional perspectives
    supporting, 174
Action planning, 50–51, 225–227
Advanced strategies for making maps more useful,
    233–247
    bridges, 233–234
    core and belt, 235–236
    inter-mapper consistency, 244–245
    off the shelf model, 245–246
    from optimism to reality, 238–239
    reducing redundancy, 242–243
    scale of abstraction, 240–242
    sub-structures, 236–238
    time, 234
    unanticipated consequences, 243–244
Advisory groups, 8, 55
Agosto-Rosario, Moisés, 71
Alecxih, L., 271
American Evaluation Association, 24, 176
American Management Association, 176
American Psychological Association, 176
Applied research, **3**
Arrows
    how to use on maps, 217
    loops and causal arrows, 158
    in logic models, 103
    showing causal relationships, 12
ASK MATT game, 59–61, 202
    case study using, 61–63
ASK MATT Solutions, 60
Atomistic concepts, 161, 162

Atomistic redundancy, 242
Atomistic structures, 236
Authorship, of research results, 24
Avoiding harm from research, 22
Axelrod, Robert, 142

Before-and-after design, 268
Belt of knowledge map, 235–236
Berk, R., 265
Bias
    gender, 126
    researcher, 122, 126
Bibliographic information for literature review,
    77–79
Big data, 3
Bing search engine, 75
Blinding, 266
Branching structure, 238
Breadth, **147**, 148–153
    breadth of integrated theory, 181
    ranking theories according to, 186, 188
    unanticipated consequences and, 244
Bridges, 233–234
Bridging, 179, 180

Case studies, 275, **275**
    collaboration among researchers, 182–195
    evaluating the structure of entrepreneurship
        theories, 153–157
    Howard University PAC-Involved evaluation (see Howard
        University *PAC-Involved: Engaging Students in PAC
        (Physics, Astronomy, Cosmology) Learning Through
        Repurposing of Popular Media*)
    IAMO (Leibniz Institute of Agricultural Development in
        Transition Economies), 90–93
    mapping a regional energy coalition, 61–63
    mapping from program materials, 90–93

map of an academic research institution's
strategic plan, 99
NMAC Strong Communities project, 70, 71, 72, 87–89,
90, 249–259
Case Study, 275
Categorization, 160
Causal arrows. *See* Arrows
Causal coding, **86**
Causal connections, xxiii, 12–14, 142.
See also Propositions
abstract example of, 14
better understanding of topic and decision making
and, 35
clarifying in interviews, 123, 127
computer modeling and, 272
core of knowledge map and, 235
"detail pictures" of, 249
in knowledge appraisal matrix, 17, 18, 21
logic and, 19
logic model example and, 104
mapping, 128, 130, 190
mapping in Kumu, 208, 209
substructures and, 236
unstructured conversation and, 58
Causality, **12**, 12–14
Causal knowledge maps, 7. *See also* Knowledge
maps (KMs)
integrated through collaborative effort, 186
sample, 130, 131
tips for creating, 132
visualizing data on, 134–135
Causal link monitoring (CLM), 275–276, **276**
Causal logic, 12
Causal relationships, examples of simple, 13
Causal statements, 80, 82, 85, 89. *See also* Propositions
Causation, correlation *vs.*, 143
Charts, 140–142
Chin, M. H., 82
Circular structure, 237
Class activities
choosing a topic, 145
clustering and categorizing, 160
collectively creating a map, 49
considering options presented by maps, 55
creating an online map, 213–215
creating maps from related studies, 87–88
evaluating evidence, 19–21
evaluating the structure of a map, 148

gap analysis, 163
integrating multiple maps, 192
interview practice, 126
mapping from program materials, 93–94
mapping from research findings, 132–134
practicing facilitation for choosing a topic, 44
thinking about multiple methods, 111–112
Closed-ended survey questions, 109, 262–263
Clustering, 159–160
Coding, **85**, 86
causal, 86, **86**
Collaboration, **34**
Collaboration with other researchers, 169–198
across industries, 176–177
case study, 182–195
challenges to interdisciplinary, 193–195
communication between disciplines, 172
cycle of, 174–177
finding people, finding maps, 177–182
integration, acceleration, solution and, 173–177
team development and, 194–195
Collaborative action paths, 53
Collaborative decisions, 224–225
Collaborative mapping, 7, 33–67
case study, 61–63
collaboration over consensus, 35–36
collaborative mapping session, 44–49
dealing with difficult dynamics, 55–58
finding opportunities for, 51
gamified approach to, 59–61
from mapping to action, 50–51
milestones on road to, 39–55
preparation for mapping session, 39–44
reaching results, 52–55
relevance, 36–37
revisiting map each year, 54
uses for, 37–39
Command and control management theory
integrative propositional analysis scores on, 188, 190
part of map from, 189
Common good and equity, research and, 24
Communication, between disciplines, 171, 172
Community forum, 7
Community institutional review boards, 25, **25**
Competence, of evaluators, 24
Complex problems
innovative approaches to, 4–5
maps for solving, 2–5

Computer modeling, 272

Concept charts, 140–141

Concept mapping, knowledge mapping *vs.*, 26

Concept maps, 5

Concepts, xxiii, **7**, 34

  abstract example of, 14

  actionable, 51

  identifying, 6–7

  mapping, 130

  at overlap between stakeholder groups, 36–37

  questions to prompt, 45

  research questions for measuring, 105–106

  transformative, 47, 48, 51

  use by stakeholders, 34–35

Confidentiality, research and, 23

Connections on map, research questions for measuring, 105–106

Consensus, collaborative mapping and, 35–36

Consortial benchmarking (CB), 176–177

Contribution analysis, 276–277, **277**

  steps of, 277

Convenience sample, 115

Conversations

  guiding, 222–225

  unstructured, 57–58

Core of knowledge map, 235–236

Correlation, causation *vs.*, 143

Cost analysis studies, 269, **269**

Cost-benefit analysis, 269

Cost-effectiveness analysis, 269

Cost utility analysis, 269

Cover page, sample, 250

Creating Maps from Text handout, 88

Crowd sourcing, 55

Cultural differences among stakeholder groups, 41

Cultural responsiveness, research and, 23

Culture gap, interview participants and, 117

Data, 9–11, **11**. *See also* Related research and materials, mapping from

  analysis of knowledge map's, 18–19

  Knowledge Appraisal Matrix and, 17

  limitations of, 10–11

  presenting with maps, 216–222

  putting together with meaning and logic, 14, 15–21

  qualitative, **314**

  quantitative, **265**

  research strategies for collecting, 262–272

sources of, 10

  in study appraisal checklist, 84

  techniques for capturing interview, 119

  visualizing on map, 134–135

Date of publication, inclusion criteria for research review and, 73

Decisions, collaborative, 224–225

Deconstruction, 161

Delphi method, 263–264, **264**

Deming, W. Edwards, 188, 190

Depth, **147**, 147–153

  of integrated theory, 181

  ranking theories according to, 186, 188

  unanticipated consequences and, 244

Desktop tools for making maps, 202–203

  useful features and possible downsides of, 203

Destination quadrant, 150

Detailed findings section of research report, 128

Detail maps, sample, 254, 256

  text explaining, 255, 257

Diagrams, 140–142

Duck Duck Go, 75

Economic evaluation, 269

Eisen, Saul, 119

Elements worksheet, 209

Elimination of items that do not work on map, 162

Entrepreneurship theory

  evaluating the structure of, 153–157

  partial map of, 151

Environment, in knowledge map, 5

ERIC, 76

Evaluation questions (EQs), **72**, 102–103, 105, 106

  examples, 107

  interview questions and, 121–122

  types of, 105

Evaluators' Ethical Guiding Principles, 24

Evidence, evaluating, 19–21

Excel

  Data Validation feature, 209

  Kumu and, 208, 209

Existing research, 70

Experiments

  field, **267**

  quasi-experiments, 267–268, **268**

  randomized, 265–266, **266**

Expertise, collaboration and, 175

Experts, identifying, 177–178

Explanation, 179–180

Explanatory text, 241

Face-to-face interviews, 118

Facilitating conversations around a map, 222–225

Facilitator, **36**

Fake journals, 74

Feedback loops, 51, 190, 239

Ferretti, Marco, 182, 184–185

Field experiment, **267**

Fink, Gerhard, 188, 190, 191, 192

Flowcharts, 140, 142

Focus groups, 109, 110, 273

    interviews using, 7, 113

Format, interview, 118

    Fragmentation in the social sciences, 170–171

Franklin, Benjamin, 50

Gamification, **59**

Gamified approach to collaborative mapping, 59–61

Gap analysis, 162–163

Gender bias, 126

Geographic location, inclusion criteria for research review and, 73

Global Positioning Systems (GPS), 2

Glossary, 283–288

Goals

    research question, 103

    short-term and long-term, 226

Google, 75

    Search Tips, 76

Google Scholar, 75, 76, 170, 193

Government reports, 74

Graceful Systems, ASK MATT game and, 60, 61–63

Graphic recording, 140–142

Groupthink, 9

Hairball map, 217, 218, 235

Handouts

    creating maps from text, 88

    interview planning checklist, 123

    making basic knowledge map and measuring breadth and depth of a knowledge map, 149

    participants' guide to knowledge mapping, 49

    tips for creating causal knowledge maps from research findings, 132

    tips for facilitating group, 49

Hawthorne effect, 274

Health Systems Evidence, 76

Hierarchical linear model (HLM), 271

Holmes, T. J., 154, 155

Howard University *PAC-Involved: Engaging Students in PAC (Physics, Astronomy, Cosmology) Learning Through Repurposing of Popular Media*, 93–94, 102

    causal knowledge map, 131

    causal relationship with less evidence, 134

    causal relationship with more evidence, 135

    creating online map for, 213–215

    discussion guide, 124–125

    evaluation questions, 106, 107

    interview guide, 121

    interviews with project team and participants, 103, 117–118

    interview timing, 118–119

    logic model, 104

    methods for answering example evaluative questions, 112

    possibilities for collaboration map, 224

    recruitment message, 116

    research methods used in, 109

Human-centered design, 4

IAMO (Leibniz Institute of Agricultural Development in Transition Economies), 90–93

Implementation science, 4, 108

Improvement science, 108

Incentives for interview participants, 117

Industrial organizational psychology, 226–227

Industries, collaboration across, 176–177

Inferential leap, 143

Information-gathering, on topic, 7–8

Informed consent, 23, 120

Insightmaker.com, 203–204

    sample map from, 204

    useful features and possible downsides of, 204

Institutional review boards (IRBs), **24**, 24–25, 120

    community, 25

    private, 24–25

Integration

    bridging and explaining to support, 179–181

    of multiple maps, 87–89

    sample map, 191

    showing results, 181–182

    steps to, 178–179

Integrative complexity, 144

Integrative propositional analysis (IPA), 145–148
　case study, 186, 187, 188
　for nine theories of entrepreneurship, 154, 155–156
　scores for four theories of power in organizations, 188, 190

Integrity of evaluators, 24

Interactive poster presentations, 201

Interdisciplinary collaboration. *See also* Collaboration with other researchers
　challenges to, 193–195
　communication between disciplines, 172
　fragmentation in the social sciences and, 170–171

Interdisciplinary research, 4

Interdisciplinary research cycle, 175

Inter-mapper consistency, 244–245

Internet, inclusion criteria for research review and, 75

Interrupted time series, 268

Interview data
　analysis of, 127
　techniques for capturing, 119

Interview discussion guide, 120–127
　sample, 124–125

Interviewers, 119

Interviews, 109, 110–111, **113**, 113–127, 273
　focus group, 7, 113
　interview discussion guide, 120–127
　interview plan, 113–114
　limitations of, 113
　participant recruitment and logistics, 115–119
　planning checklist handout, 123
　procedures for protecting research participants, 120
　who to interview, 114–115

Isolated concepts, 161, 162

Iterative process, 182

Johnson, Liz, 188, 192

Journal on Policy and Complex System, 190

Journals, inclusion criteria for research review and, 76
　Predatory/fake, 74

Kemper, P., 271

Key findings report, 128, 222

Key performance indicators (KPIs), 227–228

Knowledge, **2**. *See also* Data; Logic; Meaning
　extracted from studies, 79–81
　mapping knowledge from studies, 85–89
　three dimensions of, 6–14

Knowledge Appraisal Matrix, 16, 17
　marked-up, 18

Knowledge mapping, concept mapping *vs.,* 26

Knowledge maps (KMs), xxiv, 2, **2**. *See also* Causal knowledge maps; Collaborative mapping
　concepts and causal connections on, 5, 11–12
　evolving understanding of, 140–145
　example of simple, 18
　examples from strategic plan, 91–92
　exploring new circles and arrows to expand and improve, 109
　putting meaning, data, and logic together on, 14, 15–21
　quadrants of, 150–153
　research strategies for creating and expanding, 272–277
　sample causal, 131
　steps to integrating, 178–179
　tips for creating causal, 132
　visualizing data on, 134–135

Komisar, H. L., 271

Kumu (Kumu.io), 185, 206–207, 206–215
　creating a map in, 209–213
　formatting a map in, 212
　importing data into, 212
　mapping in, 208–209
　sample knowledge map in, 213
　sample online interactive strategic knowledge map, 206
　spreadsheet with information about causal relationships, 210–211
　spreadsheet with information about concepts, 208
　useful features and possible downsides of, 207

Leadership team, collaborative mapping and circling back to, 54–55

Legend, sample, 252

Leibniz Institute of Agricultural Development in Transition Economies (IAMO), 90–93

Leverage points, 51, 158–159, 185

Limitations and conclusions, case study on entrepreneurship theories, 157

Linear redundancy, 242–243

Linear structure, 236–237

LinkedIn, 193

Literature map, 71

Literature review, 8, 183

Llosa, L., 271

Location
collaborative mapping session, 42–43
interview, 118
Logic, **11**, 11–14. *See also* Structure, evaluating;
    Structure; Substructures
analysis of knowledge map's, 18, 19
Knowledge Appraisal Matrix and, 17
limits to, 14
putting together with meaning and data,
    14, 15–21
in study appraisal checklist, 84–85
Toulminian, 25
Logic model, 5, **103**, 145
creating, 103
sample, 104
Logic structure, **11**
Logistics
collaborative mapping session, 42–43
interview participant, 117, 118–119
Loops, 47, 48, 157–158, 185
in circular structure, 237
feedback, 51, 190, 239
leverage point and, 159
optimistic, 238–239, 239
Low-tech tools for making maps, 200–202
ASK MATT tabletop game, 202
useful features and possible downsides of, 201

Magnitude of effect, assessment of study's, 83
Mapping tools. *See* Online mapping tools; Tools for
    mapping
Matched comparison group studies, 267
Meaning, **6**, 6–9. *See also* Collaborative mapping
analysis of knowledge map's, 17–18
concepts and, 35
Knowledge Appraisal Matrix and, 17
problems with relying solely on, 8–9
putting together with data and logic,
    14, 15–21
in study appraisal checklist, 84
Measurement, of structure of maps, 145–148
Merging concepts, 132
Meta studies, 177
Methods. *See* Research methods
Michigan Technological University, 60
Microsimulation modeling, 271
Mind maps, 5

Modeling
computer, 272
microsimulation, 271
Monthly meetings, to enact map actions, 52–53
Moore, C., 272
Morgan, Pamela, 61–63
Multilevel perspective (MLP), 185
Multiple maps, integrating, 87–89

Narrative documents, 109, 111
review of, 273
Natural science quadrant, 150, 151–153
Nested maps, 220–222
Newton, X. A., 271
NMAC Strong Communities project, 70, 71, 72, 87–89
sample report, 249–259

Objectivity, additional perspectives supporting, 174
Observation, **274**
qualitative, 274
quantitative, 265, **265**
Off the shelf model, 245–246
Ohm's Law, 151–152
Online mapping tools, 203–213, 229–230
insightmaker.com, 203–204
Kumu.io, 206–215
Stormboard.com, 205–206
Online mapping platforms, supporting collaborations,
    192, 193
Open-ended survey questions, 109, 274–275, **275**
Optimistic loop, 238–239
Organizational chart, 140, 141
Organizational development, 226–227
Organizations, types that might use collaborative
    mapping, 38
Orientation, at collaborative mapping session, 44–45
Overlap, **179**
connecting maps where they, 178–179
explaining concept, 179–180
identifying, 189
shifting scale of abstraction and, 180–181
Overview map, 236, 240–241
sample, 252
sample text explaining, 253

Panetti, Eva, 182, 184–185, 187
Parmentola, Adele, 182, 184–185

Participants' Guide to Knowledge Mapping handout, 49
Path diagram, 272
Peer-reviewed journal articles, 74
People with disabilities
  accessibility of collaborative mapping sessions, 42–43
  as interview participants, 117
  working with, 58
Performance story, 277
Pessimistic connections, 239
Phone book quadrant, 150, 153
Phone interviews, 118
Planning, **225**
Portland Energy Conservation, Inc., 61–63
Poster presentations, 201
Power dynamics, collaborative mapping and, 58
PowerPoint, making maps using, 202–203
Practitioner, **6**
Predatory journals, 74
Premature decision, 57
Pre-post design, 268
  retrospective, 269, **269**
Presentations, making, 216–222
  presenting data with maps, 216–222
Principal investigator (PI), **106**
  interviews and, 119
Privacy
  of interview participants, 120
  research and, 23
Private institutional review boards, 24–25
Problem statement, case study on entrepreneurship
    theories, 154
Professional associations, 193
Professional-facing map, 219, 220
Program evaluation, **4**
  choice of map topic and, 39
  conducting practical research and, 262
  map as logic model for, 35
  mapping from own research, 102, 105
  mapping from program materials and, 89
  structure of knowledge maps and, 145
Program materials, mapping from, 89
  case study, 90–93
Propositions, xxiii. *See also* Causal statements
  concepts and, 7
  mapping, 129, 130
  mapping in research findings, 129
  mapping in studies, 85–86

Proto-maps, 2, 3
Publication type, inclusion criteria for research review and,
    73–74
Public engagement, 55
Purposes for collaborative mapping, 37–39

Quadrants of knowledge map, 150–153
  destination, 150
  natural science, 150, 153
  phone book, 150, 153
  social science, 150
Qualitative data, 242
Qualitative observation, 109, 110, 274
Quantitative data, **265**
  reviewing existing, 262
Quantitative meta-analysis, 265, **265**
Quantitative observation, 265, **265**
Quasi-experiments, 267–268, **268**
Quotes, 119, 272

Randomized experiments (randomized controlled trial),
    265–266, **266**
Random sample, 115
Recording interviews, 119
Recruitment message, sample, 116
Recruitment of interview participants, 115–118
Redundancy, reducing, 242–243
References, sample report, 259
Regional energy coalition, mapping, 61–63
Regression discontinuity design, 267
Related research, **71**
Related research and materials, mapping from,
    69–99
  assessing research quality, 82–85
  case study, 90–94
  creating a table of studies, 77–79
  extracting and organizing knowledge from studies,
      79–82
  mapping from program materials, 89–93
  mapping knowledge from studies, 85–89
  searching for and choosing existing studies,
      73–77
  steps to mapping from existing research, 71–89
  uses for mapping from existing research, 70–71
Relevance, collaborative mapping and, 36–37.
    See also Meaning
Report. *See* Sample report

Reporting relationships, 226–227
Research, xxiii, **3**. *See also* Related research and materials, mapping from; Searching for research
    avoiding harm from, 22
    high quality, 15
Research, mapping from own, 101–138
    conducting interviews, 113–127
    developing research questions, 102–108
    organizing research findings, 127–128
    reporting and presenting research, 128–135
    specifying methods to answer research questions, 108–112
Researcher bias, 122, 126
Researchers
    appraising study's meaning for, 84
    differences between mapping with stakeholders and, 173–174
    different zones of focus for, 182
Research ethics, 22–25
    protecting research participants, 120
Research findings. *See also* Sample report
    organizing, 127–128
    reporting and presenting, 23–24, 128–135
ResearchGate, 75, 193
Research topic, 7–8
Research methods, **261**, 261–281
    to answer research questions, 108–112
    before-and-after design, 268
    case study, 275, **275**
    causal link monitoring, 275–276, **276**
    closed-ended survey questions, 109, 262–263
    contribution analysis, 276–277, **277**
    cost analysis studies, 269, **269**
    Delphi method, 263–264, **264**
    field experiments, **267**
    finding data, 262–272
    focus groups, 273
    interviews (*see* Interviews)
    open-ended survey questions, 109, 274–275, **275**
    qualitative observation, 109, 110, 274
    quantitative meta-analysis, 265, **265**
    quantitative observation, 265, **265**
    quasi-experiments, 267–268, **268**
    randomized experiments, 265–267, **266**
    retrospective pre-post design, 269, **269**
    reviewing existing quantitative data, 262
    review of narrative documents, 273
    social network analysis, 270, **270**
    statistical modeling, 270–272, **271**
    strategies for creating and expanding maps, 272–277
Research participants, **23**
Research quality, assessing, 82–85
Research questions (RQs), **72**
    developing, 102–108
    for expanding maps, 106–108
    for measuring concepts and connections on map, 105–106
    methods to answer, 108–112
Research utility, 23
Respect for people, conducting research with, 24
Results
    case study on entrepreneurship theories, 155–157
    sharing collaborative map, 53–54
    tracking, 227–228
Results chain, 103
Retrospective pre-post design, 269, **269**
Review of narrative documents, 273
Robert Wood Johnson Foundation, 76
Rogers, Patricia, 144–145

Sample report, 249–259
    cover page, 250
    detail maps, 254, 256
    legend/orientation for reading maps, 252
    overview map, 252
    references, 259
    report overview, 251
    summary and conclusion, 258
    text explaining overview map, 253
Samples of populations for interview participants, 114–115
    convenience, 115, 154
    least likely, 115
    maximum variation, 115
    most successful/least successful, 115
    random, 115
    strategies for selecting, 115
Scale of abstraction, 240–242
Schmitz, Jr., J. A., 154, 155
Scholarly literature databases, inclusion criteria for research review and, 75
Search engines, 75
Searching for existing or related research, 72–77
    expanding your search, 75
    scanning search results and selecting studies, 76–77
    study inclusion criteria, 73–74
    where to search, 74–76

Secondary research, 70. *See also* Related research

Seminal works, 74

Semi-structured interviews, 120

Simplicity, 161, 162

Simulation modeling, 26

Single-case design (single subject design), 268

Smartphone recording mode, 119

Social network analysis, 270, **270**

Social science quadrant, 150

Social sciences, fragmentation of, 170–171

"Special" situations, 56

Stakeholder-facing map, 219, 221

Stakeholder groups, xxii–xxiii

    surveying, 40

Stakeholders, **8**, 34

    appraising study's meaning for, 84

    concepts at overlap between, 36–37

    concepts that are meaningful for, 7–8

    differences between mapping with researchers and,
        173–174

    inviting to participate in collaborative mapping,
        40–42

    overlap between stakeholders' perspectives, 52

    use of concepts, 34–35

Stakeholder subgroups, 41–42

Statistical matching techniques, 267

Statistical modeling, 270–272, **271**

Stories, adding to maps, 272. *See also* Narrative
    documents

Stormboard.com, 205–206

    sample strategic knowledge map, 206

    useful features and possible downsides of, 205

Strategic niche management (SNM), 185

Strategic plan, knowledge map from, 91–92

Structure, **11**. *See also* Substructures; Logic

Structure, evaluating, 139–167

    abstraction/categorization, 160

    case study, 153–157

    clustering, 159–160

    comparing and improving maps, 148–153

    deconstruction, 161

    early techniques for understanding, 144–145

    eliminating what does not work, 162

    evolving understanding of knowledge maps,
        140–145

    inferential leap and, 143

    leverage points, 158–159

    loops, 157–158

    measuring structure of maps, 145–148

    showing the invisible/gap analysis, 162–163

    simplicity, 161, 162

Structured equation modeling, 271–272

Structured interviews, 120

Structure of decisions, 142

Study appraisal checklist, 83–85

Study findings, organizing, 81–82

Study inclusion criteria, 73–74

Study limitations, 79

Subgroups of stakeholders, 41–42

Submaps, 217–220, 219, 240–241

Substructures, 236–238

    atomistic, 236

    branching, 238

    circular, 237

    linear, 236–237

    transformative, 238

Summary and conclusion, example, 258

Super connectors, collaborative mapping and, 57

Super talkers, collaborative mapping and, 56–57

Surveying stakeholder groups, 40

Survey questions

    closed-ended, 109, 262–263

    open-ended, 109, 274–275, **275**

Surveys, 109, 110

    Delphi method, 263–264

    limitations of, 263

    social network analysis and, 270

Survival analysis, 272

Synthesis. *See* Integration

Systematic inquiry, 24

Systems thinking, 4

Table of studies, creating, 77–79

Tabletop mapping

    ASK MATT tabletop game, 202

    bridges and, 233–234

Team development, 194–195

Team LMI, ASK MATT game and, 59

Text explaining sample detail maps, 255, 257

Text explaining sample overview map, 253

Theory maps, integrated with bridging, 180

Theory of change, 5, 103, 276

Time, indicating passage of, 234

Timing, interview, 118–119

Tips for Creating Causal Knowledge Maps from Research
    Findings handout, 132

Tips for Facilitating Group handout, 49
Tools for making maps, 5, 200–215
    desktop, 202–203
    low-tech, 200–202
    online mapping (see Online mapping tools)
Topic
    choosing map, 34, 35, 39–40
    going off, 56
    researching, 7–8
Topic-specific repositories, inclusion criteria for research
    review and, 76
Toulminian logic, 25
"Tower of Babel" effect, 171
Town hall meetings, 55
Tracking results, 227–228
Transformative concepts, 51
    encouraging, 47, 48
    identifying, 147
Transformative logic structure, 238
Transition management (TM), 185
Transitions in technology, 185
Transportation for interview participants, 117
Trust, mapping and, 174
Tuskegee Syphilis study, 22

Unanticipated consequences, 239, 243–244
U.S. Centers for Disease Control and Prevention, 22
    website, 76
U.S. Public Health Service Syphilis Study, 22
University of Naples-Parthenope, 184
Unleased Consulting, ASK MATT game and, 60
Unstructured conversation, 57–58

Unstructured interviews, 120
Useful knowledge, promotion of, 50

Variable, 7. See also Concept
Venn diagrams, 140, 141
Video interviews, 118
Visualizing data on map, 134–135

Wallis, Steven
    about, xxvii
    collaboration among researchers case study, 182,
        184–185, 187, 190, 192
    evaluating entrepreneurship theories case study,
        153–157
    mapping from program materials case study, 90–93
Waypoints, 2, 3
Websites
    inclusion criteria for research review and, 75
    publishers', 193
    university/research center, 193
Whiteboard and sticky notes presentation, 201
Word software, making maps using, 202
Worksheets
    elements, 209
    for making basic knowledge map and measuring
        breadth and depth of a knowledge map handout,
        149
Wrap-up, interview, 122–123
Wright, Bernadette, 70, 153–157
    about, xxvii

Yahoo Search, 75